Working with Evidence 1

The Industrial Revolution

Peter & Mary Speed

Oxford University Press 1985

To the Teacher

Oxford University Press, Walton Street, Oxford OX2 6DP

Oxford London
New York Toronto Melbourne Auckland
Kuala Lumpur Singapore Hong Kong Tokyo
Delhi Bombay Calcutta Madras Karachi
Nairobi Dar es Salaam Cape Town

and associated companies in
Beirut Berlin Ibadan Mexico City Nicosia

First published 1985
ISBN 0 19 917067 3

Typeset by MS Filmsetting Limited, Frome, Somerset
Printed in Great Britain by Butler & Tanner Ltd, Frome

Acknowledgements

The publishers would like to thank the following for permission to reproduce the illustrations:

Aerofilms, p 3 left; Revd Wm P Allen, Christian Brothers O'Connell School, Dublin, p 134; Archives Nationales du Québec, Collection Initiale, p 142; BBC Hulton Picture Library, pp 16, 33, 47 top, 70, 88, 95, 100, 122, 133, 139; Bodleian Library Oxford, UK Copyright, pp 107, 108; British Library and Weidenfeld and Nicolson Archives, p 132; British Schools Museum (Jill E Grey Collection) pp 96, 98; The Syndics of the Cambridge University Library, p 90 from Sir Frederick Morton Eden *The State of the Poor* volume I, 1797; Chubb Security Services Ltd, p 44; John Cornwell, p 23 bottom; Crown Copyright, pp 55, 56, 60; Crown Copyright material from the Public Record Office appears by permission of the Controller of HMSO, p 126 bottom; Crown Copyright, Science Museum, pp 14, 38, 49, 69, 71, 75, 77, 78, 79, 80, 123, 126 top; The Living Steam Museum p 53; Mary Evans Picture Library, pp 24, 25, 26, 31, 35, 36, 39, 58, 82, 83, 87, 89, 102, 105, 137; Marke Girouard *Life in the English Country House* Yale University Press, p 7; Greater London Council Record Office, Print Collection, p 100; Guildhall Library, City of London, pp 117, 124; Helmshore Local History Society, pp 29, 34; Hertfordshire Constabulary, pp 85, 86; The Illustrated London News Picture Library, p 130 bottom; 'Our World' Wallchart, *Inland Waterways* Macmillan Children's Books, p 65; The Manchester Local History Library, pp 27, 28, 41, 91, 93; Mansell Collection, pp 8, 17, 103, 104, 141; National Institute of Agricultural Botany, p 130 top; Norfolk County Library, pp 19, 20; The Science Museum, London p 49; The Tate Gallery, London, p 5; University of Reading, Institute of Agricultural History and Museum of English Rural Life, pp 3 right, 12, 13, 15, 109; Verity Press, p 22; Board of Trustees of the Victoria and Albert Museum, copyright, p 2; Library and Museum Services Department, Walsall, pp 45, 47; Trustees of the Wedgwood Museum, Barlaston, Staffordshire, p 63; Welholme Galleries, p 18; Wellcome Institute Library, London, pp 111, 115; Wolverhampton Public Libraries, p 43.

Almost every good history course is written for children that are average – average in their ability, the interest they show, and the effort that they are prepared to make. This is as it should be, but it does make problems for enthusiastic pupils. While they can gain much from a general course, they will master it quickly and easily, and then demand more. *Working with Evidence* fills that need. It is a collection of sources for the young student to interpret, with the help of questions. There are exercises to challenge the more able, but at the same time, most of the tasks are within the grasp of anyone of sound ability.

The books have a number of aims. The first is to encourage the enthusiasm for history which we hope is already present. To that end, we have avoided anything dour, like Acts of Parliament, but have chosen sources which are interesting, and some even amusing. However, no source has been included just because it is entertaining; each one makes a serious contribution.

Secondly, we want to encourage study in depth. This should not be at the expense of study in breadth, but once they have covered a general history course, pupils will gain far more if they then look at a few topics in some detail.

Our third aim is to give some idea of the nature of historical evidence. Pupils often ask how we know what happened in the past and using the sources is the best way for them to find the answer. They should soon learn that sources support, complement or contradict each other and can, indeed, do all of these things at the same time.

Finally, we hope our readers will develop a number of skills, useful not only in history, but elsewhere. They will be asked to do the following:

1 Understand thoroughly each of the sources.
2 Evaluate the sources, compare them, and, where necessary, decide between them.
3 Extract from the sources what seem to be the most useful ideas and facts.
4 Synthesise the information so gained in a piece of writing.
5 Follow this work with further research and study.

The two books in this series were written to complement the *Oxford Junior History*, Books 4–6, but they could be used alongside any similar course. They are meant for children aged from about 10–13, but those preparing for external examinations will find them a useful introduction to the study of documents.

Cover *coal wagon* – The President and Council of the North of England Institute of Mining and Mechanical Engineers
artefacts – A. R. Griffin BA, Ph. D., Curator, National Mining Museum, Lound Hall, Retford, Notts.

Contents

Chapter 1 *Farming*

Enclosing the Common Land

When the Saxons arrived in England, from the fifth century onwards, they built villages and cleared the land around them to grow food. Beyond the fields was a belt of land which was called the 'common'. Though it was not cultivated, it was useful for the villagers in all sorts of ways. Mainly, they grazed their animals on it, during the summer, when the grass was growing.

In the eighteenth century there were still a great many villages which had commons. They did not produce much food. Sometimes, they were swampy and, in places, they grew fairly useless plants like brambles and bracken. Some farmers wanted to cultivate them properly, but as the commons belonged to the whole village, they could only do so if everyone agreed. It was very difficult to persuade the more backward folk to do so. Often, the only way was for Parliament to pass an Enclosure Act to compel them.

During the eighteenth century there were a great many of these Enclosure Acts. Usually, it was the squire and the more important farmers who asked for the Act. After it was passed, the common was enclosed. Everyone who had had the right to put animals on it, was, instead, given a share of it. He then put an 'enclosure' round his plot, to show it was truly his. An enclosure might be a wall, or a fence, or, more likely, a bank with a hedge on it. Almost always the wealthier farmers were given much more of the common than their poor neighbours.

We can draw a comparison with your school playground. At present it is not enclosed, so all of you can play all over it. If it were enclosed, each of you would have a tiny plot, with a fence round it, while most of the yard was taken by the teachers for a car park.

In this section we are going to see how the enclosure of the commons affected village people.

The Sussex Downs This was one kind of common, wide open spaces on the tops of hills. The other kind lay in a fringe, perhaps a quarter or half a mile wide, round the cultivated land of the village. Some of the first kind is still not enclosed, especially where the soil is poor, as on the top of Dartmoor. Practically none of the second kind remains.

Enclosures The ploughed land of the village was enclosed as well as the common. This had been in huge fields about a mile across. The photograph covers, roughly, a third of one such field. Each farmer had strips scattered everywhere. You can gain some idea of these from the photograph, for each was made from two or three of the ridges. You can also see the enclosures that were made, probably, in the eighteenth or early nineteenth century.

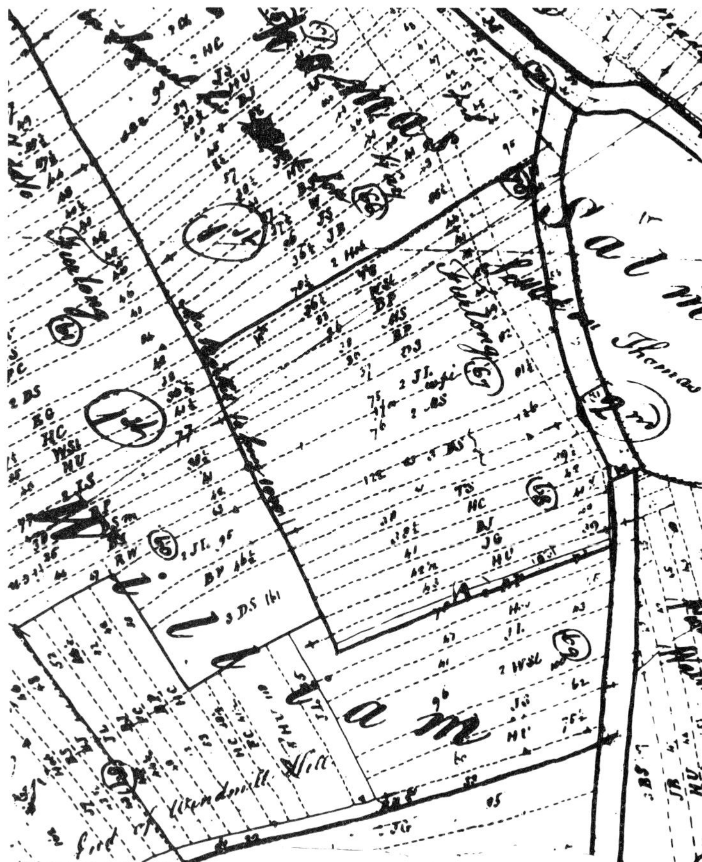

An Enclosure Map A surveyor has measured all the strips and drawn them on the map. The initials on the strips stand for the names of their owners. How many can you find that belonged to one man, say H.U.? After enclosure, every man will have his land in one place. The heavy black lines show where the new enclosures will run. You can see two complete new fields on this section of map. How many of the old strips are there in each of them?

To start with, here are three extracts which show how the common was used before enclosure. The first is from a book by Stephen Addington. He is writing not only about the common, but also the cultivated land which the villagers had:

> The cottagers have little parcels of land in the ploughed fields, with a right of common for a cow and three or four sheep, by the assistance of which, and with the profits of a little trade or their daily labour, they procure a very comfortable living. Their ploughed land furnishes them with wheat and barley for bread, and, in many places, with beans or peas to feed a hog or two for meat; with the straw they thatch their cottage, and winter their cow, which gives a breakfast and supper of milk, nine or ten months in the year. They have likewise a right to cut turf, roots and furze on the common, which must be a great advantage to those who have not money to purchase other fuel.
>
> *Reasons For and Against Enclosing Open Fields*, 1772

1 Draw up two lists showing what the villagers have **a** from their ploughed land **b** from the common. Which of their animals depends on both?

2 What happens to almost all the food produced by a modern farmer? What happened to the food produced by the people Addington described?

This is what William Cobbett said about the Forest of Dean:

> The people look hearty and well, just as they do round the forests in Hampshire. Every cottage has a pig or two. These graze in the forest, and, in the fall, eat acorns and beech-nuts and the seed of the ash. Some of these foresters keep cows, and all of them have bits of ground, cribbed, of course, at different times, from the forest; and to what better use can the ground be put? I saw several wheat stubbles from 40 to 10 rods. I asked one man how much wheat he had from about ten rods. He said more

than two bushels. Here is bread for three weeks, or more, perhaps; and a winter's straw for the pig besides. Are these things nothing? The dead limbs and old roots of the forest give fuel; and how happy are these people, compared with the poor creatures about Great Bedwyn and Cricklade, where they have neither land nor shelter, and where I saw girls carrying home bean and wheat stubble for fuel!

Rural Rides, 1821

1 Find the Forest of Dean on a map.
2 Find out what a 'rod' and a 'bushel' are.
3 What does Cobbett mean by saying land has been 'cribbed' from the forest? What does Cobbett think of 'cribbing'?
4 Why does Cobbett say the people of Great Bedwyn and Cricklade are unlucky, compared with those of the Forest of Dean?

In some places there were people called 'squatters'. They were not members of the village, and so they were not allowed to live in it. They were, though, given permission to stay out on the common where they built themselves little huts. They had no legal right to be there, and could be ordered to leave at any time. Here, Arthur Young describes some squatters near Aldershot:

Jacob Johnson has about three rods of land, and no cow, only a pig. Edward Smith has two cows and a heifer. William Farr has a pig and very fine potatoes. Dolly has two cows and a heifer, and about two acres of land.

They said the common was a very good one for feeding cows. Dolly has had 4 lb of butter per week from one little Welsh cow that had the common only. They buy hay in winter, or hop bines, and straw, managing in this respect as well as they can.

Annals of Agriculture, Vol 36, 1801

1 What use are these squatters making of the common?
2 What problem do they have in winter?

We must now see what happened when commons were enclosed. William Howitt wrote:

One would naturally have supposed that in a *Christian* country, there would have been a desire to provide for those who had nothing. That in every parish the common should have been divided among those who had most need of it. The rule has always been exactly the reverse: and the consequence has been that our poor villagers, robbed of their old common rights, have been thrown upon the parish: their little flock of sheep, their few cows, their geese, their pigs, all gone: and no help left them to eke out their small earnings: and in the case of loss of work, or sickness, nothing but the parish – the evil influence upon the character of the rural population has been enormous.

Rural Life of England, 1838

1 How does Howitt say commons should be divided?
2 What, in fact, happens?
3 How do the villagers suffer? What does Howitt mean when he says they are 'thrown upon the parish'? (See page 88).
4 What do you suppose happened to any squatters, when a common was enclosed?

This little poem was written in about 1830:

The fault is great in man or woman,
Who steals a goose from off the common:
But who can plead that man's excuse,
Who steals the common from the goose?

1 What does the writer mean by 'stealing the common from the goose?'

Here are reports on enclosures from different parts of England:

Tutvy, Bedfordshire Before the enclosure the poor inhabitants had no difficulty in finding milk for their children: since, it is with the utmost difficulty that they can find milk at all. Cows lessened from 110 to 40.

Letcomb, Berkshire The poor seem the greatest sufferers: they can no longer keep a cow, which before many of them did, and they are therefore now maintained by the parish.

Cranage, Cheshire Poor men's cows and sheep have no place, or any being.

Rutcliffe, Leicestershire A great decline in cheese and pigs, caused mainly by taking away the land from the cottager.

General Report on Enclosures, Board of Agriculture, 1808

1 List the ways the poor suffered as the result of enclosure in these villages.

William Cobbett wrote:

It is miserable work where fuel is to be bought and where, as at Salisbury, the poor take by turns the making of fires at their houses to boil four or five tea-kettles. What a winter-life must these lead whose turn it is not to make the fire! At Launceston in Cornwall a man told me that the people in general could not afford to have fire and that he himself had paid threepence (1p) for boiling a

Farm labourers drinking How did Arthur Young feel about scenes like this? (See below). What impression is the painter trying to give?

leg of mutton at another man's fire!
Rural Rides, 1822

1 How has the enclosure of the commons affected these people?

This is what Arthur Young said:

Go to an alehouse kitchen of an old enclosed country, and there you will see the origin of poverty and poor rates. For whom are they to be sober? For whom are they to save? (Such are their questions) For the parish? If I am diligent shall I have leave to build a cottage? If I am sober, shall I have land for a cow? If I am frugal shall I have half an acre of potatoes? You offer no motives: you have nothing but a parish officer and a workhouse! – Bring me another pot!
Annals of Agriculture, Vol. 36 1801

1 How does Arthur Young say the poor spend their money?
2 What does he suggest they would rather spend it on?
3 Why do they not do so?

William Howitt wrote:

Shut us up in towns, or in never ending hedges and ditches and we shall cease to be the high-souled people we are. We must have some openness, some freedom, some breathing spaces left us. The sick; the overworn in spirit; the followers of a summer's recreation, all seek our hills and sea-coasts and plains, where the peace or magnificence of nature is to be found. If we knew how many make a summer excursion to the sea-side, or to our moorland and mountain districts, it would be amazing.

I do not mean to say that no waste lands should be henceforth enclosed. There are plenty that have no particular grace or interest about them. Let them be hedged or ditched as soon as you please; but as for the village green, the common lying near a town, the forest and the moorland that has a poetical charm about it – may the axe and the spade that are lifted up against them be shivered to atoms.
Rural Life of England, 1838

1 Why does Howitt say plenty of land should stay unenclosed?
2 What land, according to him, could be enclosed? Would Cobbett and Young have agreed with him?

Note: Howitt makes the mistake of thinking that commons are there for all and sundry. Common land is the property of the local people; folk who come from other places and wander all over it are usually trespassing.

Here now are some other results of enclosures. The first extract was written by William Stevenson:

At Beaminster seven hundred acres of common land were enclosed by an Act obtained in 1807; persons having common rights used to let them for half-a-crown ($12\frac{1}{2}$p) a year: the allotments for these were more than half an acre each, and some of the ground is now let for near £5 an acre, a year.

Agriculture of Dorset, 1812

1 'Common right' was the right a villager had to feed beasts on the common. What was one of these rights worth before enclosure?
2 When the land was enclosed, how much was given to each villager having a common right?
3 How much were some of these plots worth a year?
4 How many times had the villagers' property increased in value?

The following extract is about Wedmore, in Somerset. Here the land is very close to sea level and almost completely flat:

Within twenty years there have been enclosed upwards of 3,000 acres of rich moor land. Before, when it was in commons, it was useless because of flooding six or seven months in the year; when used as pasture for the remaining months, it was of little value, because too many animals were put on it; which land is now let from 30s to 60s (£1.50–£3) per acre. These enclosures are made by ditches, which by annual cleansing and spreading the contents over the surface, afford an excellent manure. This has also created work whereby the poor-rate has been reduced.

General Report on Enclosures, Board of Agriculture, 1808

1 Why were the Wedmore commons worth very little before enclosure?
2 How much was the land worth after enclosure?
3 How were the enclosures made in this area? Why was this method chosen, do you suppose?
4 How did these enclosures create jobs? Would other enclosures e.g. hedgerows have created work as well?

Arthur Young wrote a book on Norfolk. Here are three extracts from it:

1 The fame of the country in general was not heard of until the vast improvements of heaths, wastes, sheep-walks and warrens by enclosure and marling were undertaken by Lord Townshend, and others, which were in the first thirty years of the last century. They were happily imitated by many others and estates that had been too insignificant to be known, were talked of even in London.

2 Mr Salter of Winborough is one of the most spirited improvers in the county; he rented 800 acres in a state not far removed from waste; and by ditching, draining, marling and good farming of various kinds has brought it to be one of the most productive farms in Norfolk.

3 In several parliamentary enclosures the effect has been at least the doubling of the produce.

Agriculture of Norfolk, 1813

1 What was much of the land of Norfolk like in the old days?
2 Who began to make improvements? When?
3 In what ways has the land of Norfolk been improved? (Look up 'marling' in a dictionary).
4 Why would farmers not have made these improvements without first enclosing their land?
5 How much extra food was sometimes grown on land, after it had been enclosed?
6 Contrast what Young says here with the extract from his *Annals of Agriculture* on page 5. Is Young in favour of enclosures, or is he against them?

These figures are of the population of England and Wales:

1695	5.5 million	1801	9.3 million
1750	6.0 million	1851	17.9 million

1 Draw a graph to show how the population of England and Wales increased.
2 How, do you suppose, did the growth of population encourage landowners and farmers to make enclosures?

Written Work

1 You are a rich landowner who has asked Parliament to pass an Enclosure Act for your village. Explain why you did so.
2 Now pretend you are a poor villager. Say what you fear will happen when your village common is enclosed.

Research

1 Find out more about Viscount ('Turnip') Townshend, Arthur Young and William Cobbett.
2 Find out more about the improvements made in farming during the eighteenth and early nineteenth centuries.

The Aristocracy

Until the end of the nineteenth century, the richest and most important people in Britain were the aristocrats, or nobles. Most of them had titles, such as duke, marquis or earl and all of them owned a great deal of land. They made their money by letting their land to farmers, who paid them rent. Aristocrats were wealthy. In 1800, the one with the largest income was the Duke of Devonshire. He had £50,000 a year. The one with the least money was probably the Earl of Clarendon and he had £3,000 a year. Many of them had £10,000 a year or more. It is difficult to say how much all this would be worth now, but it helps to look at wages. In 1800 the average man earned £50 a year. Today he earns £7,000, or 140 times as much. If you multiply the Duke of Devonshire's income by the same figure, how much does that make?

Dinner party What impression is the artist trying to give of these people? Do you think either William Howitt or Prince Puckler-Muskau would have agreed with him?

In this section we are going to see how aristocrats lived. Here, first of all, is what William Howitt said about them:

> Imagine the owner of a noble estate coming down to receive his friends there. When he enters his own neighbourhood, he enters his own kingdom. The very market town through which he last passes is probably all, or three quarters of it, his property. On all sides he sees signs of welcome. Wherever he looks, they are the woods, the parks, the fields of his ancestors, and now his own, that meet his eyes. Here he is sole lord and master: and from him, he feels, flow the good of his dependent people, and the pleasures of his distinguished guests. The hamlet, which shows its thatched roofs and lowly smoking chimneys near, is all his own; nay, the rustic church is part and parcel of the family estate. It was probably built and endowed by his ancestors. The living is in his gift, and is perhaps enjoyed by a relative or college friend. The sabbath-bell rings, and he enters that

Hunting party Which of the things mentioned by Prince Puckler-Muskau can you see here? (See page opposite).

old porch with his guests; he sees the banner of some brave ancestor float above his head, and the tombs of others on the walls. What can be more flattering to all the feelings of a human creature: what lot can be more perfect?

Rural Life of England, 1838

1 As you saw in the introduction, noblemen owned land. What else does Howitt say they owned?
2 Why is the church part of the estate?
3 What do you think Howitt means by saying 'the living is in his gift'? (Look up 'living' in a dictionary).
4 According to Howitt, what are the feelings a nobleman is likely to have as he goes to church?
5 What, in your opinion, should people think about as they go to church?

Here now is what it was like to be a visitor at a nobleman's house. The writer is a German, Prince Puckler-Muskau:

Strangers have generally only one room allotted to them. Englishmen seldom go into this room, except to sleep, and to dress twice a day; for all meals are taken in company and anyone who wants to write does it in the library. There, also, those who wish to converse arrange to meet, and you have an opportunity of gossiping for hours with the young ladies. Many a marriage is thus arranged or destroyed among the law books.

Ten or eleven is the hour for breakfast. It is, of course, very elegant and complete. The ladies do the honours very agreeably. If you come down later, when the breakfast is removed, a servant brings you what you want. In many houses he is on watch until one o'clock, or even later, to see the stragglers do not starve. Half-a-dozen newspapers lie on the table for everyone to read. The men now either go out hunting or shooting, or on business; the host does the same without troubling himself in the least about his guests (the truest kindness and good-breeding), and about half-an-hour before dinner the company meets again in the drawing room dressed most elegantly.

The course and order of the dinner I have already described to you. (Puckler-Muskau gives a long description of a dinner elsewhere in his book. You can find part of this description on page 104. When the meal was over, the ladies left to go to the drawing room; the men stayed at table for a time, talking and drinking.)

When the men have drunk as much as they wish, they go in search of tea, coffee, and the ladies, and remain for some hours with them, though without mixing much. Today, for instance, I observed the company was distributed in the following manner. Our suffering host lay on the sofa, dozing a little; five ladies and gentlemen were very attentively reading in various sorts of books; another had been playing for a quarter of an hour with a long-suffering dog; two old Members of Parliament were arguing violently about the Corn Bill; and the rest of the company was in a dimly-lighted room adjoining, where a pretty girl was playing on the piano, and another, with a most perforating voice, singing ballads.

A light supper of cold meats and fruits is brought, at which everyone helps himself, and shortly after midnight all retire.

At night, I had a most excellent chintz bed with a canopy. It was so enormously large that I lay like an icicle in it, for the distant fire was too remote to give me any feeling of warmth.

A Regency Visitor, The English Tour of Prince Puckler-Muskau, 1826–1828

1 How does a guest use his room?
2 Up until what time is it possible to have breakfast?
3 How would you expect a library to be used? How does Puckler-Muskau say the library of a great house is used?
4 How do the men spend the day?
5 What does the host do for his guests during the day? How does Puckler-Muskau feel about this? Do you agree with him?
6 Where does everyone go after dinner? What do they do there?
7 Why was Puckler-Muskau uncomfortable in bed?

Here is what William Howitt said about the way rich people enjoyed themselves:

If a gentleman is fond of field sports, racing, hunting, coursing, shooting, fishing, all offer themselves to his choice; the country sports, as everything else in English life, are so well organised; all their necessary equipment and implements are brought to such perfection, that the pleasures of the sportsman are made complete, and take place all the year round. Hunting, coursing, shooting each has its own season, its own particular horses, dogs and weapons.

Rural Life in England, 1838

1 Which sports does Howitt mention? What is 'coursing'? (Look up 'to course' in a dictionary.)
2 In what ways are field sports well-organised?
3 How can you tell that Howitt is a little too proud of his country?

Here is Puckler-Muskau's account of a day's hunting:

We had a fine day's hunting here. The weather was remarkably clear and sunny, and at least a hundred red coats took the field. Such a sight is certainly full of interest, the many fine horses; the elegantly dressed huntsmen; fifty or sixty beautiful hounds following Reynard over stock and stone; the wild, mounted troop behind; the rapid change of wood and hill and valley; the cries and shouts – it is miniature war.

The country here is very hilly, and at one time the hounds ran up so steep and long a hill, that most of the horses were unable to follow them, and those that did, panted like the bellows of a smithy. But when we had once reached the top, the view was glorious: you looked down upon the whole, from the fox to the last straggler, with one glance; and besides that, over the rich valley to the left, which extends to London, and to the right over the sea gleaming like a mirror beneath the bright sun.

The most striking thing, however, to German eyes, is the sight of the black-coated parsons, flying over hedge and ditch. I am told they often go to the church, ready booted and spurred, with the hunting whip in their hands, throw on the surplice, marry, christen or bury as fast as they can, jump on their horse at the church door and off – tally ho! They told me of a famous clergyman fox-hunter who always carried a tame fox in his pocket, so that if they did not find a wild one, they might be sure of a run. The animal was so well trained that he amused the hounds for a time; and when he was tired, took refuge in his safe hiding place – which was none other than the altar of the parish church. There was a hole broken for him in the church wall, and a comfortable bed made under the steps. This is right English religion.

A Regency Visitor, The English Tour of Prince Puckler-Muskau, 1826–1828

1 How can you tell Puckler-Muskau enjoyed his day's hunting?
2 What does he say about fox-hunting parsons? Do you think he approves of these men or not?

The best fox-hunting country in Britain was in Leicestershire. In 1822 Charles Apperley wrote:

Melton Mowbray generally contains from two to three hundred hunting horses, the average number being ten to each sportsman living there, although some who ride

Wife and son of an Aristocrat This is a painting of Frances Anne, Marchioness of Londonderry, by Sir Thomas Lawrence, 1827.

a lot, and have long purses, have from fourteen to twenty for their own use. The stud of the Earl of Plymouth for many years exceeded the last mentioned number. It may seem strange that one man should need so many horses just for his personal use; and it must be admitted that it is not necessary in many counties. In Leicestershire, however, every sportsman always has two horses in the field on the same day. This is found more economical in the long run as it is exhaustion from long-continued, severe work that most injures the health of horses. It must also be borne in mind that there is hunting every day of the week, that one horse out of every six is, upon an average, lame or otherwise unfit for work, and that a horse should always have at least seven or eight days' rest after a severe run with the hounds. It will not seem surprising, therefore, that ten or twelve hunters should be the minimum for a regular Leicestershire sportsman.

The sum total of expenses attending a stud of twelve hunters at Melton is, as nearly as can be estimated, one thousand pounds per annum. In all stables the average outlay for the purchase of horses is great – at least two hundred guineas each hunter; and, in some, the annual amount of wear and tear of horse flesh is considerable.

Charles James Apperley, alias 'Nimrod', *The Chase*. Article in the *'Quarterly Review'*, Vol 47 1822

1 Which Leicestershire town is the main centre for fox-hunting?
2 How many horses is a huntsman likely to have?
3 Explain why he needs so many.
4 Look at the wages of ordinary working folk on page 21. How long would each of them have to work to earn the money a nobleman might spend on hunting in one year?
5 How much was a hunter? Give the modern equivalent price by multiplying by 100.
6 What did Apperley mean by saying the 'wear and tear of horseflesh is considerable'?

During the winter, rich people went to fashionable towns like Bath, Cheltenham and Brighton. There they enjoyed themselves in all sorts of ways, but especially by going to balls. Here Puckler-Muskau describes some balls he attended at Brighton:

There are now private balls every evening; and in rooms to which a respectable German citizen would not invite twelve people, some hundreds are here packed like negro slaves. A ball without a crowd would be despised; and a visitor of any fashion who found the staircase empty, would probably drive away from the door.

When you are once in, however, I must confess that nowhere do you see a greater number of pretty girls, against whom you are squeezed, than here. Some of them have been educated for a year or two in France, and dress rather better than the others. Many of them speak German. A man may have as many invitations to parties of this sort as he likes, but if he does not stay long, he does not so much as see the hostess. Certainly she does not know half the people present. At one o'clock a very choice cold supper is served. The supper room is usually on the ground floor, and the table cannot contain above twenty persons at a time, so the company goes down in troops, and meets, pushing and elbowing on the narrow staircase. If you manage to find a seat you may rest a little, and many take advantage of this, without bothering about people waiting behind them; little attention is paid to giving place to the ladies. On the other hand, the servants are very active in replacing the dishes and bottles as soon as they are emptied.

In order to see the whole thing, I stayed till four in the morning in one of the best houses and found the end of the party, after most of the visitors were gone, the most agreeable; the more so as the daughters of the house were remarkably pretty, friendly girls. There were, however, some strange people at the ball; among others a fat lady of at least fifty-five, dressed in black velvet with white trimmings, and a turban with floating ostrich feathers, who waltzed like a Bacchante whenever she could find room. Her very pretty daughters tried in vain to rival their mamma.

The music in most of these balls was extremely meagre and bad. The musicians, however, contrive to produce such a noise with such instruments as they have, that you cannot hear yourself speak near them.

A Regency Visitor, The English Tour of Prince Puckler-Muskau, 1826–1828

1 What things does Puckler-Muskau dislike about English balls?
2 What does he like about them?
3 Why did the middle aged lady catch Puckler-Muskau's eye? What was her dancing like? (A 'Bacchante' is a follower of Bacchus, the god of wine.)

Written Work

You have been spending some time in the company of a great noble. Describe your experiences.

Research

1 Find out about some of the less desirable ways the English aristocrats enjoyed themselves e.g. gambling and duelling.
2 Some aristocrats were very serious minded. Read, for example, about Thomas William Coke, First Earl of Leicester and Anthony Ashley Cooper, Seventh Earl of Shaftesbury.

Prosperous Farmers

It is possible that in a Saxon village each farm was roughly a virgate of land. This was about 30 acres, which was enough for a family to grow all the food it needed. As time went on, though, some of the farms grew bigger, while others became smaller.

This was the position at Laxton, in Nottinghamshire in 1635:

Size in Acres	*Number of Farms*
Under 5	33
5–9	16
9–20	20
20–40	13
40–70	12
70–200	9
Over 200	3

1 How many Laxton farmers still had, roughly, a virgate of land in 1635?
2 How many had a good deal less than a virgate?
3 How many had a good deal more?
4 Show the information in the table in a bar diagram.
5 Why did farms change in size over the centuries, do you suppose?

A man with a large farm grew more food than he and his family could eat, so he sold his surplus. A man with a small farm could not grow enough food, so he worked part-time for a richer neighbour.

Then came the enclosure movement of the eighteenth and early nineteenth centuries. When that was over, most villages were no longer a mixture of farms of all sizes. For the most part, only large and medium ones remained and these were held by rich men. Nearly all the small farms vanished, and the men who had held them became full-time labourers.

Note: You can discover how that happened if you read *Oxford Junior History*, Book 4 *Britain becomes a Great Power*, Chapter One, Sections 5 and 6.

Here, we shall see what people thought of the change and also what kind of men the rich farmers were.

Farmer and Ploughman What is the cartoonist trying to say about farmers and the way they treat their labourers?

This is what William Cobbett wrote about a village in Hampshire:

The little village of Stoke Charity once contained ten farms, and it now contains but two. There used to be ten well-fed families in this parish at any rate; these, taking five to a family, made fifty well-fed people. And now all are half-starved, except the curate and the two families.
Rural Rides, 1822

1 How many farms were there in Stoke Charity? How many are there now?
2 How has the change affected the people of the village?

Cobbett also wrote:

I went to a sale at a farm, which the farmer is quitting. Here I had a view of what has long been going on all over the country. The farm had been held by a man of the name of Charington.

Everything about this farm-house was formerly the scene of plain manners and plentiful living. Oak clothes chests, oak bedsteads, oak chests of drawers, and oak tables to eat on, long, strong and well supplied with joint stools. Some of these things were many hundreds of years old. But all appeared to be in a state of decay and disuse. There appeared to have been hardly any family in that house, where formerly there were, in all probability, from ten to fifteen men, boys, and maids; and, which was the worst of all, there was a parlour. Aye, and a carpet and bell-pull too! One end of the front of this once plain and substantial house had been made into a 'parlour'! And there was the mahogany table, and the fine chairs, and the fine glass, and there were the decanters, the glasses, the dinner-set of crockery-ware. I dare say it had been *Squire* Charington and the *Miss* Charington's; and not plain Master Charington, and his son Hodge, and his daughter Betty Charington, all of whom this accursed system has turned into mock gentlefolks, while it has ground the labourers down into real slaves.

The land produces what it always produced, but that produce is now shared differently. Why do not farmers now feed and lodge their work-people, as they did formerly? Because it costs more to feed them, than to pay them wages. This is the real cause of the change. This Squire Charington's father used, I dare say, to sit at the head of the oak table along with his men, say grace to them, and cut up the meat and pudding. He might take a cup of strong beer to himself, when they had done; but that was pretty nearly all the difference in their manner of living. So that *all* lived well. But the squire had many wine decanters and wine glasses and a 'dinner set' and a 'breakfast set' and dessert knives. Paying for the fine meals that went with them meant there was not enough money to feed the workers at the long oak table. That long table could not share in the work of the decanters and the dinner set. Therefore, it became almost untenanted; the labourers retreated to hovels called cottages; and instead of board and lodging, they got money; so little of it as to enable the employer to drink wine.

When the old farm-houses are down (and down they must come in time) what a miserable thing the country will be! Those that are now erected are mere painted shells, with a mistress within, who is stuck up in a place she calls a parlour, with, if she have children, 'young ladies and gentlemen' about her; some showy chairs and a sofa; half a dozen prints in gilt frames hanging up: some book shelves with novels and tracts upon them: a dinner brought in by a girl that is perhaps better 'educated' than she: two or three nick-nacks to eat instead of a piece of bacon and a pudding: the house too neat for a dirty shoed carter to be allowed to come into: and everything proclaiming that there is here a wish to make a *show*. The children are all too clever to work: they are all to be gentlefolks. Go to plough! Good God! What, 'young gentlemen' go to plough! They become *clerks*, or some skimmy-dish thing or other. They flee from the dirty work as cunning horses do from the bridle.

Rural Rides, 1822

1 Cobbett is making a contrast between the old days and his own times. What changes have taken place? Deal with this question under the headings:

a Farm house furniture
b The farm house building
c Inhabitants of the farm house
d Meals in the farm house
e Occupations of the farmer's sons.

Threshing by machine What three pieces of equipment are in use? How many men are at work? They will finish threshing in three days. To thresh the wheat with the flail would take six men three months. The farmer pays a man 10p a day. How much have the machines saved him in wages? During the 'Swing Riots' of 1830 many threshing machines were smashed. Who broke them, do you think, and why?

2 Read the account of the farm worker's breakfast on page 103. Would Cobbett have approved of this? Give reasons for your answer.
3 Make a list of the things which Cobbett disliked about the Charingtons.
4 How many of them seem wrong to you? (You and your family may be guilty of some of them!)
5 Why did Cobbett object to them? (Look especially at the end of the second paragraph).

Arthur Young wrote this after a visit to Norfolk:

In talking with Mr. Thurtell, on the size of farms, he remarked that nothing could, in his opinion, be more absurd than the prejudice against large farms. From what he had seen, large farms produce on every acre much more food for people to eat than small ones; that improvements, if they arise at all, must be from large farmers, who are able, and now-a-days willing, to make experiments.

The vast improvements that have been made in Norfolk by converting boundless heaths, sheep walks and warrens, into well-cultivated districts, by enclosing and marling, are such as were never yet made by small farmers. Great farmers have converted in this country, three or four hundred thousand acres of wastes into fertile land; little farmers have never, in any country that I know, produced equal effects.

Agriculture of Norfolk, 1813

1 Why, according to Mr. Thurtell, are large farms better than small ones?
2 What improvements have large farmers made in Norfolk?
3 Does Arthur Young think small farmers could have done as well?

In 1811 a Scottish farmer called Robert Brown wrote a book on farming. In it he said:

An improved system of farming requires that the farm upon which it is to be carried on should be of a good size, otherwise there is not enough room for all the crops that are necessary for proper management. The farmer who practises husbandry in the proper way, should not only have his fields under all sorts of grain, but likewise enough grass and winter crops to keep his cattle and sheep through all the different seasons of the year.

Treatise on Rural Affairs, 1811

1 Why does Robert Brown think that large farms are necessary?

The following extract is part of an agreement signed by a man called George Fry when he rented a farm of 110 acres in Dorset:

The arable lands are to be managed according to the four field System which is as follows. That not more than one fourth part of the arable Lands shall be sown with wheat in any one year, and that after such a crop shall have been so taken, the same Lands shall be sown with Oats. And with such oats shall be sown to each acre of the said land not less than 3 bushels of Rye Grass seeds and ten pounds weight of good broad-leafed clover seeds, this shall remain in lay for the space of one year before the same be broken up. When the same be again broken up such Land shall be summer fallowed and the same system again pursued thereon. But if the Tenant chooses to sow any part of the summer fallow to Turnips and feed the same off when green with sheep in time to sow the Land to Wheat, he shall be at Liberty to do so.

Lease of Snelling Farm, near Blandford, 1830

Notes: 'Lay' is grassland which is ploughed for crops after a short time.

'Fallow' is land which is not growing anything, but is having a rest for a year, or most of a year.

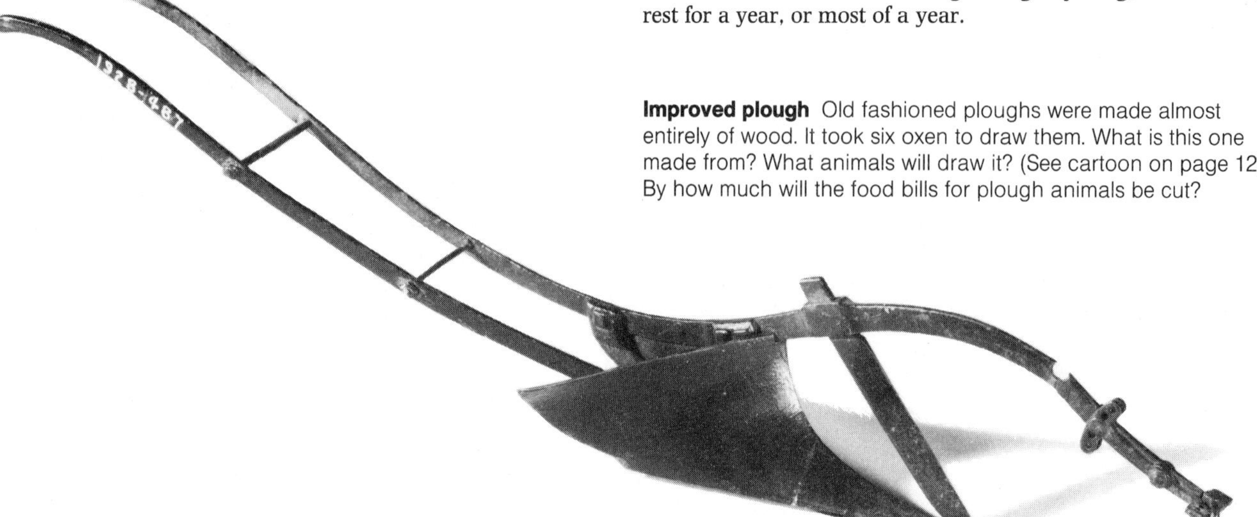

Improved plough Old fashioned ploughs were made almost entirely of wood. It took six oxen to draw them. What is this one made from? What animals will draw it? (See cartoon on page 12). By how much will the food bills for plough animals be cut?

Steam ploughing Here is another use for the steam engine which you saw on page 13. How does the system work? What will happen when the plough reaches the right hand side of the field?

1 What crops does George Fry promise to grow?
2 In what order must he grow them on any one field?
3 Which crop would he have sold? Which crops would he have kept to feed to his cattle?
4 Does this lease bear out what Robert Brown said, in the last document?

Here now is a description of the farm of Sir John Conroy in Berkshire. The writer is James Caird:

The farm of Sir John Conroy, at Arborfield Hall, about four miles to the south-east of Reading, comprises about 320 acres, exclusive of the park surrounding the mansion. Four years ago every acre of the land was drained with pipes laid four feet deep, the drains being 15 feet apart. Immediately following the drainers, the whole farm was trenched by forks to a depth of 22 inches. The cost of both operations, drainage and trenching, was nearly £12 an acre – so that, if there has been a great improvement, it must not be forgotten that it has been done at great cost. Farm roads were made at the same time and commodious farm buildings were also erected.

Next the rickyard is the barn, the whole machinery of which is driven by a ten-horse steam engine. The thrashing machine is fitted with an excellent shaker by Garrett, which at once separates the grain from the straw. The straw is then passed to a cutter by which it is cut either into 4 inch lengths for litter, or into $\frac{1}{2}$ inch lengths for food. A corn and cake bruiser and turnip cutter are also attached to the engine when required.

An eating-room, with benches and a table, is provided for the people to eat their midday meal. Here there is a fire for cooking and a washhand basin in the corner. The workers are managed with as much order and precision as the rest of the farm. They are engaged by the week, the present rate of wages being ten shillings (50p). They are paid every Saturday in small silver so that they have no need to go for change to the public house. A serious fault is never passed over: no quarrelling or swearing is permitted to any person engaged on the farm. Should there be any serious misconduct or neglect of duty, the offender receives with his pay on Saturday, a notice that his services are no longer needed. All over-time is paid for and every man made to feel that while he must do exactly as he is told, he is, at the same time, treated with perfect fairness. I can bear witness to the intelligent appearance of the men, and the cheerful spirit they were showing.

English Agriculture, 1850–1851

1 What sort of house did Sir John Conroy have? What would Cobbett have said about that?
2 How did Sir John Conroy improve his land?
3 How much did this cost him in all? How much would that be in modern money? (Multiply by 100).
4 How else did he improve his farm?
5 What machinery is there in the barn?
6 Could a small farmer, with much less money, have been as efficient as Sir John Conroy?
7 What has Sir John Conroy provided for his workers?
8 How much does he pay them?
9 How does he make sure they behave themselves and work hard?
10 How do Sir John Conroy's men feel about working for him?
11 How do you think Sir John Conroy would have answered Cobbett's criticism of the Charingtons? (Pages 12–13).

Farmer and farm worker Compare and contrast this drawing with the cartoon on page 12. Which do you think Mary Russell Mitford would approve of?

Finally, here is a description of a large farm and its owner written by Mary Russell Mitford:

Passing up the lane we used first to meet a thick, solid suburb of ricks, of all sorts, shapes and dimensions. Then came the farm, like a town; a magnificient series of buildings, stables, cart-houses, cow-houses, granaries and barns, that might hold half the corn of the parish, placed at all angles towards each other, and mixed with smaller habitations for pigs, dogs and poultry. They formed, together with the old farm-house, a sort of amphitheatre, looking over a beautiful meadow, richly set with hedge-row timber, oak, ash and elm. Both the meadow and the farm-yard swarmed with horses, oxen, cows, calves, heifers, sheep and pigs; beautiful grey-hounds, all manner of poultry, a tame goat and a pet donkey.

The master of this land of plenty was well fitted to preside over it; a thick, stout man of middle height, and middle aged, with a healthy, ruddy, square face, all alive with intelligence and good humour. He wore his dark, shining hair, combed straight over his forehead, and had a trick, when particularly merry, of stroking it down with his hand. The moment his hand approached his head, out flew a jest. He had always leisure to receive his friends at home, or to visit them abroad; to take journeys to London or make excursions to the sea-side; was as punctual in pleasure as in business, and thought being happy and making happy as much the purpose of his life as getting rich.

His wife was like her husband, with a difference. Like him in looks, only thinner and paler; like him in voice and phrase, only not so loud; like him in merriment and good humour, like him in her talent of welcoming and making happy, and being kind.

Her pets were her cows, her poultry, her bees and her flowers. The farm yard swarmed with peacocks, turkeys, geese, tame and wild ducks, fowls, guinea-hens and pigeons; besides a brood or two of favourite bantams in the green court before the door.

Next to her poultry, our good farmer's wife loved her flower-garden; and indeed it was of the very best. She was a real, genuine florist. I liked the bees' garden the best; the plot of ground immediately round their hives, filled with common flowers for their use.

To come back to our farm. Within doors everything went as well as without. It was closely packed with favourite arm-chairs, favourite sofas, favourite tables, and a side-board decorated with the prize cups and collars of the greyhounds, and generally loaded with substantial work baskets, jars of flowers, great pyramids of home-made cakes, and sparkling bottles of gooseberry wine, famous all over the country. The walls were covered with portraits of half-a-dozen greyhounds, a brace of spaniels as large as life, an old pony and the master and mistress of the house in half-length.

Our Village, 1848

1 To what does Miss Mitford compare the rick yard and the farm?
2 What farm buildings were there?
3 What animals were there?
4 What kind of man was the farmer?
5 What kind of woman was his wife? What did she enjoy doing?
6 What things were there in the farm house?
7 In what way is Miss Mitford's account the same as Cobbett's?
8 How are the two accounts different?

Written Work

1 Write your own description of a large farm in the early nineteenth century. Use the headings:
   - **a** Fields and their crops.
   - **b** Animals.
   - **c** Farm buildings.
   - **d** The farm house.
   - **e** The farmer and his family. Include the way he treats his workers.

   Remember that there are some different points of view in the documents, so you must decide between them.
2 How did large farms help the country as a whole, more than small ones would have done? (Look at the population figures on page 6).

Research

The period 1850–1875 has been called the 'Golden Age of British Farming'. Find out what you can about it.

Farm Labourers

Very few of the people living in the countryside were great landowners or rich farmers. Most of them were humble farm labourers. Their numbers were growing, especially between about 1750 and 1850. There were two reasons for this. In the first place the population of Britain was increasing. It was the towns which grew the fastest, it is true, but there were plenty more people in the countryside as well. Secondly, small farmers found it difficult to make a living in competition with men like Sir John Conroy, whom you read about in the previous section. As a result, many of them gave up their farms, and became labourers. In this section we will see how farm labourers lived.

In 1842, a doctor wrote this about Cerne Abbas which, today, is one of the most beautiful villages in Dorset:

Most of the cottages are of the worst kind; some were mud hovels with cesspools or piles of filth close to the doors. The mud floors of many are much below the level of the road and in wet seasons are little better than so much clay. In many of the cottages I visited, the beds stood on the ground floor, which was damp three parts of the year; scarcely one had a fireplace in the bedroom, and one had a single, small pane of glass stuck in the mud wall as its only window, with a large heap of wet and dirty potatoes in one corner. Persons living in such cottages are generally very poor, very dirty and usually in rags, living almost wholly on bread and potatoes.

I have often seen springs bursting through the mud floors of some of the cottages, and little channels cut from the centre under the doorways to carry off the water,

Dorset farm labourer's living room Probably the cottage would have only one other room, the bedroom. How does this cottage compare with those at Cerne Abbas? (See the extract on this page).

whilst the door had been removed from its hinges for the children to put their feet on whilst making buttons.

Report on the Sanitary Condition of the Labouring Population of Great Britain, Edwin Chadwick, 1842

1 Make a list of the reasons why the cottages of Cerne Abbas were uncomfortable and unhealthy.
2 What did the inhabitants wear? What did they eat?

In the 1840's, Lord Ashley, later the Seventh Earl of Shaftesbury, was having a great deal to say about the bad state of the towns. He strongly criticised the slum houses in which factory workers had to live. Then, in 1843, a Poor Law official visited a cottage in the village of Stourpaine in Dorset, which belonged to Lord Ashley's father, the Sixth Earl of Shaftesbury. It became famous all over England, for certain factory owners made sure that the report on it was published in the newspapers. The cottage had only a living room and a bedroom. This is what the bedroom was like:

The room was ten feet square, not reckoning the two recesses by the sides of the chimney, about 18 inches deep. The roof was of thatch, the middle of the chamber being about seven feet high. Opposite the fire-place was a small window, about 15 inches square, the only one to the room. Bed *A* was occupied by the father and mother, a little boy, Jeremiah, aged $1\frac{1}{2}$ years and an infant, aged four months. Bed *B* was occupied by the three daughters – the two eldest, Sarah and Elizabeth, twins, aged 20; and Mary, aged 7. Bed *C* was occupied by the four sons – Silas, aged 17; John, aged 15; James, aged 14; and Elias, aged 10.

Report on the Employment of Women and Children in Agriculture, 1843

1 How many people slept in this bedroom?
2 How many square feet was the room?
3 How many square feet were there for each person? How many square feet do you have for yourself in your own bedroom?
4 Why did the factory owners want everyone in England to know about this cottage, do you suppose?

Cobbett described some labourers he saw in Wiltshire:

The labourers along here seem very poor indeed. Farm houses with twenty ricks round each, besides those standing in the fields; pieces of wheat 50, 60 or 100 acres in a piece; but a group of women labourers presented

Gleaning These children have been gleaning. What is that? How does it compare with the other jobs children had to do?

such an assemblage of rags as I never before saw. I never before saw country people so miserable in appearance as these. There were some very pretty girls, but ragged as colts and pale as ashes. The day was cold too, and frost hardly off the ground; and their blue arms and lips would have made any heart ache.

Rural Rides, November 1821

1 Why were these labourers miserable?
2 Why does Cobbett mention the ricks and wheat fields?

Here is another extract from Cobbett:

I have seen no wretchedness in Sussex: nothing to be at all compared to that which I have seen in other parts: and as to thcsc villagcs in the South Downs, they are beautiful to behold. There is an appearance of comfort about the dwellings of the labourers all along here. The gardens are neat and full of vegetables of the best kinds. I see very few of 'Ireland's lazy root'. As I came along between Upwaltham and Eastdean, I called to me a young man, who, along with other turnip-hoers, was sitting under a hedge at breakfast. He came running to me with his victuals in his hand; and I was glad to see that his food consisted of a good lump of household bread, and a not very small piece of bacon.

I saw, and with great delight, a pig at almost every labourer's house. The houses are good and warm; and the gardens some of the best I have seen in England. What a difference! Good God! what a difference between this country and the neighbourhood of those corrupt places Great Bedwyn and Cricklade! What sort of *breakfast* would this man have had in a mess of *cold potatoes*? Could he have *worked*, and worked in the wet, too, with such food? Monstrous! No society ought to exist where the labourers live in a hog-like sort of way.

Rural Rides, August 1823

1 Which part of England is Cobbett describing?
2 What does he say about the cottages and their gardens?
3 What food was the farm worker eating? What did Cobbett think of it for a breakfast?
4 What does Cobbett think of potatoes? Find out what food value potatoes have and decide whether he was right.
5 What does he mean by labourers living 'in a hog-like sort of way'?

Here now is a statement made by Robert Bowman, a farmer from Calne, in Wiltshire:

In my opinion, the very best thing for a young boy, the child of a farm labourer, is to be employed on the same farm with his father: he is learning his work, and is well looked after by both father and master. Nothing can happen to a young boy so advantageous as to be so placed out.

I have always had a boy or two to work for me. I think the work improves their health. I generally take them about seven years old, and keep them till twelve, and then if they can get a more profitable place elsewhere, I let them go. At twelve they have learned a deal of useful knowledge when they are in good hands.

Looking at what boys learn at school, and seeing that now they learn as much at seven or eight as some years ago they did at twelve or fourteen, I think that putting them to work at seven or eight is the very best thing for them, though it necessarily takes them from the day school. They lose school instruction, certainly, but I think the knowledge they get of their future occupation quitc compensates for such loss. According to my experience, I find a boy beginning as early as seven or eight gets a more thorough knowledge of every part of the work wanted about a farm. When he grows up, he can turn his hand to everything that is wanted. But a boy who begins at thirteen, fourteen or fifteen, never gets beyond a common labourer.

From the time I take a young boy, he works the same hours as a man, but his work is very light; it can hardly be called work; it is only some little matter to occupy him.

Pulling beet This was always hard, miserable work. When would it be particularly unpleasant?

I begin by paying him 1/6 (7½p) a week. His wages go on increasing, till at 12 years old I give him 2/6 (12½p) a week. From the first of his coming to me he is, you may say, off his father's hands. In the great majority of cases the labourer's family has only the man's wages, 8/- or 9/- (40p or 45p) a week to live on. It is a great thing, therefore, for the family if one or more of the children are employed.

Report on the Employment of Women and Children in Agriculture, 1843

1 What ages are the boys Robert Bowman employs?
2 Why does he say it is good for boys to go to work?
3 How does he feel about them missing school?
4 What wages does Bowman pay his boys?
5 How does he say their wages help their families?
6 Do you think we should believe everything Bowman says? Give your reasons for your answer.

Next, we have a statement made by a farm boy from Kent. His name is James Orton and he is 14. James's statement reads a little strangely in some places, because he is answering questions which are not printed in the document. With a little imagination you can guess what they were:

My father is dead. I work in the fields when I can get work. The day before yesterday I was digging; I dig from daylight till dark. I have an hour for dinner in the middle of the day. I breakfast before I start, and earn 8d (3p) in the day. In the summer, when the wheat is up, I weed the corn; I get 6d (2½p) a day for that. I sometimes lead the horse at plough, and get 8d. I get 6d only for couching; it is not so hard as digging or leading the horse at plough. I could not get any bird scaring this year; 6d is the price of that a day. I get 8d at poling, for laying the poles. I picked hops; I do not know how much I got for that. I have had no digging in the hop-grounds since my father died. I cut wheat and beans this year with my mother; I do not know how much my mother got; I have set potatoes for 8d a day. I keep sheep sometimes for 6d. I don't remember what I got for clearing the ground for hops. Last summer I got 3/6 (17½p) a week for keeping cows in the stables, milking and feeding them. I have got 6d a day for topping and pulling up turnips. My mother has relief from the parish; I do not know how much. I have always three meals in the day; I have bread and meat for dinner, and bread and cheese for breakfast, and bread and cheese for supper. When I am not at work I do not often get bread and meat for dinner. It is ever so long

Women harvesting The reaper has cut the wheat. What are the women going to do with it? Why does no-one do this work today? How many people can you see in the field? How many would there be at harvest time today? It used to be very unfashionable to have a suntan. How can you tell that?

since I went to school. I left off going to school before my father died, when I was about eight years old. I cannot read. I do not know the names of the months. I have good health; I have never any pains. When I do not work, I go out to play; I had rather work than play. You get more victuals when you work.

Report on the Employment of Women and Children in Agriculture, 1843

Note: 'Couching' means pulling up a weed called 'couch grass'. Having 'relief from the parish' was like drawing National Assistance today.

1 Make a list of the jobs which James has done and say, where possible, how much he earned for each.
2 What hours does he work?
3 What food does he have?
4 Does James prefer to work or play? Why?
5 From what James says, was Robert Bowman right about children's education?

Here is a statement by Mrs. Britton, the wife of a farm labourer from Calne:

My husband is an agricultural labourer. I have seven children, all boys. The oldest is fourteen, the youngest nine months old. My husband is a good workman, and earns from 9/- to 10/- (45p to 50p) a week pretty constantly, but finds his own tools, – his wheelbarrow, which cost £1, pickaxe, which cost 3/- (15p) and scoop which cost 3/-.

I have worked in the fields and when I went out I left the children in the care of the eldest boy, and frequently carried the baby with me, as I could not go home to nurse it. I have worked at hay-making and harvest, and at other times in weeding and keeping the ground clean. I generally work from half-past seven till five or half-past. When at work in the spring I have received 10d (4p) a day, but that is higher than the wages of women in general; 8d or 9d is more common. I am always better when I can get out to work in the fields. I intend to do so next year if I can. Last year I could not go out owing to the birth of the baby. My eldest boy gets a little to do; he don't earn more than 9d a week; he has not enough to do. My husband has 40 lugs of land for which he pays 10/- a year. We grow potatoes and a few cabbages, but not enough for our family; for that we should like to have 40 lugs more. We have to buy potatoes. One of the children is a cripple and the guardians allow us two gallons of bread a week for him. We buy two gallons more according as the money is. Nine people can't do with less than four gallons of bread a week. We could eat more bread if we could get it; sometimes we can afford only one gallon a week. We very rarely buy butcher's meat, certainly not oftener than once a week, and not more than six penny worth. I like my husband to have a bit of meat now he has left off drinking. I buy ½lb of butter a week, 10oz tea, ½lb sugar. The rest of our food is potatoes, with a little fat. The rent of our cottage is 1/6 (7½p) a week; there are two rooms in it. We all sleep in one room, under the tiles. Sometimes we receive private assistance, especially in clothing.

Report on the Employment of Women and Children in Agriculture, 1843

Notes: 'Lug' is a dialect word meaning a rod, pole or perch. The 'guardians' were the poor law authorities. The help they gave was like the National Assistance we have today. A 'gallon loaf' weighed about 9 pounds.

1 How many people are there in the Britton family?
2 How much does Mr. Britton earn? What expenses has he?
3 What work does Mrs. Britton do? What hours does she work?
4 What does the family have to live on, apart from Mr. and Mrs. Britton's wages? (What does Mrs. Britton mean by 'private assistance'?)
5 What expense does the family no longer have?
6 How does their house compare with the ones described earlier?

This is the weekly budget of Robert Crick and his family (converted to modern currency). Robert was a farm worker from Suffolk:

	Age	*Earnings*	*Expenses*	
Robert Crick	42	45p	Bread	45p
Wife	40	4p	Potatoes	5p
Boy	12	10p	Butter	2p
Boy	11	5p	Cheese	1p
Boy	8	5p	Tea	1p
Girl	6	nil	Sugar	1½p
Boy	4	nil	Salt	¼p
			Soap	1p
Total		69p	Blue	¼p
			Thread etc.	1p
			Candles	1p
			Coal and wood	4p
			Rent	6p
			Total	69p

Report on the Employment of Women and Children in Agriculture, 1843

Note: 'Blue' was used in washing. White articles look brighter if they are very slightly blue in colour.

Hedging The man would say he was 'laying' the hedge? Why? Some of the people who objected to enclosures said they caused unemployment. What does this picture suggest? Why are modern farmers grubbing up their hedges?

1 Would you say, from what is in the other documents, that this budget is correct?
2 What proportion of the family income is earned by the children?
3 How long does Robert Crick have to work to pay for the family's bread? How long does your father or mother have to work to pay for your family's bread?
4 Draw a pie diagram to show what proportions of the Crick's money went on food, other household goods, heating and lighting, and rent.
5 Ask your parents if they will draw a similar pie diagram for their own expenses. (They may have a mortgage instead of paying rent).
6 What important item is missing from the Crick's budget?
7 Which of Robert Bowman's remarks (pages 19–20) does this budget confirm?

Written Work

Write a description of how farm labourers lived in the early nineteenth century. First of all decide on suitable headings, such as houses, clothes, food etc. Then gather together all the information you can from the documents, and arrange it under your headings.

Research

1 Find out what you can about
   a The 'Swing Riots' of 1830.
   b The Tolpuddle Martyrs.
   c Joseph Arch and the National Agricultural Labourers' Union.
2 Find out how well-off farm workers are today, compared with workers in industry.

Chapter 2 *Industry*

Children in the Coal Mines

Today, coal is very important, especially as fuel for power stations. In the early nineteenth century there was no oil or North Sea gas, so coal was even more important then. You can see some of its uses in this and the next chapter.

Coal lies in the ground in seams, rather like the layers of cream in a sponge. The diagram shows you how it was mined:

a Shaft. This is the way in and out of the mine. It could be anything up to 2,000 feet deep. (St. Paul's Cathedral is 365 feet high).

b Underground tunnels, known as 'gates' in the north of England. They grow longer as more coal is dug. They are as high as the coal seams, which is anything from eighteen inches to six feet or more.

c Coal face. This is where the coal is dug.

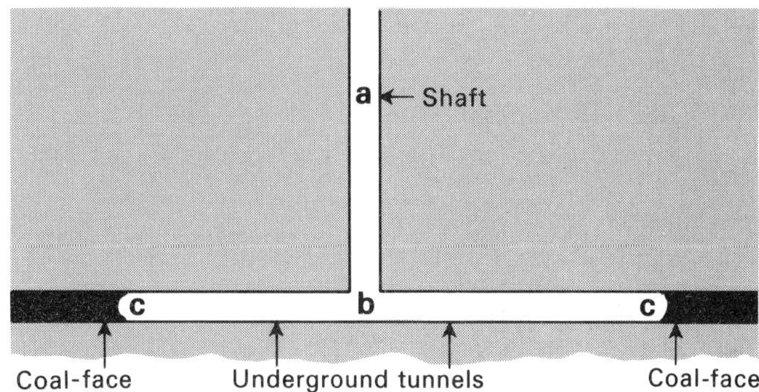

Diagram of a Coal Mine

Winning coal The man is undercutting the coal with his pick axe. The boy is drilling a hole at the top of the seam. When they have finished they will put a small charge of gunpowder in the hole and explode it. What will this do? What will their next job be?

Lord Shaftesbury visiting a mine The boy is a 'hurrier'. What is his job? (See below). What kind of report did Lord Shaftesbury make of his visit, do you suppose?

The man who owned the coal mine hired 'hewers' to work for him. They dug the coal and loaded it into little trucks called 'corves'. Hurriers then dragged them to the bottom of the shaft and they were wound to the surface. The hurriers were the wives and children of the hewers. They had to work hard, because the hewers were paid by the amount of coal they sent out of the pit. There were unpleasant rumours about what went on in the mines so in 1842 Parliament appointed some inspectors to visit them and write a report. This is what a boy called William Dyson told an inspector:

'I am a hurrier. I am fourteen years old and I have been employed ever since I was six. I come to work at seven o'clock, and sometimes leave at four, five or six in the evening in summer, and in the winter near seven. I live half a mile from the pit. I get my breakfast before I go to the pit and take my dinner with me, which is a dry muffin. I have not time to get my dinner in the pit, but eat it on my way home. I have nothing to drink. When I get home I sometimes get potatoes and meat. Our workings from the shaft are 500 yards and I have to hurry the corves full that distance and bring them back empty. I have to hurry so many corves a day, depending on orders for coal.

We have but one girl working with us, by name Ann Ambler. She gets 6/- (30p) a week. She hurries by herself and has to hurry the same weight and distance as I have; there is not a bit of difference between any of us. I have seen her thrashed many times when she does not please the hewers: they rap her in the face and knock her down. She does not like the work, she does not that. I have seen her cry many times.'

Report of Children's Employment Commission (Mines), 1842

1. At what age did William Dyson start work?
2. What are his hours of work? Why are they longer in winter do you suppose?
3. How far does he live from the pit?
4. What problem does he have with meals?
5. How far does he take the corves?
6. Why is he busier some days than others?
7. What are Ann Ambler's wages?
8. How does her work compare with William's?
9. Why do you think the hewers might be angry with Ann? (Remember how they were paid).
10. In what ways is the hurrier's work unpleasant?

A Turn Wheel The cutaway illustration shows Ann Ambler and William Dyson being wound up the shaft.

One of the inspectors who visited the mines was called Scriver. This is what he said about the gates, or tunnels, along which the children hauled coal:

'I know but two gates large enough to allow the use of horses, which is why children have to do the work. In some of them I have had to creep upon my hands and knees the whole distance, the height being barely twenty inches, and then have gone still lower upon my breast and crawled like a turtle. In others I have been able to make my journey by stooping.

They are sometimes of great length. In the Booth Town Pit, I walked and crept 1,800 yards to one of the nearest faces. The floor of this gate was every here and there three or four inches deep in water and muddy throughout.

The roofs and walls are at some places even, at others rough, rocky and loose, needing proppings to support them: despite, however, every care, large masses sometimes fall, burying the children.'

1. Why do children rather than horses haul the coal?
2. How long are some of the gates? (How many yards are there in a mile?).
3. Why was it unpleasant to go along the gates?
4. Why was it dangerous?

The larger mines had steam engines to wind coal and people up the shaft. A small mine would have a turn-wheel, like the one shown in the picture. Here is what Scriver said about it:

'The turn wheel is certainly dangerous as you depend all the time on the man or woman who works it. The unfortunate case of David Pellett who was drawn over the roller by his own uncle and grandfather just at the moment when a passing funeral caught their attention shows how unsafe it is.

The sketch shows Ann Ambler and William Dyson being drawn up on the clatch iron. As soon as they arrived at the top, the handle was made fast by a bolt drawn from the upright post; the woman then grasped a hand of both at the same time and by main force brought them to land'.

1. How was David Pellett killed?
2. What happened when Ann and William reached the top of the shaft?
3. What danger were they in at that moment?
4. What would happen if the rope was jerked and they started to swing on the way up?

A woman coal bearer This way of carrying coal was common in Scotland. The basket is called a 'creel' and to stop it slipping a 'tug' passes round the woman's forehead. How much do you think the coal weighs? Probably, it is the woman's husband who has put this coal on her back. Fathers loaded their daughters in the same way.

As you have seen, miners faced many dangers, but what they dreaded most was an explosion. If a pit was not well ventilated it might fill with a gas called methane, or 'fire damp.' This is what could happen as a result:

> 'Explosions from fire damp are common in deep mines. One which happened near Newcastle was very remarkable: 70 men were blown out of the pit and a large piece of timber about ten yards long and ten inches thick was blown a considerable distance and stuck into the side of a hill.'
>
> *A Treatise on Coal Mines*, Dr. William Sharp, 1769

Now study this table:

Deaths in Mines in Great Britain 1838

	Age		
Cause of Death	Under 13	13–18	Over 18
Fell down shaft	14	16	36
Drawn over pulley	3	—	3
Fall of stone down the shaft	1	—	3
Drowned	3	4	15
Fall of stones or coal	14	14	69
Crushed	—	1	1
Explosion of gas	13	18	49
Suffocated	—	2	6
Explosions of gunpowder	—	1	3
By tram waggons	4	5	12

1 Add up the number of people killed for each cause.
2 Arrange the totals in numerical order of importance.
3 How many people died in all?

Written Work

Describe the life of a child coal miner in the early nineteenth century. You should say what it was like down a coal mine, what work children did, what their hours and wages were, and what dangers they faced.

Research

1 What invention did Sir Humphry Davy make in 1815? (See front cover).
2 After it received the report of the *Children's Employment Commission (Mines)* in 1842, Parliament passed a Mines Act in the same year. Find out what it said.
3 If you live in a mining district find out what you can about your local coal mines especially their history. Are there any reminders of accidents, such as graves in the churchyard?

The Cotton Factories

Before the nineteenth century, most of the goods produced in Britain were made by people working in their own homes, or in small workshops. Then in the late eighteenth and early nineteenth centuries a number of machines were invented to spin and weave cotton. They needed powerful water wheels or steam engines to drive them which, of course, people could not have at home. As a result, cotton manufacturers began to build factories.

Manchester cotton factory, about 1830 How does this factory compare with those we have today? Why did the owner choose to build his factory here, do you suppose?

Today, we are used to factories, but in the early nineteenth century they were new. Never before had there been huge buildings in which hundreds of people worked regular hours, tending machines. Almost everyone was interested, some were suspicious, and some, hostile. William Cobbett who had never seen any factories, gave a popular idea of them:

> Some of these lords of the loom have in their employ thousands of miserable creatures. In the cotton spinning work these creatures are kept fourteen hours in each day, locked up, summer and winter, in a heat of 80 to 84 degrees. The rules which they are subjected to are such as no negro slaves were ever subjected to.
>
> Observe, too, that these poor creatures have no cool

room to retreat to, not a moment to wipe off the sweat, and not a breath of air to come between them and infection. The door of the place wherein they work is locked, except half an hour at tea time; the workpeople are not allowed to send for water to drink. If any spinner be found with his window open, he is to pay a fine of a shilling.

Not only is there not a breath of sweet air in these truly infernal scenes but, for a large part of the time, there is the abominable stink of the gas, mixed with the steam, there are the dust and what is called cotton flyings, which the unfortunate creatures have to inhale: and the fact is, the notorious fact is, that well constituted men are rendered old and past labour at forty years of age, and that children are rendered decrepit and deformed, and thousands of them are slaughtered by consumption before they arrive at the age of sixteen.

William Cobbett, *Political Register* Volume 152, November 20th, 1824

1 How many people does Cobbett say one manufacturer may employ?
2 Make a list of the ways in which Cobbett says the factories are unpleasant.
3 What rules does Cobbett say the workers must obey? Can you find them in the rules on the opposite page?
4 What does he say happens to many people, as a result of working in the factories?
5 What does Cobbett think of factory owners?

Parliament was worried about the new factories, and appointed several Commissions of Inquiry. Members of the Commissions visited factories and wrote reports. Here is what two of the workers told a Commissioner. Their employer was Archibald Buchanan, whose mill was at Catrine, near Ayr:

I have been a great many years in the dressing room. There are fanners (extractor fans) in it, but there is a good deal of dust in taking out the coarse cotton. My breath is away sometimes with the cough, and it is especially bad in the night.

Evidence of Mary Black

I have been 26 years overseer of the web dressing apartment in the power-loom weaving mill: the heat required for the work of that room is from 80 degrees to 90 degrees, but I have seen the thermometer rise to 92. There are eight women in the apartment and nine children. I think the effect of the heat is to make the females a little pale like, while they are in. I do not think their general health is affected by the heat.

Evidence of James Skinan

1 Which two problems are mentioned here?
2 Had the owner of the mill done anything about either problem?
3 How far would these two workers have agreed with Cobbett?

Scutching This is the first job in the factory. The cotton arrives, packed tightly in bales, and this machine loosens it.

RULES
TO BE OBSERVED
By the Hands Employed in
THIS MILL.

RULE 1. All the Overlookers shall be on the premises first and last.

2. Any Person coming too late shall be fined as follows:—for 5 minutes 2d, 10 minutes 4d, and 15 minutes 6d, &c.

3. For any Bobbins found on the floor 1d for each Bobbin.

4. For single Drawing, Slubbing, or Roving 2d for each single end.

5. For Waste on the floor 2d.

6. For any Oil wasted or spilled on the floor 2d each offence, besides paying for the value of the Oil.

7. For any broken Bobbins, they shall be paid for according to their value, and if there is any difficulty in ascertaining the guilty party, the same shall be paid for by the whole using such Bobbins.

8. Any person neglecting to Oil at the proper times shall be fined 2d.

9. Any person leaving their Work and found Talking with any of the other workpeople shall be fined 2d for each offence.

10. For every Oath or insolent language, 3d for the first offence, and if repeated they shall be dismissed.

11. The Machinery shall be swept and cleaned down every meal time.

12. All persons in our employ shall serve Four Weeks' Notice before leaving their employ; but L. WHITAKER & SONS, shall and will turn any person off without notice being given.

13. If two persons are known to be in one Necessary together they shall be fined 3d each; and if any Man or Boy go into the Women's Necessary he shall be instantly dismissed.

14. Any person wilfully or negligently breaking the Machinery, damaging the Brushes, making too much Waste, &c., they shall pay for the same to its full value.

15. Any person hanging anything on the Gas Pendants will be fined 2d.

16. The Masters would recommend that all their workpeople Wash themselves every morning, but they shall Wash themselves at least twice every week, Monday Morning and Thursday morning; and any found not washed will be fined 3d for each offence.

17. The Grinders, Drawers, Slubbers and Rovers shall sweep at least eight times in the day as follows, in the Morning at 7½, 9½, 11 and 12; and in the Afternoon at 1½, 2½, 3½, 4½ and 5½ o'clock; and to notice the Board hung up, when the black side is turned that is the time to sweep, and only quarter of an hour will be allowed for sweeping. The Spinners shall sweep as follows, in the Morning at 7½, 10 and 12; in the Afternoon at 3 and 5½ o'clock. Any neglecting to sweep at the time will be fined 2d for each offence.

18. Any persons found Smoking on the premises will be instantly dismissed.

19. Any person found away from their usual place of work, except for necessary purposes, or Talking with any one out of their own Alley will be fined 2d for each offence.

20. Any person bringing dirty Bobbins will be fined 1d for each Bobbin.

21. Any person wilfully damaging this Notice will be dismissed.

The Overlookers are strictly enjoined to attend to these Rules, and they will be responsible to the Masters for the Workpeople observing them.

WATER-FOOT MILL, NEAR HASLINGDEN,
SEPTEMBER, 1851.

J. Read, Printer, and Bookbinder, Haslingden.

Here now is what Archibald Buchanan, the factory owner, said in conversation with a Commissioner:

What is the highest degree of heat you have in your works?
We have no occasion for heat above seventy.
Do you, in summer, keep the windows open?
We do.
Do you know at what temperature your works are, in the winter?
It is very difficult to say: we have difficulty in getting the people to keep their rooms as cool as we should wish.
Who are the people that will not keep the works cool?
The work-people generally; it is the most difficult part of my management to make them keep the rooms properly aired.

Evidence of Archibald Buchanan

1 How does Buchanan disagree with his own workers?
2 How would he have disagreed with Cobbett?
3 According to Buchanan, who is to blame if the mill is not properly ventilated?

When he had spoken to Buchanan and a number of workers, the Commissioner wrote his report. This is what he said:

'I had great pleasure in walking through the eighteen apartments of the mill and seeing the admirable order of the works, and the happiness of the people employed, which is quite remarkable. No artificial heat is required, except in the web dressing room of the power-loom weaving mill: the windows open from the top: the rooms are thoroughly ventilated, there is a clock and a thermometer in every room: no unpleasant smell in any part of the works, and the utmost cleanness and neatness everywhere.

There are plenty of fanners in the preparing rooms: but the dust is not removed as thoroughly as in the new mill at Deanstown.

There are between 800 and 900 workers, all occupying houses built by the company.

Although we were only a few hours at Catrine, we saw enough to satisfy us of the great respect in which Mr. Buchanan is held by his workers.

Factories Inquiry Commission, 1833

1 What does the Commissioner think of the mill?
2 What does he think of Buchanan?
3 What does he say about the problems mentioned by the two workers?
4 Why does he not think them too important, do you suppose? (For one reason you should look at the number of workers in the web dressing room, and the total number in the mill).
5 How would the Commissioner have answered Cobbett, do you suppose?

After it had received the report of the Factories Inquiry Commission in 1833, Parliament passed the Factories Regulation Act. Among other things, it appointed factory inspectors. One of these was Leonard Horner. In 1834, he inspected Buchanan's mill, and this is what he wrote to his daughter:

Catrine, which was only a farm-house with a water mill and blacksmith's shop adjoining, has risen into a village with a population of two thousand seven hundred. On Sunday, I went to the chapel, built by the owners of the works, where there was a large and most respectable congregation, and I afterwards called on Mr. Buchanan, who has a very handsome house, prettily situated in ornamental grounds, half a mile from the works.

On Monday, I spent the whole morning in my examination of the works: I find them in the highest order, and every arrangement that could be desired for the comfort and welfare of the people.

A great many of the workers have houses belonging to themselves, which they have purchased out of their savings: I visited several of them, and was struck by their extraordinary neatness, cleanliness and handsome furniture. One of the mechanics (those who make and mend the machinery) a man of forty years of age, who earns twenty-five shillings (£1.25) a week, lives in a house which cost him £200 and which he paid for out of his savings. It is of two stories, with a nice garden, full of fruit trees and vegetables, and the rooms are most handsomely furnished. I do not think there can be a happier population, and it is quite delightful to see Mr. Buchanan among his people, who seem to look up to him as a father.

Memoir of Leonard Horner, 1834

1 Which of the points made by the Commissioner in 1833, does Horner also make?
2 What extra information does Horner give us?
3 Does Horner contradict the Commissioner in any way?
4 If William Cobbett read this letter of Horner's, what do you think he would say?

Here now are two different descriptions of mill workers:

Any man who has stood at the exit of a great cotton mill must admit that an uglier set of men and women, or boys and girls, it would be impossible to find. Their complexion is sallow and pallid, with a peculiar flatness of the features. Their stature is low, the average height of 400 men being 5′ 6″. A very general bowing of the legs. Great numbers of girls and women walking lamely or awk-

Factory girls What was the age of the youngest of these girls, do you think?

What is this artist trying to tell us about factory girls? Does he agree more with Gaskell or with Ure? (See below).

wardly. Nearly all have flat feet. Hair thin and straight, many of the men having but little beard and that in patches of a few hairs. A spiritless and dejected air, a sprawling and wide action of the legs and an appearance, taken as a whole, giving the world but 'little assurance of a man'.

The Manufacturing Population of England, 1833, P. Gaskell.

So much nonsense has been written about the deformities and diseases of factory people that some of my readers may not believe me when I say I have never seen among a like number of young women, so many pleasing faces and handsome figures as I saw on Mr. Ashton's weaving galleries. Their light labour and erect posture in tending the looms gives them generally a graceful carriage. Many of them have adopted tasteful modes of wearing neat handkerchiefs on their heads, and have a great deal of the Grecian style of beauty.

Philosophy of Manufactures, 1835, Andrew Ure

1. List the things which Gaskell says are wrong with mill workers. Use your own words.
2. What does Ure say is attractive about Ashton's factory girls?
3. How has their work been good for them?
4. Do you suppose all the jobs in a cotton factory were good for the workers?
5. Which writer do you think Cobbett would have believed?
6. Do you think either, or both, of these writers exaggerates at all?

In Derbyshire, there were some mills belonging to the Strutt family. If one of their workers did anything wrong, a small sum of money was deducted from his or her wages. Here is a list of offences for which workers were fined:

Fines at Strutts' Mills, Derbyshire 1805–1813 (inclusive)

1 **Absence from work without leave**
   Leaving work without giving notice
   Running away
   Being off drinking
   Going to Derby Fair
   Going off without leave with soldiers

2 **Theft of Mill Property**
   Stealing packthread
   Stealing Oil, Candles etc.
   Stealing yarn
   Stealing a pair of pincers

3 **Destruction or Damage of Mill Property**
   Breaking a Drawing Frame
   Setting fire to a lamp cupboard
   Stuffing a stove tunnel up
   Breaking a pair of scales

4 **Failing to do Work as Required**
   Having 20 spindles idle without need for any
   Making waste of good yarn
   Spoiling a parcel of cotton upon machine
   Neglecting cleaning, oiling etc.
   Leaving her machine dirty
   Weighing sorts wrong and being saucy when told of it
   Counting hanks wrong
   Damping her cotton

5 **Failure to Comply with Mill Discipline**
   Idleness and looking through the window
   Calling thro' windows to some soldiers
   Riding on each others' backs
   Going out of the room in which she works to abuse the hands in other room
   Telling lies
   Fighting
   Throwing water on Ann Gregory very frequently
   Sending for ale into the room
   Terrifying S. Pearson with her ugly face
   Beating William Smith Junior
   Throwing bobbins at people

6 **Misconduct Outside Working Hours**
   Putting Joshua Haynes's dog into a bucket of hot water
   Taking James Ludlum's coat
   Rubbing their faces with blood and going about the town to frighten people
   Stealing gun-flints

1 Do you think it was right to punish workers for the offences listed here?
2 How many years are covered by the list? How many people were fined, on an average, in any one year? How does this compare with the number punished in your school?
3 Write a list of the rules which you think the Strutts had for their mills. Compare your lists with the one on page 29.
4 Look again at what Cobbett said about the rules which mill workers had to obey. Do you think he was right?

Written Work

Write two descriptions of your town or village. One should make it sound a very pleasant place, and the other should make it sound unpleasant. Neither, though, is to say anything which is completely untrue. From this exercise, and from reading the extracts in this section, you will realise one of the main problems of writing history. It is that different sources give us different impressions of the same thing.

Read through the documents again and see what they say about the following:

The factories – ventilation, temperature, dust, discipline.

Factory owners.

Factory workers.

Now try to decide which sources are the most reliable. You already know that Cobbett had never seen a factory, but does the other evidence suggest he was wrong in everything? Can you rely entirely on the word of a factory owner or a factory worker? Can you trust a Parliamentary Commissioner or an inspector of factories? Do you think that both Gaskell and Ure (pages 30–31) had seen the factory workers they described? If so, why did they write such different things about them?

When you have looked at all this evidence, write what you think is an honest account of the cotton factories, their owners and their workers.

Research

Find out all you can about:

1 The spinning and weaving inventions of the eighteenth and nineteenth centuries.
2 The buildings and machines of a cotton factory of the early nineteenth century.

Oxford Junior History, Book 4, *Britain becomes a Great Power*, Chapter Two, will help you.

Children in Factories

Before there were any factories, people made cloth in their own homes. Children did not go to school. They helped their parents, or else they were sent as apprentices to other families. When cotton factories were built, children went to work in them, with the adults. There were plenty of jobs they could do, but the two most usual were 'piecing' and 'scavenging'. One machine might be spinning as many as a thousand threads, and from time to time some of them broke. It was the work of the 'piecer' to join the ends. The 'scavenger' had to brush up the dust, and keep the room clean.

Soon, there were tales that factory children were being badly treated. It was largely because of this that Parliament appointed the Factory Inquiry Commissions you read about in the previous section.

Children helping a spinner The girl is a 'piecer'. Her job is to mend any threads that break. The boy is a 'scavenger'. What is he doing? Compare this work with that done by children in coal mines.

Here is the story which Thomas Clarke of Leicester told the Commission of 1833:

> I am aged eleven. I work at Cooper's factory. I spin there. I was in Ross's factory before that. I was a piecer there. I pieced for Joseph Badder one while, then for George Castle. I was very nigh nine years of age when I first went to piece. I got 2/6d ($12\frac{1}{2}$p) at first. I think I was a good hand at it. When I had been there half a year I got 3/-d (15p). Badder used to strap me some odd times. Some odd times he'd catch me over the head, but it was mostly on the back. He made me sing out. He would strap us about twelve times at once. He used to strap us sometimes over the head. I used sometimes to fall asleep. The boy next to me often fell asleep; he got many a stroke. They always strapped us if we fell asleep. Castle used to get a rope about us as thick as my thumb, and double it, and put knots in it, and lick us with that. That

was a good bit worse than the strap. I ran away because Thorpe used to come and strap me. He did not know what he was strapping me for: it was just as he was in his humours. I never saw such a man; he would strap anyone as did not please him. I didn't like it and I ran away.

I never complained to the master about it. I don't know why I did not. I never told my mother but one time, and that was when there were marks on me. She told me not to mind; she'd give me a halfpenny to go again and be a good boy. I showed her my back. I told her I was very bad and she would look. She found bruises and marks of straps. She wanted to know was she to go down and tell them about it and I told her, no. I thought I should catch it the worse. When I ran away, my mother ran after me and would have beat me if she could have catched me. She said she would give me it if I did not get back to the factory. I always paid my wages to my mother. My father takes my wages from the paytable and gives it to me to take home to my mother. My mother used sometimes to give me a halfpenny or a penny again, she said to buy me apples for me to eat on Sunday. I used to go to the factory a little before six, sometimes at five, and work on till nine at night. We never came away before nine, without (unless) they were on the spree of it, getting a drop. We had half an hour at breakfast, an hour at dinner, and half an hour at tea. We did not always have full meal-times. They sometimes rang the bell before the time and we were forced to go.

Factories Inquiry Commission, 1833

1 How old was Thomas Clarke when he started work?
2 How much did he earn?
3 Why did Badder strap him and the other boy?
4 Why did Thorpe strap him? What did Thomas do as a result?
5 What did Thomas's mother say when he complained to her about the beating?
6 What did she say and do when he ran away from the factory? Why was this do you suppose?
7 How many hours a day did Thomas work?
8 What sometimes happened to meal breaks?

Cartoon of cotton factory Which of the extracts support this view of the factory? Which do not? The Peels were important cotton manufacturers, and Sir Robert was a leading Tory politician. What was the purpose of this cartoon, do you suppose?

Factory Inspector After 1833, it was illegal to employ children below the age of nine in factories. Inspectors went round to see the law was obeyed. It was not easy, since in those days, children did not have birth certificates.

Here now is Joseph Badder's evidence:

I have always found it more difficult to keep my piecers awake the last hours of a winter's evening. I have told the master, and I have been told by him that I did not beat them half enough. This was when they were working from six to eight.

I have seen them fall asleep, and they have been performing their work with their hands while they were asleep, after the billy had stopped, when their work was over. I have stopped and looked at them for two minutes, going through the motions of piecing fast asleep.

I know Thorpe has been up before the magistrate half a dozen times or more, on the complaints of the parents. He has been before the bench, and I have seen him when he came back, and told the parents they had better take the children away. After that he has been sometimes half drunk perhaps, and in a passion, and would strap them for the least thing, more than he did before. I remember once that he was fined; it is about two years ago; it was for beating a little girl; he was fined 10/- (50p). I have seen him strap the women when they took the part of the children. The master complained he was not strict enough. I know from Thorpe that the master always paid his expenses when he was before the magistrate. I believe they generally do, in all the factories.

I have frequently had complaints against myself by the parents of children for beating them. I told them I was very sorry after I had done it, but I was forced to do it. The master expected me to do my work, and I could not do mine unless they did theirs.

Thomas Thorpe was the foreman; he is living in this town now, but he is very ill. I believe his illness has been brought on by over-work and drinking, which he took to keep up his spirits; ale and spirits, and smoking and chewing tobacco. I hardly ever saw him without a quid or a pipe in his mouth for some years. I knew him before he took to these hard hours. He was not a hard drinking man then. He was a comber in Mr. Ross's employ. He was a trustworthy servant. He worked for them for many years. He took to his bed from their work. I believe he is now but just alive. His wife and children are going to the workhouse; he got a little better and went down to his work, and next night he got tipsy and they turned him away. He was not able to go to his work next day, and I think not all the week, and they sent for the key and told him he need not come again.

In 1825 they (Ross's) built a mill. Sometimes my mother, sometimes my brothers brought my meals. I could take my meals and mind the machine at the same time. I went to work at six a.m. on Monday and came home at eleven on Tuesday night, and came again at six on Wednesday morning, and worked till eleven on Thursday night. Then on Friday morning at six till Saturday evening about seven or eight. Then begin on Monday as before. I worked these hours for several weeks together. I was then about seventeen. My parents saw an alteration in me, and wished me to leave; I was then receiving 12/- (60p); that is the rate for nine days. I felt over-worked enough. One night I fell asleep, and slipped on to the carding engine when it was running. I ran down off the engine without being hurt, I hardly know how. That determined me to leave.

Factories Inquiry Commission, 1833

1. What problems does Badder say he had with his piecers?
2. What did the factory owner say about it?
3. What did the children sometimes do when work was over?
4. Why was Thorpe sometimes taken before the magistrate? How did he behave afterwards?
5. What did the employer do for Thorpe when he was taken to court?
6. What excuse did Badder give the parents when he beat their children?
7. What does Badder think caused Thorpe's illness?
8. What did the employer do when Thorpe fell ill?

9 What hours was Badder working in 1825? How much did he earn? How much was that an hour?
10 Why did he leave Ross's factory?

Here is the evidence of Henry Ross, the factory owner. Formerly, he employed and paid the piecers himself. Now he gives the spinners extra money, and lets them employ the piecers themselves. This was what usually happened in factories.

I am the owner here. It is nearly a year since I made the change of putting the children under the spinners. The main reason for the change was that they were dissatisfied with the number of piecers we allowed them. They pay the piecers by the week, in the same way I should have done. I don't think there is any difference in the amount. Since the change I have heard that the spinners punished the piecers too much. The overlooker said, 'No sir, nothing to hurt!' But I think they might do without any, if they always spoke severely to them. I think the spinners might keep the children without any beating if they would be steady with them.

Our last overlooker, (Thorpe) was not a good-tempered man; he was honest and hard-working, but bad-tempered.

Factories Inquiry Commission, 1833

1 Why did Ross put the piecers under the control of the spinners?
2 Has the change been good for the children?
3 What two things is Ross not sure about, in his own factory?
4 How does he think the spinners could avoid beating the children?
5 What does Ross say about Thorpe?
6 What sort of man do you think Ross was? Make up your mind from his own evidence and from Badder's.

The next extract is from a book by Andrew Ure:

If there is cruelty of any kind, the adult workers are the only culprits. The following piece of evidence will confirm this:
'Who is it that beats the children?'
'The spinner'
'Not the master?'
'No, the masters have nothing to do with the children. They don't employ them'
'Do you (a spinner) pay and employ your own piecers?'
'Yes, it is the general rule in Manchester, but our master is very strict with us that we don't employ them under age.'
'Are the children ever beaten?'
'Sometimes they get beat, but not severely; for sometimes

Child factory worker What seems to be this girl's problem?

they make the stuff to waste, and then punishment is needful; but that is unknown to the master – he does not allow beating at all.'

No master would wish to have wayward children in his factory, who do not work unless they are beaten, and he usually fines or turns away any spinners who maltreat their assistants. Hence ill-treatment of any kind is very rare. I have visited many factories in Manchester, entering the spinning rooms unexpectedly at different times of the day, and I never once saw a child being chastised, nor indeed did I ever see children in ill-humour. They always seemed to be cheerful and alert, taking pleasure in the light play of their muscles. It was delightful to see the nimbleness with which they pieced the broken ends, and to see them at leisure after a few seconds exercise of their tiny fingers. The work of these lively elves seemed to resemble a sport, in which habit gave them a pleasing skill.

The Philosophy of Manufactures, 1835, Andrew Ure

1 Who, according to Ure, is cruel to children in factories?
2 What does he say the employers feel about the beating of children? Do you think this was true of Henry Ross?
3 How much cruelty is there in the factories, according to Ure? What evidence does he give for this?
4 How does he find the children when he visits factories?
5 What does he say about the piecers' work?
6 Where would **a** Thomas Clarke, **b** Joseph Badder **c** Henry Ross probably agree with Ure? Where would each of them disagree with him, if at all?

Here is part of a Commissioner's report on Scotland:

If ever there is too much punishment, it is in the smaller mills where quite often the overseer has a strap; but I doubt very much whether any such abuse exists in any degree worthy of notice. I have the strong impression that country schoolmasters in Scotland are far more likely than mill owners or overseers to exert their authority by using the strap too severely.

Factories Inquiry Commission, 1833

1 According to the Commissioner, in which factories are the children punished most?
2 How serious does he think the problem is?
3 Which places are worse than factories?

Finally, here is an extract from a book by W. Cooke Taylor:

We are gravely told that 'juvenile labour in all circumstances is wrong'. I never believed this. I am sure that my own fagging at school was worse than any which I ever saw in a cotton mill. But let us grant that juvenile labour is wrong, there is something still worse, and that is juvenile starvation. I have seen with some pain, the little piecers and cleaners employed in their dull work, when the sun was high in the heaven: I thought how much more delightful would have been the gambol of free limbs on the hillside, the inhaling of the fresh breeze, the sight of the green meadow, with its spangles of buttercups and daisies, the song of the bird, and the humming of the bee. But I have seen other sights. I have seen children perishing from sheer hunger in the mud hovel, or in the ditch by the way-side. I have seen the juvenile beggar and the juvenile tramp with famine in their cheeks and despair in their hearts. I have seen the juvenile delinquent, his conscience seared by misery. I would rather see boys and girls earning their living in the mill, than starving by the roadside, shivering on the pavement or carried in a van to prison.

Notes of a Tour in the Manufacturing Districts of Lancashire

1 How does Cooke Taylor think his school compared with a cotton mill?
2 What does he say about children's work in factories?
3 What would he rather see children doing?
4 Name three things which he says might happen to a child who is not at work.
5 Where would Andrew Ure disagree with Cooke Taylor? Where might he agree with him?

Written Work

1 Imagine it is 1835. Write a report on cruelty to children in factories. Say **a** what form it takes, **b** who is responsible **c** how serious the problem is.
2 Write the story of Thomas Thorpe's life. You have the most important facts in the extracts, and for the rest you must use your imagination. Probably he started work as a piecer like Thomas Clarke, and then became a spinner like Joseph Badder.

Research

1 Find out what laws Parliament made to protect factory children.
2 Read about the Ten Hours Movement.

The Handloom Weavers

In the eighteenth century cloth was woven by handloom weavers. You can see why they had this name if you look at the pictures below and on page 41.

Handloom weavers worked at home, but even so they had employers. Each employer kept a warehouse, from which his weavers collected the yarn they needed. They took it home and when they had woven it into cloth, they returned it to the warehouse. Their employer then paid them for their work.

Possibly you may know someone who has a simple handloom, or there may be one in your school. If so, try to find out how it works. It will help if you understand what 'warp' and 'weft' are. Warp threads run the whole length of a piece of cloth. The weft is woven into the warp, and runs from side to side.

There had been handlooms of a kind since prehistoric times. Then, in the late eighteenth and early nineteenth centuries a number of inventors developed the power loom. That was a loom driven by a steam engine. People could not have power looms and steam engines in their homes, so factories were built to take them. This happened in Lancashire and Lanarkshire in the 1820's and 1830's.

A writer called Edward Baines explained why he thought power looms were better than hand looms:

> A very good handloom weaver, 25 or 30 years of age, will weave two pieces of shirtings per week, each 24 yards long, containing 100 shoots of weft in an inch.
>
> In 1833, a power loom weaver, from 15 to 20 years of age, attending to four looms, can weave eighteen similar pieces in a week; some can weave twenty.
>
> *History of the Cotton Manufacture of Great Britain*, 1837

1 How many yards of cloth can a handloom weaver make in a week? How many can a powerloom weaver make?

2 Why does a powerloom weaver make a lot more?

Handloom Weavers and Spinner These people are working in a room in their house. The young man on the right may be the weaver's apprentice, or his son. The woman is his wife or, perhaps, his daughter. She cannot possibly supply all the thread for the two men. At least three spinners were needed to keep one weaver busy.

Power Looms These, and all the other machines in the factory, are driven by a pair of steam engines. Find the driving shaft. Why do the belts go round large drums? What accidents might the workers have, if they are not careful?

3 Why can powerloom weavers be younger than handloom weavers, do you suppose?
4 Why would employers prefer young workmen?

Here is what happened to handloom weavers' wages over the years:

Wages paid for weaving a length of cambric on a handloom

1800	25/–	(£1.25p)
1810	19/6d	($97\frac{1}{2}$p)
1820	9/–	(45p)
1830	5/6d	($27\frac{1}{2}$p)

1 Draw a graph on squared paper to show how wages fell.
2 How much harder, roughly, would a weaver have to work in 1830 in order to make as much money as he did in 1800?

In 1840 a weaver called John Duce described weavers' lives in the old days, and how things had changed:

> When I was young, Monday was generally a day of rest; Tuesday was not severe labour: Saturday was a day to go to the warehouse, and that was an easy day for the weaver. In those times we could afford to go and have balls, and to go and spend money at fairs, and we could afford to take our wives and families to a tea-garden; but it is as much as we can do now, working hard all the week, and sometimes on Sunday besides, to be able to get a bare living; and such as work so many hours destroy their health and strength.
>
> *John Duce's evidence to the Handloom Weavers' Commissioners*, 1840

A *When John Duce was a young man:*
1 What did the weavers do on Monday, Tuesday and Saturday?
2 What do you suppose they did on Sunday?
3 How many days did that leave them for reasonably hard work at their looms?

4 How did weavers and their families enjoy themselves?

B *In 1840:*
1 How many days a week did weavers work?
2 Why was this necessary?
3 What happened to the weavers as a result?

Here now is an interview with another weaver, called John Brennan. It took place in 1834:

You are a weaver? Yes.
What are your wages? Seven shillings and sixpence ($37\frac{1}{2}$p) a week.
How long have you been a weaver? Twenty-three years.
What did you earn when you began work? I was only a boy then, but I could earn 12/- (60p) a week.
How does the fall in wages affect you? It robs me of all the comforts of life. I can get nothing but the worst of food and less of it than I used to.
What do you do for clothing? As well as I can. Sometimes I have some and sometimes very little.
What do you do for furniture? I have never bought any in my life.
How does your wife do for clothes? Just as I do – quite as bad.
Have your children any stock of clothes? No, they have just enough to put on clean on Sunday; they have one dress on and one off.
What do you do for cooking utensils? I have never bought any since I was born. I live in the same place where my father and mother lived; they are dead and the utensils they had, I have still. I never had it in my power to buy any.
Do you belong to any friendly society?* No, I do not. I could not pay for it. I have all my children, my wife and myself, in a penny club for burial.
How do you pay the doctor when you are ill? I have to work myself well again.
What do you pay for your church seat? I am not prepared to go. I would if I had got decent clothing. When I was a young man I did get more wages. I had three suits of clothes, and a good watch in my pocket, and two or three pairs of shoes, and one or two good hats.
What does your wife earn? About 5/- (25p) per week.
Does she go to a cotton factory? Yes.
Is it not painful to you to have to send your wife to a factory? Yes, it causes great grief to me.

Select Committee on Hand-loom Weavers, 1834

* A friendly society was a bit like an insurance company. Members paid a few pence a week, and then had sick pay if they fell ill.

Handloom weaver In the 1840's weavers had to work for up to sixteen hours a day to make a bare living. This man is using a 'flying shuttle'. You can read about that, and about the weavers in their prosperous times in *Oxford Junior History*, Book 4, page 24.

1 How much does John Brennan earn?
2 How much did he earn when he was a boy?
3 What does he say about his family's food and clothing?
4 What things has he never bought?
5 To what club does he pay money?
6 What do you imagine he expects to happen to his children?
7 What does he do when he is ill?
8 Why does he stay away from church?
9 How much does Mrs. Brennan earn?
10 Where does she work? How does John feel about this?

Here now is another point of view:

There are many complaints of stealing. As proof of this, an employer told me that he had gone to the house of a weaver to ask about some work that was overdue. As the weaver was not at home he went upstairs and the first thing he saw was seven 'widows' hanging over a clothes line.

A 'widow' is the term they use for the unsaleable warp when divorced from the weft, which it is possible to sell and which the weaver had stolen.

Report: Handloom Weavers' Commissioners, 1840

1 What complaint is made about weavers?
2 How was this particular weaver caught?
3 What is a 'widow' in real life? What does 'widow' mean here? (Explain in your own words.)

Now an employer who has bought some steam looms explains why he has done so:

I can ask a higher price for my cloth by its being more regular in the weaving and better made. I am not robbed of my weft. I can now take an order and know when I can deliver it, which, when I employed handloom weavers, I never could.

Report: Handloom Weavers' Commissioners, 1840

1 Give three reasons why this employer prefers steam looms.

In the factories a skilled man could earn 30/- (£1.50) a week. Why, then, did the handloom weavers not find factory jobs? Edward Baines, in his book on the cotton industry, said this about them:

> Since they work in their own cottages, their time is their own. They may begin and leave off work at their pleasure: they are not bound punctually to obey the call of the factory bell: if they feel like it they can leave their loom for the public house, or to lounge in the street, or to do some other job, then, when they have to, they may make up for lost time by a lot of hard work. In short, they have more freedom than factory workers; they receive their materials, and sometimes do not take back the cloth for several weeks: and they are able, if they are short of money to steal a few cops of their employers' weft in order to buy bread or beer. All this makes the weavers' work more attractive to men of idle, irregular and wasteful habits than other occupations. It is a dear-bought miserable freedom, but like poaching or smuggling, some would sooner have it than work regular hours in a factory for twice the money.
>
> Edward Baines, *History of the Cotton Manufacture of Great Britain*, 1837

1 How does Baines say the handloom weavers spend their time?
2 What bad habits does he say they have?
3 What criminals does he compare them with?
4 What does he suggest they would most dislike about factories?

Another writer called Gaskell had this to say:

> People who blame handloom weavers for being obstinate and not taking jobs in factories do not understand the problem. It is well-known that power looms do not need an adult worker, but they are managed entirely by young women and girls. There is no room for the male handloom weaver. The factories are closed against him.

1 Why, according to Gaskell, do handloom weavers not find work in factories?
2 Does the picture on page 39, or any other document in this section, support his opinion?
3 Which writer is more sympathetic to the handloom weavers, Baines or Gaskell? Give reasons for your answer.

This is what happened to the price of cloth:

Price of Calico, per yard

Year	*1815*	*1820*	*1825*	*1830*
Price	4p	$2\frac{1}{2}$p	$1\frac{1}{2}$p	1p

1 Farm labourers earned, on average, 1p an hour. A dress took seven yards of material. How long did a farm labourer have to work to buy his wife the material for a dress in 1815 and 1830?
2 How do you suppose ordinary people, like farm labourers, felt about power looms?

Written Work

1 Imagine you are living in 1840. Write an article for a newspaper to try and make people sorry for handloom weavers.
2 Now pretend you are a factory owner. Write a reply to the article and be critical of handloom weavers. Say also why you have bought power looms.

Research

1 Find out more about the history of the loom. For example:
What were prehistoric looms like?
What did John Kay invent?
What did Joseph Jacquard invent?
Who invented the first power loom? Who improved it so that it could be used in factories?
2 Many handloom weavers became Chartists. Find out what you can about them.

Oxford Junior History, Book 4, Chapter Two, will help you answer some of these questions.

The Locksmiths of South Staffordshire in the 1840's

In the last two sections we have been looking at cotton factories. Factories, though, were new, and until the end of the nineteenth century most people worked at home. Almost every county had its handicraft trades. For example, there were button making and rope spinning in Dorset, lace making in Devon, stocking weaving and lace making again in Nottinghamshire. In this section we are going to learn about the locksmiths of Wolverhampton and Willenhall in South Staffordshire.

You have already seen that Parliament appointed Commissions of Inquiry to see how children were treated in the factories. It also wanted to know what was happening to those who worked in the homes of their parents or employers. So, in 1842, it appointed the Children's Employment Commission. The Commissioner who went to South Staffordshire was R. H. Horne, and all the extracts in this section were written by him. For reasons which you will see for yourself, Horne's reports became famous, so much so that Benjamin Disraeli took a lot of material from them for his novel *Sybil.*

This is what Horne said about Wolverhampton, and the lockmaker's workshops:

> In the smaller and dirtier streets of the town, where the working classes live, there are narrow passages, at intervals of every eight or ten houses. Having made your way through the passage, you find yourself in a space varying in size with the number of houses, hutches or hovels it contains. They are nearly all crowded. Out of this space there are other narrow passages sometimes, leading to other similar hovels. These are the dwellings and workshops of the poorest of the working classes. They have the appearance, after going through the dark passage or burrow, of a sort of rabbit warren.

Locksmiths' houses, Wolverhampton What does the look of these houses tell you about their inhabitants? Where were the workshops? (See top of page 44). Note the pump which supplied all the houses with their water. The deep gutter was called a 'kennel'. It was their only sewer.

Inside of a lock The locksmith's work consisted mainly of filing the parts to shape.

There are scarcely any workshops in front of the street. Most of the work of the town is carried on in shops at the backs of the houses. You might pass along a street fifty times, up passages and court yards in which there were shops containing nests full of young children, and never know it. They are as much out of sight as birds' nests. Almost all the little workshops have the same things in common, namely, want of space in the shop; want of ventilation; and the shop itself is in some cramped, dirty locality, at the back of squalid houses and close to a pile of filth.

The worker has what is aptly called a 'standing', for he seldom has more than just enough room. Each shop contains as many as it will hold: I could seldom pass from one end of a small master's shop to another, without disturbing each workman as I passed.

Many of the shops are very dirty and dilapidated, sometimes being no more than little broken sheds. Their floor is generally the earth. Their windows are often a mere hole in the wall, into which a shutter is fitted at night. They must be wretched places in winter, especially for the feet of all those who stand from day to day at the vice.

Locks are made by forging, pressing and filing. Filing is the most common of these processes. Children are placed standing upon blocks so as to be able to reach the vice, and set to work with a file almost as soon as they can hold one.

1 Draw a plan of part of Wolverhampton, using Horne's description and your own imagination.
2 Where are most of the workshops?
3 Make a list of the ways in which the workshops are unpleasant.
4 What jobs are done in them? Which is the most common? When do children learn to do it?

Here, Horne describes the locksmith's week:

The majority of the working classes do not work at all on Monday. Half of them do not work much on Tuesday. Wednesday is the market-day, and this is an excuse for many to do only half a day's work; and as a result of attending the market they are often very unfit for work on Thursday morning. Lights are seen in the shops of many of the small masters as late as 10 and 11 o'clock at night, on Thursday. During the whole of Friday, the town is silent in all the main streets and thoroughfares, and seems to have been depopulated. Lights appear in the workshops to a late hour in the night – sometimes till morning. All Saturday morning the streets present the same barren and silent appearance. Everybody is working for his life. The wives, children and apprentices are being almost worked to death. Kicks, cuffs, curses and blows are abundantly administered to the children at this crisis of the week. The small master does not spare himself, but works incessantly without leaving off even at meal times. If they do not work half the night, they are sure to begin at four or five in the morning, till, with every effort, that may be said to amount to a ferocity of labour, added to the highest skill, they finish the required amount of work 'for the week'.

About 2 o'clock therefore, on Saturday, some of those who did some work on Tuesday begin to appear in the streets; and large masses issue forth between four and five o'clock. The wives and older girls go to market; the husbands and other adults to the beer-shops. By 7 or 8 o'clock the market is full; the streets are all alive; the beer-shops and gin-shops are full; and all the other shops are full. The manufacturers are stretching their limbs, expanding their souls to the utmost, and spending their money as fast as they possibly can. No-one ever thinks of saving a shilling.

1 Estimate the number of hours a locksmith would work, on an average, each day of the week. Show this information on a bar diagram.
2 How do the locksmiths' families suffer? When? Why?
3 What happens on Saturday?

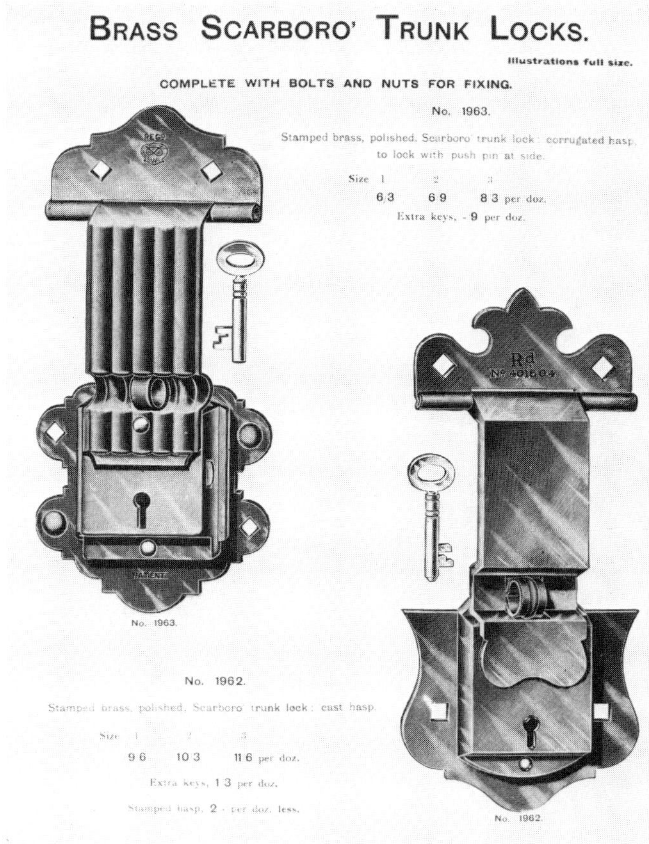

BRASS SCARBORO' TRUNK LOCKS.
Illustrations full size.
COMPLETE WITH BOLTS AND NUTS FOR FIXING.
No. 1963.
Stamped brass, polished. Scarboro' trunk lock: corrugated hasp, to lock with push pin at side.
Size 1 2 3
6/3 6/9 8/3 per doz.
Extra keys, -9 per doz.
No. 1963.
No. 1962.
Stamped brass, polished. Scarboro' trunk lock: cast hasp.
Size 1 2 3
9/6 10/3 11/6 per doz.
Extra keys, 1/3 per doz.
Stamped hasp, 2/- per doz. less.
No. 1962.

A Trunk Lock

Here is Horne's description of the locksmiths themselves:

Their most common complaint is hernia. I am assured that one third of the adult workmen in town are ruptured. The truss-maker has made a fortune. There are also many cases of distortion of joints owing to long standing at the vice, and long holding the file. The right shoulder blade is displaced, and the right leg crooks and bends inwards at the knee, like the letter K. The right hand also, is often twisted. Almost everything it holds takes the position of the file. If the poor man carries a limp lettuce or a limp mackerel from market, they are never dangled, but held like the file. If he carries nothing, his right hand is in just the same position.

They are haggard, dirty, lank and rickety. They look smokedried and grim. The mouth hangs open in despair: the eye, when not lit up by drink is sunken, dull and unobserving. The faces of the younger men are often bloated with liquor: but those of the old men are hard, dry, angular and inflexible. After a life spent looking at the inner works of locks, the face has become just like them.

1 What is the most common complaint the locksmiths have?
2 How are many of them deformed?
3 Describe their faces, using your own words.
4 From this, and the last extract, explain why the locksmiths look as they do.

Horne said this about the money the locksmiths earned:

The cheapness of their work beats anything of the kind made anywhere else; the padlock which is sold at the ironmongers in London for 1/- (5p) is made and sold by the Willenhall men for $1\frac{3}{4}$d, including all the material, labour, everything, or 1/9 ($8\frac{1}{2}$p) per dozen; the factors sell them to the London ironmongers at 2/- (10p) per dozen. The price of iron is now double what it was formerly, in 1830 and 1831, yet the Willenhall men sell even for less money than formerly. Their abject state compels them to sell for almost anything in competition with each other; they all compete together; it is all for ready money; and this they must have at any sacrifice.

1 How much is a locksmith paid for a dozen locks? How much does the factor sell them for? How much will a London ironmonger sell them for? What percentage profit is made by the ironmonger?
2 Explain why the locksmiths cannot get a better price for their locks.
3 Why are they worse off than in 1830?

Here is what a locksmith, William Kempson, told Horne:

I am aged 31 or 32, somewhere thereabouts. I am a padlock maker. I have one apprentice, and one son as works, and another as runs errands. I can't get on. I have four children. I hardly ever know how to get another bit of work after my last lot is done. I make up very tidy locks, but I canna do, I'm sure I canna. Sometimes I'm obliged to go without meals. The factors know I'm so poor I must have the money somehow, and must sell for whatever they choose to give. I canna stand agen them. I shan't have any dinner today until I've been to the factors at Walsall, three miles from here. I canna send my children to school. I canna clothe my children nor myself. These are my best clothes – all torn. My shoes are all to pieces.

1 Who does William Kempson have working for him?
2 How does he say the factors take advantage of him?
3 What is he too poor to afford?

Like William Kempson, nearly all locksmiths had apprentices. Most of these came from the work-houses. Guardians, that is the people in charge of workhouses, tried to bind children as apprentices as soon as they could, so that they no longer had the expense of keeping them. To persuade employers to take them, they often paid a sum of money called a 'premium' with each child.

The apprentice had his keep, but no wages. He could not leave his master before he was 21 so, until then, he was little better than a slave.

Horne says this about apprentices:

Most of the boys are brought from other parishes – Coventry, Tamworth, Walsall etc. The master receives a premium varying from £2 to £5 with each apprentice, and often a suit or two suits of clothes. But as soon as the master has got the boy, or rather the premium, he cares no more about him, but sets him to all manner of domestic drudgery, to run errands, pick up horse dung, nurse children etc, besides helping in the workshop, if strong enough to be of any use.

The premium often allows the master to pay the rent. When not used in this way, it often allows the master to get drunk for a whole week. The clothes of the boy, given him by the parish, have sometimes been taken away and given to the master's son. Sometimes the master has contented himself with pawning the boy's Sunday clothes every Monday morning and taking them out again on Saturday night.

A boy of 13 years of age was recently sold for 10/- (50p). The bargain was made while the men were drinking and the boy is now the apprentice of the purchaser.

1 Where do the apprentices come from?
2 What suggests that boys were apprentices when they were very young?
3 What premium does a master have for taking an apprentice?
4 How does the master spend the premium?
5 What may happen to the clothes the apprentice brings with him?
6 How might a master get rid of an apprentice?

This evidence was given by William Benton. He was William Kempson's apprentice:

William Benton is my name. I can't spell it rightly. I don't know my age exactly. My mother says I'm turned 18. I was bound apprentice about nine years and a half old; they didn't know exactly; the lawyer put my age down by guess. I have got to serve until I am 21. I work from six or seven in the morning till ten or eleven at night. I don't work after my master leaves off; we work equal times. I sometimes have an hour in the day for meals, sometimes not, according as trade is. I have enough to eat when my master has got it, and the children. When *they* are obliged to go short, *I* am obliged to go short. I have no wages – nothing but what I get by working over-hours, that is, after ten o'clock at night. My master behaves well to me; that is, as well as he can. I have the same as they have.

1 How old is William Benton? How old was he when he became an apprentice? How old will he be when he finishes his apprenticeship? How many years is that altogether?
2 What hours does he say he works? Do you suppose he does this every day? (Look at page 44).
3 When does he have enough to eat? When does he go hungry?
4 What is the only way he can have any money of his own?
5 How does he say his master treats him? What evidence does he give for this?

This is the evidence of John Putnam, a constable at Willenhall:

A boy of about 13 years of age, a locksmith's apprentice, once came to me, crying and all over blood. He said his master had been beating him because he would not let his mistress taken his shoes off to go and pawn them; the boy's head was cut open. He slept on a bed which was so filthy I would be sorry to send a dog to sleep upon it. The woman had several very young children, and she used to pitch them upon the boy's bed to lie all day, and they made it in a state not fit to mention; the boy had to creep into this at night. The master and his wife had a bad disease, and they flung filthy rags and bandages about the boy's bedroom, in the fireplace and about. The magistrate freed the boy from his apprenticeship and the master was imprisoned in Stafford gaol for two months.

I think that most of the poorer masters are in as bad a state as the apprentices and children. But the adults are older and better able to bear difficulties and distress.

1 In what ways did the locksmith and his wife ill-treat their apprentice?
2 Why did the boy go to the constable?
3 What happened to the locksmith?
4 What does the constable say about most of the poor masters? Would William Benton have agreed with him?
5 Why does the constable say life is worse for the children than the adults?

Locksmith There are no good pictures of the interior of a locksmith's workshop, but this travelling locksmith did just the same work. How would standing in this position for many hours a day affect a man? (see page 45).

Bottle Lock This was fitted to a bottle to stop dishonest servants stealing the drink.

Here is the evidence of James Hughes. He is a journeyman, that is an adult worker. He is not bound to a master, like an apprentice, and he is paid wages. This is the kind of life which is waiting for most of the boys of South Staffordshire, when they have finished their apprenticeships:

> I am 47. I have worked for a master, but could not get a living out of him, because if I earned 12/- (60p) a week, the master took 3/2 (16p) discount. When I had paid 2/- (10p) a week to the book – the money I had borrowed from the master – and 2/- for my rent, then 3/2 discount, I had only 4/10 (24p) to live upon a week, and keep my wife who is a cripple, and one child too weak to work. I have another child, a girl of 14, who is a cripple also. I do

not know how my wife and daughters became cripples, but the crippling came.

I have not worked now these five weeks. I think I might as well walk about idle with nothing to eat, as work from morning to night and have nothing to eat. My wife was once apprenticed to a woman who did all manner of tailoring, and as she is a cripple she gets a bit of patching given her now and then, or some old clothes to mend, and sometimes gets as much as 8d (4p) in one day. That is how we live now.

James Hughes's wife Jane said this to Horne when he visited the house:

I am a cripple. I have no clothes to cover myself at night, except what I wear in the day, and a sheet. I bought it for a penny a yard, when my last child was born. It is stuff that comes off brown sugar bags, as thin as a piece of brown paper. Fetch it down Jem! I have had 15 children – buried all but two. I have nothing in my bedroom, oh, go up and look! – its soon seen, ha! ha! ha!.

Horne himself reported:

The bedroom had nothing in it but an old broken bedstead, with an old bag upon the sacking, which had burst in the middle and hung down nearly touching the floor. The floor and stairs were perfectly clean.

1 What wages did James Hughes earn?
2 How much of these wages did the master take back?
3 What other expenses did James Hughes have?
4 What excuse does he give for not working?
5 What income does the family have?
6 How many children did James and Jane have? How many lived? What is wrong with Jane and the two daughters?
7 Describe the bedroom. What was the one good thing about it?

Horne had a poor opinion of the men of South Staffordshire, but he said this about the women:

The wives are very sober and very hard-working in looking after their homes, though probably they do not manage their money very well, and do not know what to do for the best in their very trying circumstances. Their remarkable cleanliness in the midst of such problems and want, and with such dirty and drunken husbands, is one of the most extraordinary things about the people of Willenhall.

Living in hunger and in rags, surrounded by children, and without hope, examples of long-enduring and uncomplaining courage are but too common among the wives of the poor locksmiths and key-makers – a courage that does not desert them even during a lingering and lonely death in the dark corners of hovels, in lanes and by-ways of this obscure manufacturing town.

Horne also said this about the way the women kept their homes:

I have entered the houses and hovels of journeymen, locksmiths and key-makers, and seen the utmost poverty, no furniture in the room below but a broken board for a table, and a piece of a plank laid across bricks for a seat; with the wife hungry – almost crying with hunger, and in rags, yet the floor was perfectly clean. I have gone upstairs and seen a bed where a husband, his wife and three children slept, and with no other article in the room of any kind whatever except the bed; yet the clothes on the bed were perfectly clean; so was the floor; so were the stairs; they were not merely clean, they were really white, and more resembled the boards in the dairy of a large farm-house, than anything that could have been expected of the little wretched hovel of a poor locksmith of Willenhall.

1 What problems do the women of South Staffordshire have?
2 Why does Horne admire these women?

Note: You saw that after it had seen the report of the Factories Inquiry Commission of 1833, Parliament passed a law to protect the factory children. It did nothing in 1842 to protect the workshop children in spite of Horne's report and others like it. This was because it felt that it would be impossible to make sure employers obeyed the law. You can see some of the reasons for this in the first two paragraphs of the first extract. What are they?

Written Work

1 A child from a Manchester factory meets an apprentice of a South Staffordshire locksmith. They tell each other about the lives they lead. Write what they say.
2 In what ways were the problems of the locksmiths like those of the handloom weavers?

Research

1 Read the first few chapters of *Oliver Twist* by Charles Dickens. This will tell you about the way Poor Law officials tried to apprentice workhouse children.
2 Were there any handicraft industries, like lock making, in your own area? If so, find out what you can about them.

The Steam Engine

Before the eighteenth century, the only sources of power were the muscles of people and animals, wind and water. Muscle power can be used almost everywhere, and in all sorts of ways, but it is not very strong. Windmills became amazingly efficient, but even in a good breeze did not generate more than about 8 horse power, and nothing at all in still weather. Water is an excellent source of power, and is much used today, but only to generate electricity which, in turn, can drive machines. These machines can be great distances from the turbines, hundreds of miles if necessary. Formerly, the machines were driven directly by the wheel so they, too, had to be at the water side. It is true that there were plenty of good places for little mills, but there were few indeed for factories that needed 100 horse power.

The first industry to suffer from a shortage of power was mining. Miners wanted to sink deep mines but it was impossible to pump them dry. Valuable deposits of copper and tin in Cornwall, and coal in many parts of Britain were out of reach: it looked as if they would have to stay in the ground. Then, in 1712, Thomas Newcomen invented an engine. It used steam, though as you can see from the diagram, it was the pressure of the atmosphere which actually drove it. Other inventors improved Newcomen's design, notably John Smeaton who, in 1775, built an engine of 76 horse power.

A Newcomen engine would wheeze and bang away for a hundred years, draining a deep mine, but it did have two main disadvantages. The first was that it burnt an enormous amount of fuel. The second was that it could only be used for pumping. It was not difficult, of course, to change the up and down motion to circular motion. Every cyclist does that. The real problem was that the Newcomen engine was jerky in its action, and if it drove a

Newcomen Engine This picture was taken in the late nineteenth century. The engine is being dismantled, after working well over a hundred years. The picture gives you some idea of its size. Estimate the length of the beam. Many of the working parts are below ground on the right, but you can see about half the cylinder. Compare its size with that of the man.

machine, it would make it run like a car with a cold engine. Neither of these disadvantages might bother the owner of a coal mine, but they did mean that the engine was no use to a factory owner. The man who overcame these problems was James Watt, who began to make his inventions in 1765. It took him a long time but, in the end, he built an engine that needed only a reasonable amount of fuel, and ran smoothly enough to drive delicate machines.

In contrast with Newcomen's engine, Watt's was a beautiful piece of engineering. However, through fear of explosions, Watt refused to use high pressure steam, so his engine lacked speed and power. It could not, for example, have driven a railway locomotive. Other inventors were not so timid and, in the early nineteenth century, there were high pressure engines of all kinds. They ranged from Richard Trevithick's huge 'Cornish' pumping engines, to Henry Maudslay's compact little 'table' engines which were just right for workshops.

In this section we will see some of the results which steam engines had.

This table shows how the use of steam power grew:

Steam Power in Great Britain in the Nineteenth Century

	1800	1850	1870	1907
Horsepower	20,000	300,000	1,000,000	9,700,000

1 Draw a graph to illustrate this table.
2 When was the growth of steam power most rapid?

How the Newcomen Engine worked

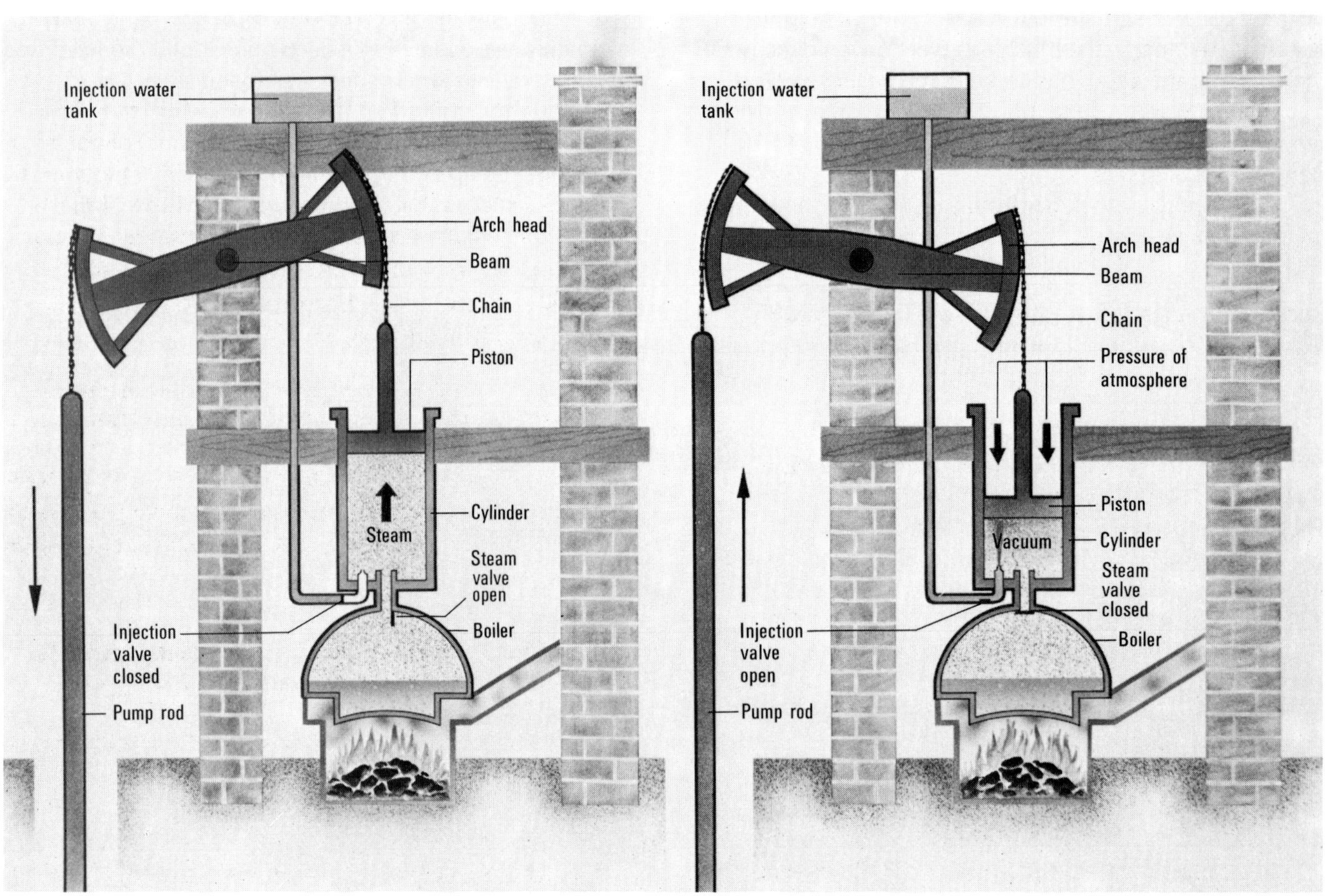

Up Stroke The steam valve is open, the injection valve is closed. The weight of the pump rod tilts the beam and raises the piston. The cylinder fills with steam.

Down Stroke When the piston is as high as it can go, the steam valve closes. The injection valve opens and cold water sprays into the cylinder. This condenses the steam and makes a partial vacuum. The pressure of the atmosphere can now push down the piston.

Note that it is atmospheric pressure which drives the engine, not steam pressure. Newcomen engines are best described as 'atmospheric engines'.

In 1827, an engineer called John Farey wrote:

In our populous towns a multitude of steam engines of all sizes, are continually at work for a great variety of purposes, such as pumping water, grinding corn, sawing timber and stone, rasping logwood, expressing oil from seeds, grinding cutlery, forming lead or copper into sheets or hollow pipes, fulling and scouring woollen cloth, twisting ropes and cables, drawing wire and for every description of laborious employment. We find them also in all extensive breweries and distilleries, in tanneries, soap manufactories, iron foundries and in the national establishments of dockyards and arsenals. Their number is daily increasing and they are continually applied to new purposes.

A Treatise on the Steam Engine

1 How many jobs that are done by the steam engine does Farey list?
2 What changes are taking place in the use of steam power?
3 Does the table on the previous page support what Farey says?

In fact, Farey did not mention the industries for which steam power was most important. He assumed everyone knew about them. We will look at a few.

Here is a description of some steam engines on the Northumberland and Durham Coalfield. It was written in 1853:

The pumping-engine at Friar's Goose colliery was at one time the largest single pumping-engine on the Tyne, being 180 horse-power. It was erected about 20 years ago. The cylinder is 6 feet in diameter, in which the stroke is nine feet. At each stroke 195 gallons of water are delivered to the surface, and as the average is six strokes per minute, 1170 gallons are delivered per minute, or 1,444,800 gallons per day. At South Hetton colliery there is a pumping engine of 300 horse-power. This engine is the most powerful one in the district.

Winding Engines are employed for raising the coal, and also for lowering the men and boys. They are quite separate from the pumping engines, which have quite enough work of their own to do.

At the Eppleton pit they raise, upon an average, 50 score of tubs of coal per day, or 333 tons, the winding engine being of 100 horse power.

At the South Hetton Colliery there are three winding engines of 90 horse-power each, adjoining the great pumping engine before named. The concentration of steam-power at this great establishment exceeds that of any other single colliery. The power of 570 horses is there constantly exerted in pumping out the water, and drawing up the coal.

Newcomen's engine was not of much value in pits which were as deep as 120 yards. Suppose these primitive engines to be all that we could now erect, what would there have been in the South Hetton shaft which is 1080 feet deep?

Our Coal Fields and our Coal Pits J. R. Leifchild

1 What power are the engines? (Give the most powerful, and the least powerful.)
2 What is meant by the 'stroke' of an engine?
3 What is the stroke of the Friar's Goose engine? What is the diameter of the cylinder?
4 How much water does the engine pump in a minute?
5 How much coal does the engine at Eppleton pit raise in a day?
6 Why would a Newcomen engine have been no use at South Hetton?
7 Check this author's arithmetic.

Iron is smelted in a blast furnace. It has this name because it needs a strong blast of air if its fuel is to burn at a high enough temperature. The only way to have the blast is from power driven bellows, and, in the early eighteenth century, ironmasters used water wheels. Here are two extracts from the diary of Richard Ford who had charge of the Coalbrookdale ironworks in Shropshire:

12 June 1733. 'ye Water is very Short wch makes ye Furnaces go on but heavily, but am still wishing for a fresh Supply.

12 July. 'Yesterday was obliged to Blow out ye New Furnace our Water being quite gone, but will put in both ye Hearths with ye utmost Expedition against Water does come.'

Much of the Coalbrookdale iron was sold at Bristol. Ford wrote to Thomas Goldney his partner there:

I will blow as soone as possible & make Piggs for 2 or 3 Weeks in ye meantime Endeavour to pacifie our Chaps for a month in wch time they shall have Piggs & afterwards constantly Supplied

Note: by Piggs, Ford meant pig iron. This is iron which comes straight from the furnace.

At the end of November, Ford wrote:

Our Water here still continues very Short wch at ye Close of ye year will prove much in our disfavour; there never was Such a Complaint at this time of ye year; I don't think there is a Forge in ye Countrey does half work, but there is no remedy but Patience.

1 What problem does Ford mention on 12 June? What does he hope will happen?
2 What did Ford have to do on 12 July?
3 What problem does Goldney have?
4 What does Ford ask him to do?
5 What promise does he make him?
6 How was the weather unusual in 1733?
7 What problem did this create for the whole of the Coalbrookdale area?
8 What, according to Ford, is the only answer?

In the end the Coalbrookdale company bought some steam engines. Study these diagrams:

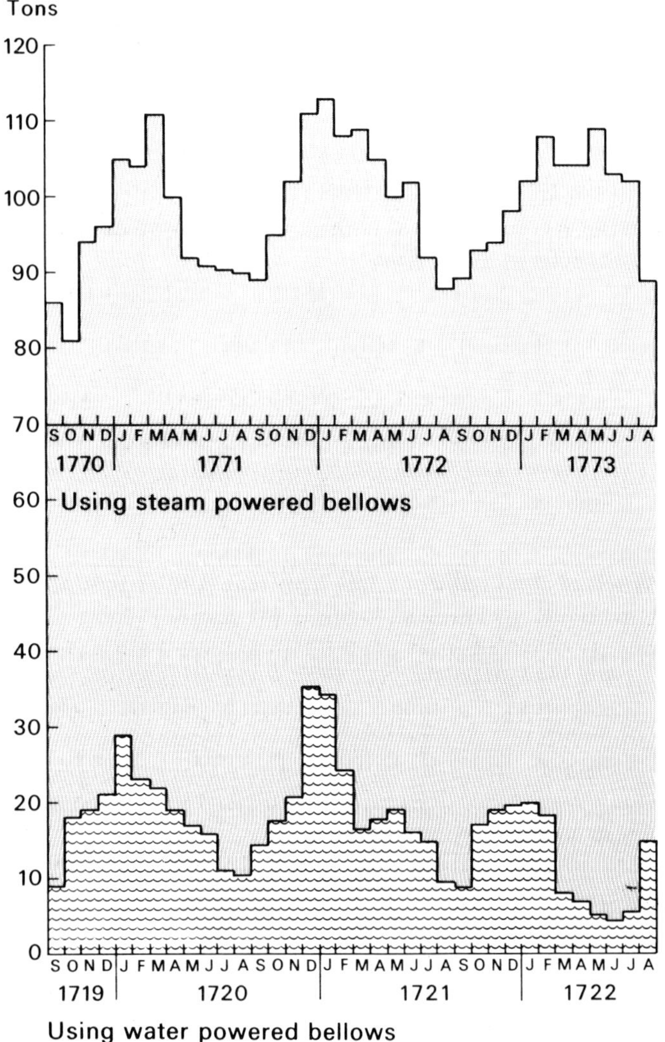

1 How did steam power help the Coalbrookdale iron company?

In 1837 a man called Edward Baines wrote a book about the cotton industry. In it he said:

It is by iron fingers, teeth and wheels, moving with exhaustless energy and devouring speed, that the cotton is opened, cleaned, spread, carded, drawn, roved, spun, wound, warped, dressed and woven. All the machines are moving at once and all derive their motion from the mighty engine: which, firmly seated in the lower part of the building, and constantly fed with water and fuel, toils through the day with the strength of perhaps a hundred horses.

The History of the Cotton Manufacture in Great Britain

1 What are the different processes that take place in a cotton factory?
2 How are the machines driven?

John Farey wrote:

A steam-engine of 100 horse power, which has the strength of 800 men, gives a rapid motion to 50,000 spindles, for spinning fine cotton threads: each spindle forms a separate thread. Although spinning is not an operation of main force, the advantages of machinery are still great, for if the threads were to be spun by the distaff and spindle in the simplest manner which was in use in Queen Elizabeth's time, each person could spin but one thread at a time, and the most diligent and expert spinner could not produce one-fourth as much thread as one of the spindles which are turned by this engine. Seven hundred and fifty people are sufficient for a cotton-mill; and by the assistance of the steam-engine they will spin as much thread as 200,000 persons could do without machinery, or one person can do as much as 266. The engine itself only requires two men to attend it, and supply it with fuel. Each spindle in a mill will produce between two and a half and three hanks (of 840 yards each) per day, which is upwards of a mile and a quarter of thread in twelve hours; so that the 50,000 spindles will produce 62,500 miles of thread every day of twelve hours, which is more than a sufficient length to go two and a half times round the globe.

A Treatise on the Steam Engine, 1827

1 How many spindles might there be in a cotton factory?
2 How many hand spinners would be needed to do the work of one factory spinner?
3 What length of thread will a factory produce in a day? How does this compare with the diameter of the world?

TO

THE ENGINEMEN AND FIREMEN

OF

STATIONARY ENGINES

THROUGHOUT THE UNITED KINGDOM

Let it be remembered that the Cornish engine requires delicate handling, for this reason, that it is a non-rotative engine, and there is no crank to measure out the length of the stroke, and that, in starting the engine, on the skill and dexterity with which the engineman manages his top and bottom handles will depend the life of the engine. Above all things the engine should be handled with confidence and not with timidity.

To the engine-driver, it may be said, remember that so long as you have the handle in your hand you are the master of the engine; you can stop her, reverse her, move her one inch or ten inches as easily as the driver of a locomotive can perform the same operation with his machine; but if you lose your head, or get frightened, at the gigantic inrush of the machine you have put in motion, you had better give up the idea of working a Cornish engine. It requires a cool head, and a strong mind.

There are a few rules for working a Cornish engine that are worth remembering:—

1. Keep the cataract well supplied with water.
2. See that the exhaust and the equilibrium handles are sound forgings, free from flaws. The breaking of either of these may wreck an engine.
3. Be satisfied that cylinder and nozzle-laggings are well lined with sawdust, or other non-conducting material; and that, if the cylinder has a case, the steam-pipe to, and the drain-pipe from, it are working freely.
4. Never institute experiments with your engine for the amusement of visitors. The engine has a regular amount of work to do, and the less you interfere with or interrupt that regularity the better the result. Stop, and start, and run at all kinds of speed, and you will cause priming to an indefinite extent.
5. When stopping an engine always secure both handles with the chain or the rods provided, and shut the governor-valve.
6. Keep your engine clean, and keep everything arranged on a system. Display as much taste in the hanging up of tools as possible. Make monograms: do something besides the bare fact of what you are expected to do. Excellence in any branch of life implies voluntary exertion.

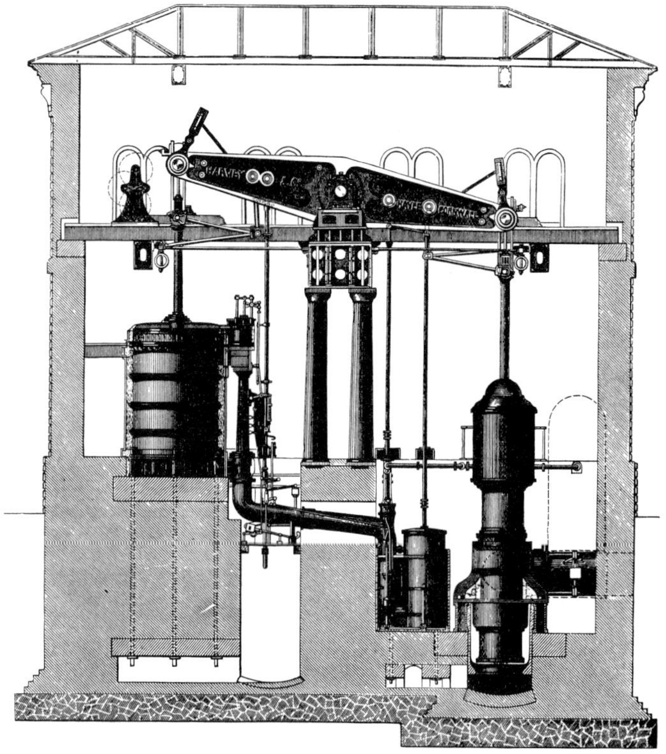

The Cornish Engine The Cornish engine was developed in the early nineteenth century. It was first meant for the tin and copper mines of Cornwall, though it was later used all over Britain. It was a pumping engine, so it had the same purpose as the Newcomen engine, and it was nearly as big. However, it was much more efficient. Also it was far more elegant. You can see that the makers have even used Greek style columns to support the beam! The large object on the right, with the dome, is the pump. Read the instructions to Enginemen and Firemen.

1 How should the engineman handle his engine?
2 What can he do, if he is skilful?
3 What should he do, if he is likely to lose his head?
4 What kind of character should an engineman have?
5 Most of the rules are technical, but you should be able to understand numbers 4 and 6. Explain, in your own words, what they are saying.

Here are two extracts from a report on coal mines written in 1842. The author describes what can happen when miners are being wound to the surface:

1 Within twenty yards of the clatch iron there is fastened a piece of rag which is intended to indicate your near approach to the surface: when this is within sight, the 'tenter' gradually turns off his steam, and you alight coolly on the bank. If, on the contrary, his attention is directed for a moment to another object, you are sent over the pulley with fearful rapidity and killed, probably, above ground: or the rope breaking you are flung with a certainty, an awful certainty, of immediate death.

2 I met with more than one instance of Children only ten years old having the lives of the colliers left to their

mercy and have seen others so inattentive to their duty as to let the corve be drawn over the pulley, and half a ton of coals thrown down the shaft.

A little more than a year since two lads were much hurt and nearly killed owing to the carelessness of the engine boy, who had the care of the engine and was only fourteen years of age, drawing them over the pulley: the engine man is obliged to be there before five in the morning, and never home before ten (p.m.), and as the butties (foremen) only allow 2/- (10p) a day for all these hours, they are therefore obliged to employ boys.

Children's Employment Commission (Mines) Parliamentary Papers 1842

1 How does the engine man know his passengers are nearing the surface?
2 What happens if his attention wanders?
3 Why do engine men sometimes leave boys to look after their engines? (Look at their hours and their wages.)

In the 1840's a man called William Dodd made a tour of the factory towns of the north of England. Here is an extract from a letter which he wrote to Lord Shaftesbury:

I had not been an hour in Bolton, before an accident occurred to a boy of the name of Samuel Skelton, of a very distressing nature, almost under my own eye. This took place in the cotton factory of Messrs Gregson and Leeming, on Thursday the 7th instant. I visited this youth, and sitting by his bed-side I took the following particulars from his weeping mother. She told me that, 'having a large family, she had been under the necessity of sending him to the cotton factory belonging to Mr. W. Garnett Taylor, at nine years of age, where he worked only a short time before he got his *right arm* entangled in the machinery, and so dreadfully crushed and torn, as to render amputation *above the elbow* necessary. In consequence of this accident, he was off work three years, during which time he had no assistance from his master! About three months ago he was again employed in the card-room of a cotton factory, belonging to the firm of Messrs. Gregson and Leeming, and on Thursday last, his left hand was caught by the machinery. By this accident he has lost the two middle fingers, and it is thought the little finger will have to be taken off; his hand also is very much torn. If he gets well, he will only have the forefinger and thumb on his left hand, and having previously lost his right arm, he will have to depend on someone for a living for the remainder of his days. I was told that Samuel Skelton's masters had done nothing for him; but I hope some public-spirited individual will take the case in hand, and try to get them to assist in some way. His father is a striker at an iron-foundry, and gets 15s. (75p) a week, when fully employed. He has a wife and eight children; one at service, one earning 5s. (25p) per week and another 2s.6d ($12\frac{1}{2}$p): this is the whole income of a family consisting of nine persons. My Lord, I am sorry to say, that a great part of the machinery in cotton factories is not guarded as it ought to be, and wants looking after.

The Factory System Illustrated

1 How did Samuel Skelton hurt himself?
2 What injuries did he suffer?
3 Whom does Dodd criticise ? Why?
4 What is your opinion of the boy's parents?
5 What does Dodd say should be done with the machinery?

Written Work

Imagine it is 1850. Write a report on the use of steam power in Great Britain, saying how it has grown, how it has helped and what problems it has caused. You will give a fuller account if you use the section on handloom weavers as well as this one.

Research

1 Calculate, roughly, how much coal the woman in the picture on page 25 could raise in a day. Assume that one load of coal would be about equal to the weight of the children and that the pit is about 300 ft deep. You must allow time for the load to be hooked on at the bottom and taken off at the top. How many women, roughly, would have been needed to do the work of the steam engine at Eppleton pit? (Page 51)
2 Calculate the capacity in cubic centimetres, of the cylinder of the Friar's Goose engine (page 51). You can take the stroke as being its height. How many strokes did the engine make in a minute? What horse power was it?
What is the cubic capacity of the engine of the average family car? How many revolutions per minute will it make? How many brake horse power will it develop? Compare these figures with those for the steam engine.
3 Find out more about the way the Watt engine worked.
4 Find out uses for the steam engine which are not mentioned in this section.
5 Visit any museum where steam engines have been restored and can be seen working.
6 Think of changes taking place in industry at the present day. Which are at all like the development of steam power in the early nineteenth century?

Chapter 3 *Transport*

Roads

Before the eighteenth century, most of the roads in Britain were no more than tracks. Village people kept them in some sort of repair themselves, and they did not care if they were rough. This was because they only used them for going to and from their fields with their carts and animals. They saw no reason to make fine roads for travellers who wanted to go long distances. In fact, there were very few of such travellers.

Nineteenth century coach

As late as 1826, William Cobbett had this conversation at East Everleigh, a village in Wiltshire:

I rode to the garden-gate of a cottage and asked a woman, who seemed to be about thirty years old, which was the way to Ludgershall, which I knew could not be more than about four miles off. She did not know! A very neat, smart and pretty woman: but she did not know the way to this town which was, I was sure, only about four

Mail coach in a drift of snow It is more important to save the horses than the coach. One horse has already been unharnessed. Why is a is a man riding away on it, do you suppose? Before turnpike roads were made there were no coach services in winter. Afterwards, coaches sometimes got into trouble, but that still happens today.

miles off! 'Well, my good woman,' said I, 'but have you been at Ludgershall?' 'No' – 'Nor at Andover?' (Six miles another way.) – 'No' – 'Nor at Marlborough?' (Nine miles another way) – 'No.' – 'Pray, were you born in this house?' – 'Yes' – 'And how far have you ever been from this house?' – 'Oh, I have been up in the parish and over to Chute'. That is to say, the utmost extent of her journeys had been about two and a half miles!

Rural Rides, 1826

1 How does Cobbett describe the woman?
2 What towns has she not visited?
3 How far away had the woman been, in her life?

A man who did have to travel a great deal was Arthur Young. He wrote about farming and went all over the country looking for information. He said this about some roads in Essex:

Of all the cursed roads that ever disgraced this kingdom, none ever equalled that from Billericay to Tilbury. It is for near twelve miles so narrow that a mouse cannot pass by any carriage: I saw a fellow creep under his waggon to assist me to lift my chaise over a hedge. The ruts are of an incredible depth. The trees everywhere overgrow the road, so that it is totally shaded from the sun, except at a few places. Add to all that the eternally meeting with chalk waggons, themselves frequently stuck fast, till 20 or 30 horses are tacked to each to draw them out, one by one.

After this description will you – can you – believe that a Turnpike was much wanted by some gentlemen, but opposed by the bruins of this county? I do not imagine that the kingdom produces such an example of detestable stupidity; and yet in this tract are found numbers of farmers who are perfectly well content with their roads.

A Six Weeks Tour through the Southern Counties of England and Wales, 1769

Notes: 1 Chalk was dug from the hills in Essex and spread on the lowland clay soils as a kind of fertiliser.
2 A Turnpike Trust would have improved the road, but at a cost.

1 What does Young say is wrong with this road?
2 Why is Young using the road? What kind of road does he want?

3 Why are the farmers using the road? What kind of road do they want?
4 What does Young say about the farmers?
5 What do you suppose the farmers might have said about Young?

During the eighteenth century more and more people wanted to travel and send goods. The roads had to be improved, and it was certain the ordinary villagers would not do the work. As a result the more important people in an area might form a Turnpike Trust. The Trust would ask Parliament to pass an Act giving it permission to take over a stretch of road. A French visitor, de Saussure describes the system:

> The Roads are magnificent being wide, smooth and well kept. It is not the custom here, as it is in France for the poor peasants to be forced to make up the high roads. In this country, everyone who makes use of the roads is obliged to contribute to the cost of keeping them up. At equal distances there are gates called 'Turnpikes', where you have to pay a penny per horse. The keeper of the turnpike gives you a ticket and a leaden mark, so that you need not pay a second time on your way back that same day.
>
> *A Foreign View of England in the Reigns of George I and George II, 1725–1730*

1 What does de Saussure think of English roads?
2 How are the main roads cared for in France?
3 Who pays for them in England?
4 How is the money collected?

Here is a list of the Turnpike Acts for the road from London to Bristol:

	Miles	*Date*
Kensington – Cranford Bridge	12	1717
Cranford Bridge – Maidenhead Bridge	14	1727
Maidenhead Bridge – Twyford	8	1718
Twyford – Reading	5	1736
Reading – Puntfield	$6\frac{1}{2}$	1714
Puntfield – Newbury	11	1728
Newbury – Marlborough	17	1726
Marlborough – Cherhill	8	1743
Cherhill – Studley Bridge	5	1707
Studley Bridge – Toghill	16	1727
Toghill – Bristol	8	1727

1 How many Turnpike trusts looked after the road between London and Bristol?
2 Which had the longest stretch of road? Which had the shortest? What was the average?

The map shows the road, with the places mentioned by the Acts:

1 Trace the map on to a piece of paper, in pencil. Mark in different colours the stretches of road that were turnpiked in each decade (ten years) between 1700 and 1750. Add a key to the map to explain what each colour means.
2 Imagine you had travelled from London to Bristol in 1720. What parts of your journey would have been on turnpiked roads? (Are things very different today? Look at a motorway map and say what you think.)

London – Bristol Turnpike Road

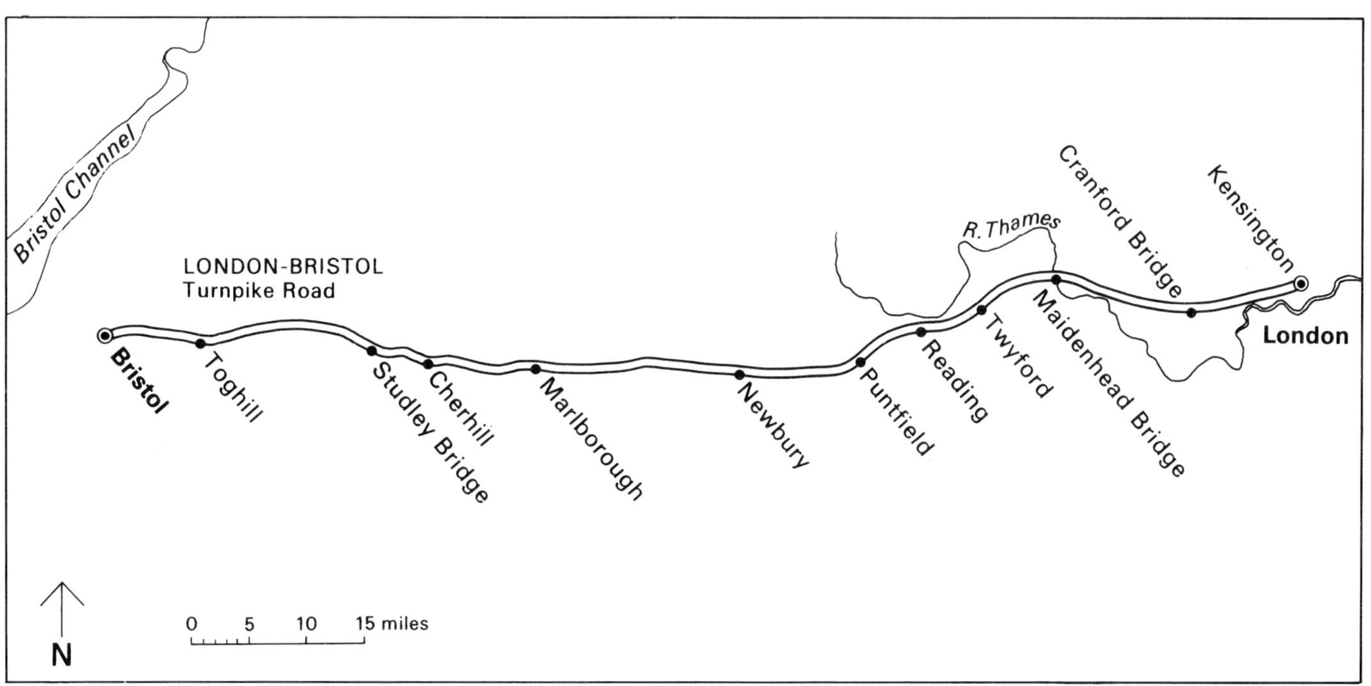

This table shows the number of Turnpike Acts passed for the whole of Great Britain in the eighteenth century:

Before 1700	5	1750–1759	170
1700–1709	10	1760–1769	170
1710–1719	23	1770–1779	75
1720–1729	45	1780–1789	34
1730–1739	25	1790–1799	71
1740–1749	37	1800–1809	59

1 Show this information with a bar diagram.
2 A certain period is known for its 'turnpike mania'. When do you think it was?
3 You will realise that the London to Bristol road was turnpiked before most of the others. Why was that do you suppose?

One of the most famous road engineers of the turnpike age was John Loudon Macadam. Here he explains his ideas on road building:

The first operation in making a road should be the reverse of digging a trench. The road should not be sunk below but rather raised above the level of the land beside it, and care should be taken that there be a sufficient fall to take off the water. This must be done by making drains to lower ground. Having secured the soil from *under* water the road-maker should next secure it from rain water by means of a solid road made of clean, dry stone or flint, so selected, prepared and laid as to be perfectly impervious to water. This cannot be done unless the greatest care be taken that no earth, clay, chalk or other matter that will hold or conduct water be mixed with the broken stone. This must be so prepared and laid as to unite by its own angles into a firm, compact body.

The thickness of such a road does not matter. The object is already attained by providing dry ground, over which the road is placed as a roof to keep it dry. Experience has shown that if water passes through to the soil, the road, whatever its thickness, loses its support and goes to pieces.

Remarks on the Present System of Road Making, 1821

Eighteenth century coach This painting was done in the nineteenth century. How does the artist give the impression that there has been a great deal of progress? (Contrast this picture with the one on page 55)

Section through a Macadam road

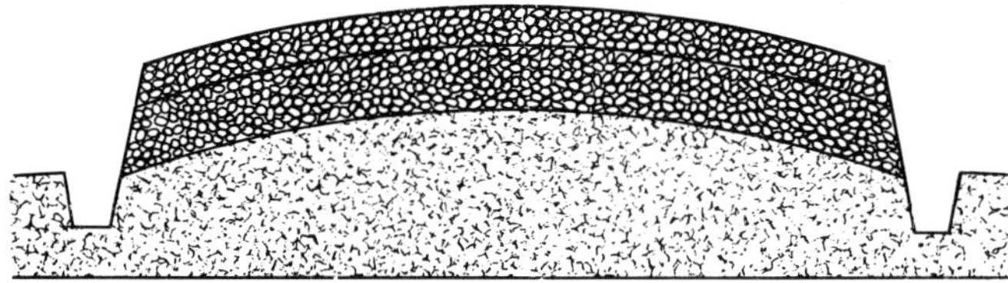

1 How does Macadam prepare the base for his road? What is he trying to ensure?
2 What materials does Macadam use in a road? How must they be laid?
3 What materials does he avoid using? Why?
4 Why does Macadam say the thickness of the road does not matter?
5 What will make a road collapse?

The turnpike trusts employed Macadam and men like him to make their roads. Arthur Young describes the road between Salisbury and Romsey which, he says, was the best he had ever found:

> Fine as their materials are, yet I have in other countries met with as fine: but never with any that were so firmly united, and kept so totally free from loose stones, ruts and water; and, when I add water, let me observe, that it is not by that vile custom of cutting grips for it to run off, to the dislocation of one's bones in crossing them: but by laying the surface so firm that carriages make no holes for it to settle in, and having everywhere a gentle fall, it runs immediately off. To conclude the whole, it is everywhere broad enough for three carriages to pass each other: and lying in straight lines, with an even edge of grass the whole way, it has more the appearance of an elegant gravel walk than of an high road.
>
> *A Six Weeks Tour through the Southern Counties of England and Wales*, 1769

Note: 'grips' were gutters that ran across a road from side to side.

1 How does Young say the road has been laid?
2 How is the surface kept free from water? What method is *not* used? Why was Young pleased about that?
3 Which of Macadam's ideas have been followed here?
4 How wide is the road?
5 To what does Young compare the road?

A retired officer, General Dyott, wrote this in his diary in 1827:

> I should imagine that travelling, as far as speed is concerned, must have reached perfection, from the very fine state of the roads and goodness of horses. We travelled ninety-nine miles, in little more than twelve hours, including a stoppage to dine. Lord Anglesey has journied from London to Beaudesert in something less than twelve hours: that is one hundred and twenty-five miles.

1 What does General Dyott think of the speed of travel? What reasons does he give for it?
2 What was the average speed he made on his journey?
3 What was the average speed Lord Anglesey made on his?

This extract is from a newspaper report of 1830 when coaching was at its peak:

> It is calculated that a person has 1500 opportunities of leaving London in the course of twenty-four hours by stage coaches. It is understood that about 300 coaches pass through Hyde Park Corner Turnpike daily. There are about forty Brighton coaches.
>
> There are 84 coaches going to Birmingham, of which 40 are daily: to Manchester 70, of which 54 are daily. In the year 1770 there belonged only two stages coaches to Manchester, one to London and one to Liverpool, and they went only twice a week: now 20 coaches pass backwards and forwards daily between Manchester and Liverpool.
>
> *The Huntingdon Gazette*, May 15th, 1830

1 How many coaches leave London every day?
2 How many coaches pass Hyde Park Corner in a day? How many passengers would they be carrying? Allow twelve to a coach. (Hazard a guess at how many people pass Hyde Park Corner by public transport today. Do not forget the Underground).
3 How many coaches go to Brighton, Birmingham and Manchester?
4 How many coaches went between Manchester and Liverpool every week in 1770? How many make this journey in 1830? (Allow a six day week). How many passengers are carried? (Allow twelve to a coach).

Study these tables:

Charges for Carriage per cwt of goods: North Yorkshire–London

1692	1727	1758
92p	80p	50p

Horses allowed per Waggon (General Highways Acts)

1667	1751
7	5

Weights allowed per Waggon in Tons (General Highways Acts)

1662		1741		1765	
Winter	Summer	Winter	Summer	Winter	Summer
1	$1\frac{1}{2}$	3	3	6	6

Note: After 1753, waggons with wheels more than 9 inches wide could carry any load they wanted.

1 Show this information on three bar diagrams.
2 In what three ways did turnpikes help the transport of goods?
3 Why do you suppose there was no limit to the weight a broad wheeled waggon could carry?

A foreign traveller in Britain described what it was like to ride on the outside of a coach:

The getting up was at the risk of one's life: and when I was up, I was obliged to sit just at the corner of the coach, with nothing to hold by, but a sort of little handle fastened on the side. I sat nearest the wheel; and the moment that we set off, I fancied that I saw certain death await me. All I could do, was to take still faster hold of the handle, and to be more and more careful to keep my balance.

The coach now rolled along with prodigious rapidity, over the stones through the town, and every moment we seemed to fly into the air: so that it was almost a miracle that we stuck to the coach and did not fall. We seemed to be thus on the wing, and to fly, as often as we passed through a village, or went down a hill.

Travels in England, 1782, C. Moritz

1 Why did Moritz find his journey frightening?

Traffic at the Elephant and Castle, London, 1826 How many vehicles are there? How many of them are stage coaches? Which of the extracts gives the same impression as this picture?

Obviously, riding on a coach, particularly outside, was unpleasant in the rain or the cold. Here is Mary Russell Mitford's description of a coach in hot, dry weather:

If we happened to meet a carriage coming along the road, what a sandy whirlwind it was! What choking! What suffocation! I shall never forget the plight in which we met the coach one evening in last August, full an hour after its time, steeds and driver, carriage and passengers, all one dust. The outsiders, and the horses, and the coachman seemed reduced to a quiet despair. They had left off trying to better their condition and taken refuge in a wise and patient hopelessness. The six insides, on the contrary, were still fighting against their fate. They were visibly grumbling at the weather, scolding at the dust, and heating themselves like a furnace by striving against the heat. How well I remember the fat gentleman without his coat, who was wiping his forehead and heaving up his wig. And that poor boy, red-hot all in a flame, whose mamma was trying to relieve his sufferings by the removal of his neckerchief – an operation which he resisted with all his might. How perfectly I remember him, as well as the pale girl, who sat fanning herself with her bonnet into an absolute fever. They vanished after a while into their own dust.

Our Village, 1848

1 Why was the journey unpleasant?
2 How were the people outside the coach behaving?
3 What were the people inside doing?

In 1861, a coachman, Thomas Cross wrote this:

In London, twenty years ago, the half-hour before the starting of perhaps five or six coaches from any of the large inns was a time of some little excitement. The neat and elegant Telegraph Coach, with its polished boot, on the hinder part of which was painted, in large letters 'The Times' 'The Independent' 'The Wonder', or some such appropriate name: the highly varnished body, the blazing Golden Cross or the Spread Eagle on the door panels: the motley crowd of people, of both sexes and all ranks, from the peer to the humble workman, some anxious to take their seats in or on these delightful conveyances: the well-groomed horses, the harness all in the nicest order: the quantity of packages issuing forth from the booking office: the instructions, not unmixed with a little good-natured banter from the booking-clerk, formed altogether a most picturesque scene.

How different the same half-hour in a provincial town today. On approaching the inn not a solitary person did I see. The dingy, half-washed coach stood by itself outside the gates, like a deserted ship; inside the yard there was a dim, dirty place set aside for the office; in it glimmered one poor mutton candle, stuck on a piece of rusty tin, that had served the ostler for a candlestick for years: by its light I entered, and could just perceive a lantern-jawed, melancholy-looking man, whose visage indicated – indeed seemed already to anticipate – the fate that awaited both him and me, leaning with his head upon his hand, inert and heedless, as most men are who have nothing to do – this was the porter. On the other side of the counter, behind an old worm-eaten desk, sat the book-keeper. The usual greeting having passed between us, I took from the desk a long sheet of white paper, which, with the exception of the heading was unsullied – not the name of a passenger or parcel was written thereon! This was what is called the 'way-bill'.

The Autobiography of a Stage-Coachman, 1861

1 What changes had there been in coaching during Thomas Cross's working life?

This table shows what it cost (in modern currency) to travel between Liverpool and Manchester in 1830:

	Fare		Time
Stage Coach	50p Inside	25p Outside	3 hours
Train	25p First Class	$17\frac{1}{2}$p Second Class	2 hours

How does the table explain the changes Thomas Cross describes?

Written Work

Write an account of road transport in the eighteenth and early nineteenth centuries. Decide first of all what headings you are going to use. Turnpike Trusts and Coach Travel could be two of them, but you will need several others.

Research

1 Find out what you can about the road engineers, especially John Metcalfe, John Loudon Macadam and Thomas Telford.
2 Find out what you can about the different types of coach and private carriage that were in use during the eighteenth and early nineteenth centuries. How did coaches change as the roads improved?
3 Read some of the very good descriptions of coach travel which you will find in Dickens. Try, *Pickwick Papers*, Chapter 28; *Martin Chuzzlewit*, Chapter 35; *David Copperfield* Chapters 19 and 55; *Nicholas Nickleby*, Chapter 5.
The Uncommercial Traveller, Chapter 24, describes an old stage coaching house that had been ruined by the railways.

Inland Waterways

In Britain there are numbers of good rivers. People have travelled and carried goods on them since prehistoric times. Moreover, they have improved them by digging cuts to avoid the larger bends, building locks and making towpaths.

Joseph Priestley, who was the manager of the Aire and Calder Navigation, wrote this about the River Trent:

> The length of this river from Burton-on-Trent, where it becomes navigable, to the Humber, is about one hundred and seventeen miles, and the fall to the low-water mark is 118 feet.
>
> This river, connecting the port of Hull, with a wide extent of agricultural, mining and manufacturing country, by means of the various rivers and canals which connect with it, affords an easy means of export for the manufactures of a large district in Lancashire; the salt from Cheshire; the produce of the potteries in Staffordshire; the coal from Derbyshire; and the agricultural produce of Nottinghamshire, Leicestershire and Lincolnshire. It also opens a link with the sea by way of Lincoln and Boston; through which channels, as well as the Humber, the goods mentioned above are carried: and in return, the interior of the country is supplied, either by Hull and Gainsborough, or Boston and Lincoln, with such goods as are required by an immense population.

Historical Account of the Navigable Rivers, Canals and Railways throughout Great Britain, 1831

1 How much of the River Trent can boats use? Which town is at the head of navigation?
2 What different parts of England does the river serve?

River Trent, and Trent and Mersey Canal Locate on the map the places mentioned by Priestley. What problem would there have been before the canals were built? The River Trent was not navigable above Wilden Ferry, but the canal builders were able to use its valley.

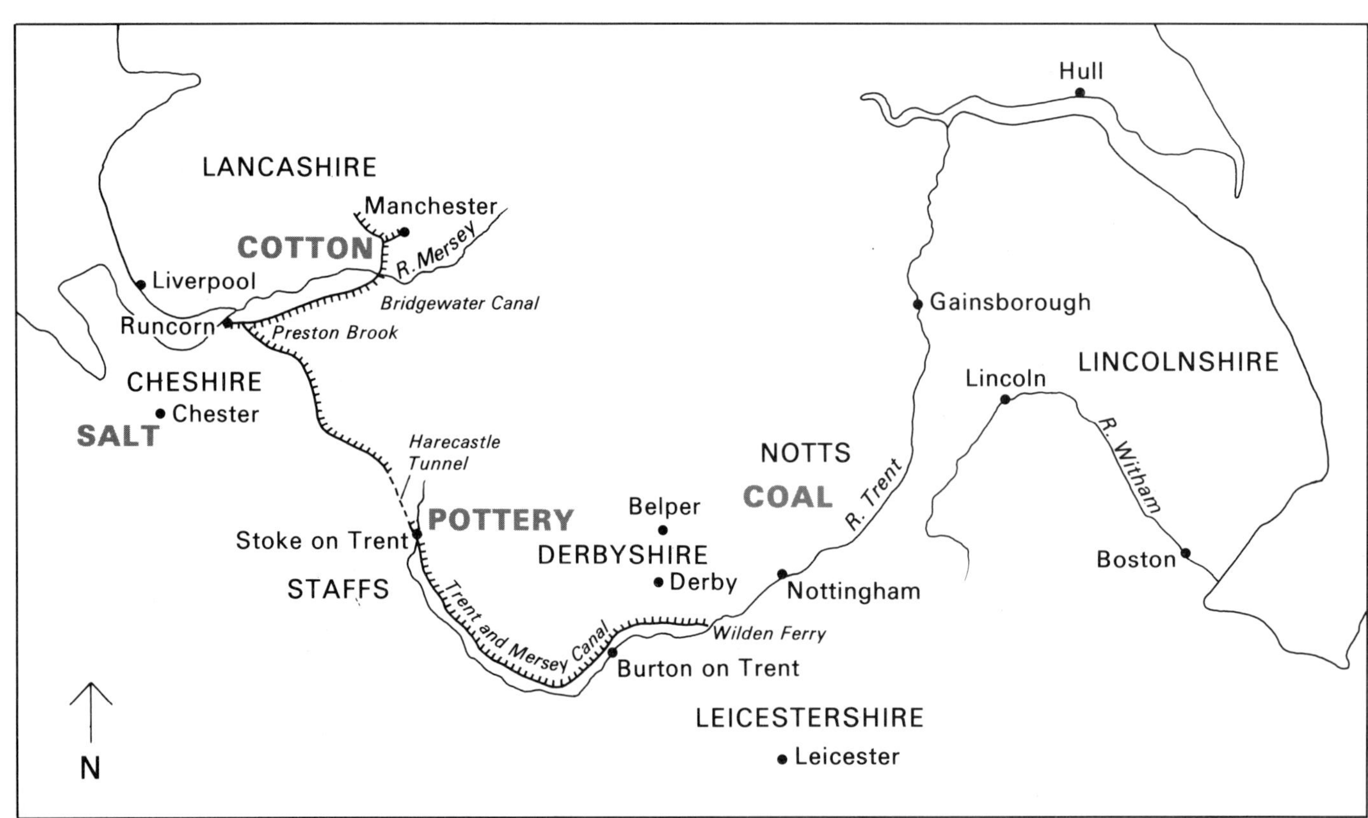

Josiah Wedgwood's Pottery Works, Etruria, near Stafford The Trent and Mersey Canal runs in front of the works. Wedgwood needed china clay which came by sea from Cornwall to Liverpool. He also needed flintstones which came from the Yorkshire hills near Hull. Why was he pleased when the Trent and Mersey Canal opened?

3 What goods does it carry?
4 What ports are on it, or near it?
5 Find the places which Priestley mentions, on the map.

One trouble with rivers is that they do not always flow where you want them, and during the eighteenth century people needed to send more and more goods by water. The answer was to dig canals.

Canals seemed very efficient. In about 1800 a group of engineers made some experiments to see what load a horse could transport in different ways.

Here are the results:

		Tons
1	Pack-horse	$\frac{1}{8}$th
2	Stage waggon, soft road	$\frac{5}{8}$ths
3	Stage waggon, Macadam road	2
4	Barge on river	30
5	Barge on canal	50
6	Waggon on iron rails	8

1 How many pack-horses would be needed to do the work of one canal horse?
2 How many stage waggon horses, working on a soft road, would be needed?
3 Draw a bar diagram to compare the work done by a canal horse, with that done by numbers 3, 4 and 6.
4 Why could a horse draw a heavier load on a canal than on a river?

Though there were numbers of canals made in the middle years of the eighteenth century, the first to catch people's imagination was the Bridgewater Canal. It had that name because its owner was the Duke of Bridgewater. The canal is nowhere near the town of Bridgewater, but is in south Lancashire. It was built in two stages. The first, from Worsley to Manchester, opened in 1771, and the second, from Manchester to Runcorn, in 1776.

Arthur Young wrote:

> The original design of the Duke of Bridgewater, was to cut a canal from Worsley, an estate of his Grace's, abounding with coal mines, to Manchester, for the easy transport of his coals to so large a market; and, in 1758–9, an Act of Parliament for that purpose was obtained. A later Act enabled the Duke greatly to extend his plan; for he now decided, and with uncommon spirit, to make his canal run not only from Worsley to Manchester, but also from part of the canal between both, to Stockport and Liverpool. The idea was a noble one, and ranks this young nobleman with the most useful geniuses of this or any other age.
>
> *A Six Months Tour through the North of England*, 1770

1 Why did the Duke of Bridgewater want to join Worsley and Manchester by canal?
2 Young says the second length of the canal ran to Liverpool. How far, in fact, did it run? Why was it not necessary to dig it all the way to Liverpool?
3 It was already possible for boats to go from Liver-

pool to Manchester for the Mersey and Irwell Navigation Company had improved those two rivers. Why did the Duke of Bridgewater think a canal would be better, do you suppose?

In 1800, the writer Robert Southey was in South Lancashire. This is what he said:

> England is now crossed in every direction by canals. This is the district in which they were first tried by the present Duke of Bridgewater, whose fortune has been greatly increased by the success of his experiment. His engineer, Brindley, was a man of real genius for this particular work who thought of nothing but locks and levels, perforating hills, and floating barges upon aqueduct bridges over unmanageable streams. When he had a plan to form he usually went to bed, and lay there working it out in his head till the design was completed. It is recorded of him that being asked why he supposed rivers were created, he answered after a pause – to feed navigable canals.
>
> *Espirella's Letters from England*

1 Why, according to Southey, was South Lancashire important for canals?
2 What problems did Brindley solve? How did he do so?
3 According to the story, why did Brindley think God had created rivers? Why did people tell this story about Brindley, do you suppose?

Joseph Priestley said this about the Bridgewater Canal:

> The whole of these canals and branches were made under the direction of Mr. Brindley, at an expense to his noble patron of £220,000: but as it all issued from his private purse, the public has no means of arriving at the exact amount, nor have they much better means of discovering the annual income, though it was estimated, some years ago, at £130,000.
>
> These navigations, although made at the private expense of the Noble Duke, and valuable as they have proved to his successors, are of much greater importance to the town of Manchester, from the ease they have afforded for the transport of goods, and in reducing the price of coal which, before, could only be obtained at double its present cost.
>
> *Historical Account of the Navigable Rivers, Canals and Railways throughout Great Britain*, 1831

Note: the Bridgewater Canal was the only one of any importance to be paid for by one man. All the others belonged to public companies, who had to publish their accounts.

Starvationers at the entrance to the mines at Worsley The 'starvationers' are the boats. Probably, they had this name because their hulls looked 'ribby' on the outside. They carried the coal from the coal face to Manchester. There were more miles of waterway underground than in the open. This was a drift mine. Since the coal seam came out of the side of the hill, there was no need for a shaft, as in the diagram on page 23.

The Bridgewater Canal The stretch from Worsley to Manchester opened in 1761 and the longer stretch, to Runcorn, in 1776.

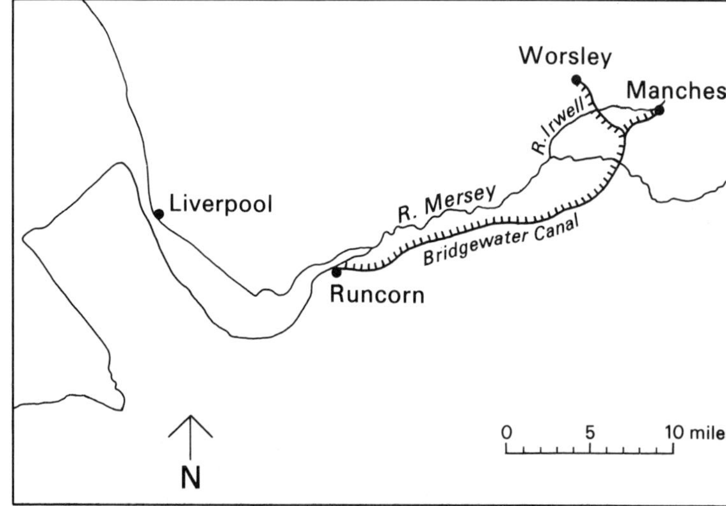

1 How much does Priestley think the Bridgewater Canal cost?
2 How much a year does he think the Duke made from it?
3 Why was the canal especially important for Manchester?

Before anyone could improve a river for navigation, or build a canal, they needed an Act of Parliament giving them permission. Here are the numbers of Acts passed for River Navigations and Canals over a period of time:

Year	*Number of Acts*	*Year*	*Number of Acts*
1750–4	3	1785–9	6
1755–9	7	1790–4	51
1760–4	3	1795–9	9
1765–9	13	1800–4	6
1770–4	7	1805–9	3
1775–9	5	1810–14	8
1780–4	4		

1 Show this information on a bar diagram.
2 It is sometimes said the Duke of Bridgewater's success with his canal encouraged others to copy him. How far do you agree? (Look back to see the dates when the two branches of the Bridgewater Canal were finished).
3 At one period there was what we call the 'canal mania'. Look at your chart and decide when that was.

An important early canal was the Trent and Mersey, sometimes known as the Grand Trunk. It was started in 1766 and finished in 1777. Priestley says:

The canal was planned by Mr. Brindley and built by him up to the time of his death, and after that by Mr. Henshall. Besides the extensive one over the Dove there are no less than one hundred and twenty-six aqueducts and culverts, ninety-one locks and six tunnels. The lockage from Harecastle Summit to the Trent, at Wilden Ferry, is 316 feet; the six locks next Wilden Ferry are 14 feet wide, enabling the river boats to come up to Burton; the rest only 7 feet; from the summit to the Duke's Canal at Preston Brook, is a lockage of 326 feet. The famous Harecastle Tunnel, two thousand eight hundred and eighty yards long, is situated upon the summit of this canal. The total length of the canal is ninety-three miles.

Historical Account of the Navigable Rivers, Canals and Railways throughout Great Britain, 1831

1 Who planned and started the Trent and Mersey Canal? Why did he not finish it?
2 How many aqueducts and culverts are there on the canal?
3 How many locks are there? How high does the canal rise at either end?
4 Why are the locks near Wilden Ferry 14 feet wide? How wide are the other locks?
5 How would the different widths of the locks cause problems?

Locks are needed on canals where boats have to change level. Gates at each end have sluices to let water in or out.

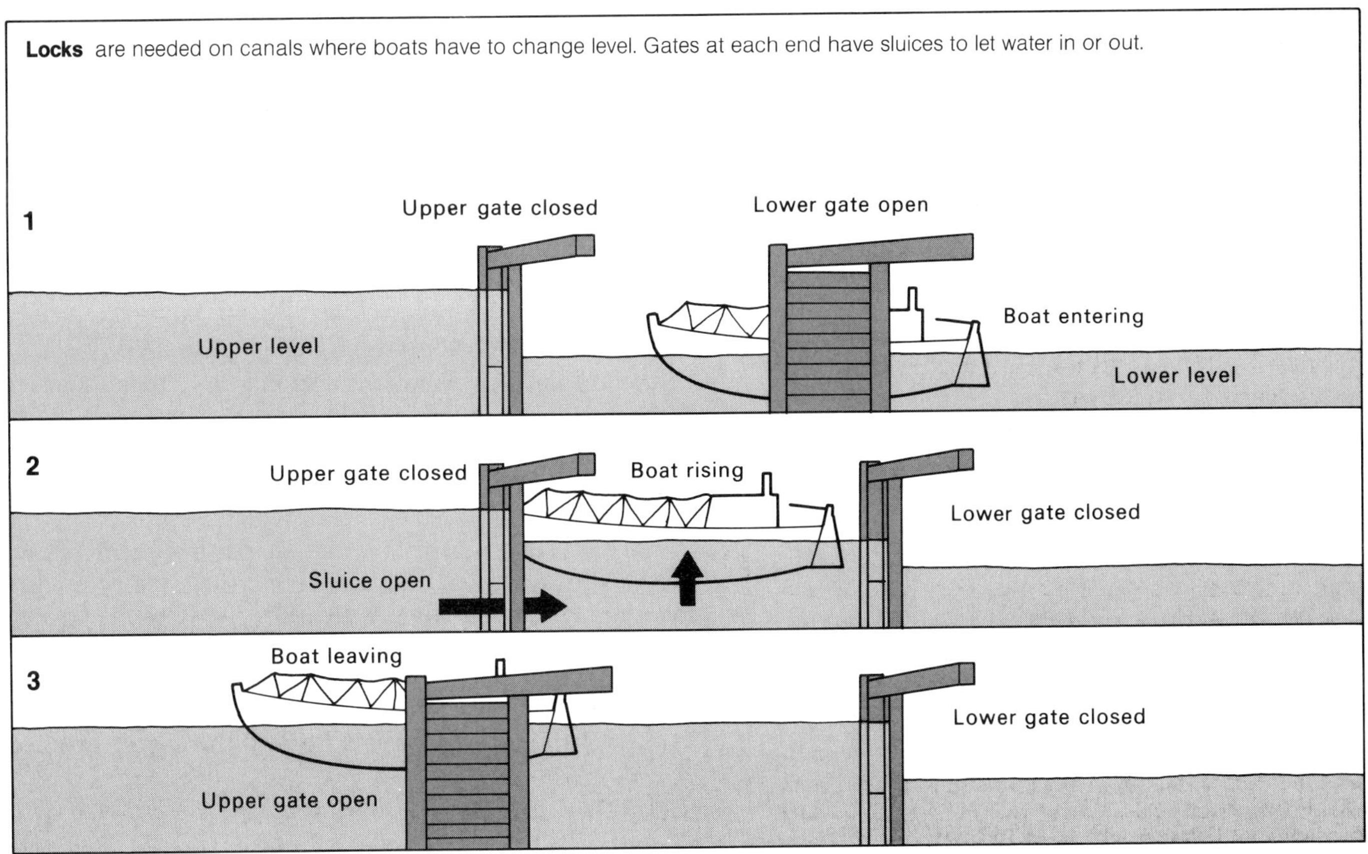

6 How many tunnels are there? Which is the most famous? How long is it?

Mostly, canals carried goods, but there were a few passenger boats as well. Robert Southey went for a ride on one:

> We left Manchester on Monday morning and embarked upon the canal in a stage-boat bound for Chester. This was a new mode of travelling and a delightful one. The boat is like a Noah's Ark, except that the roof is flatter, to carry passengers. Within this floating house are two rooms, with seats at different prices, the parlour, and the kitchen. Two horses, harnessed one before the other, tow it along at the rate of a league (three miles) an hour: the very pace which it is pleasant to keep up with when walking on the bank. The canal is just wide enough for two boats to pass; sometimes we sprang ashore, sometimes we stood or sat upon the roof – till to our surprise we were called down to dinner, and found that as good a meal had been prepared in the back part of the boat while we were going on, as would have been supplied at an inn. We joined in a wish that the same kind of travelling was possible everywhere; no time was lost; kitchen and cellar travelled with us; the movement of the boat was not noticed; we could neither be overturned nor run away with; if we sank there was no depth of water to drown us; we could read as conveniently as in a house, or sleep as quietly as in a bed.
>
> *Espriella's Letters from England*

A navigable river: a section of the River Wey For how much of its journey, roughly, would a boat be travelling by cut, and how much by river? There is a lock at the end of each cut. That is because a cut is made level, but the river goes on falling.

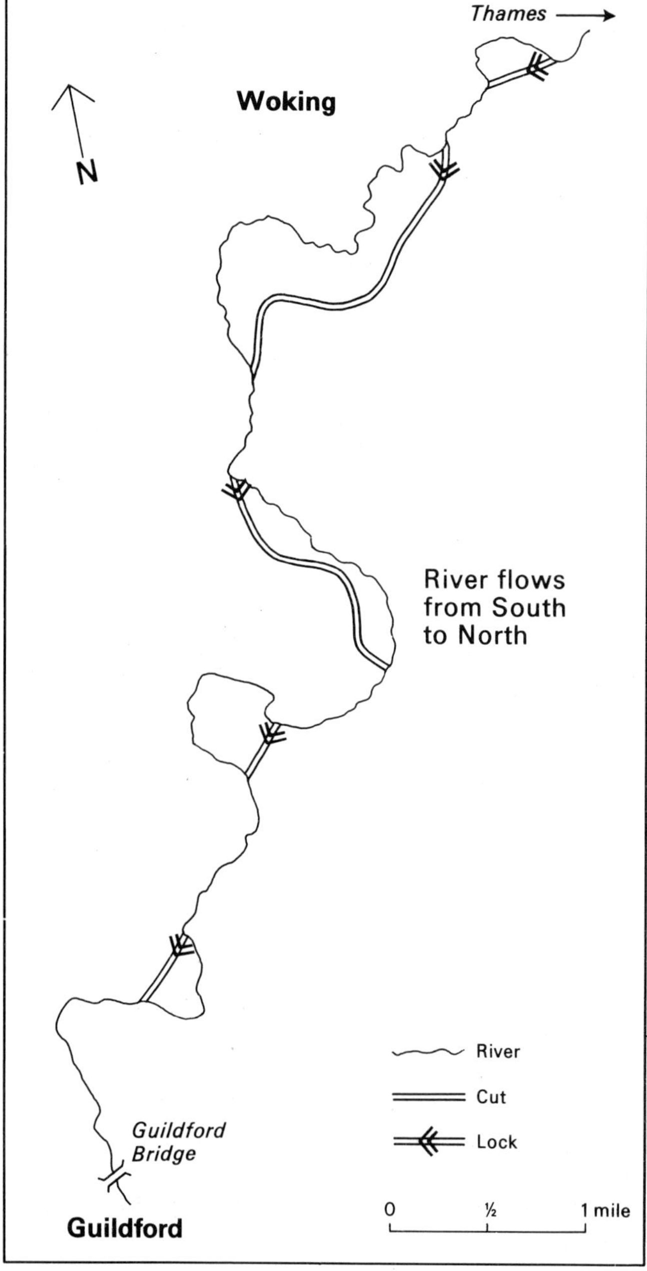

1 What canal do you suppose Southey travelled on, from Manchester?
2 How does Southey describe the canal boat?
3 How would we describe 'two rooms, with seats at different prices'?
4 What other rooms were there?
5 How did the passengers spend their time?
6 What surprised Southey about the food?
7 List all the things Southey likes about travelling by canal boat. Though he does not mention it he is comparing the boat to another form of travel. What is that?
8 Can you see one disadvantage travel by boat would have for many people? This was the reason it never became popular.

At Belper in Derbyshire there was an important cotton factory belonging to the Strutt family. They bought much of their raw cotton from London merchants. In 1826, the Strutts sent this letter to their agent in London:

> The following numbers of Sea Island Cotton are come in so shameful a condition that we must charge someone with the damage. The ropes are broken, the bags burst and the Cotton strewed about in a way we never saw before. The boatmen from Gainsborough say they received them in that state – it will be well if they can prove it, because then if you can prove the delivery in a good state, the damage is fixed on the Carrier between London and Gainsbro'.

Note: Sea Island Cotton is of the best quality. It is grown off the coast of the United States.

Flight of locks These locks led out of a branch of the Bridgewater Canal into the Manchester Ship Canal, opened in 1894.

1 Calculate, roughly, the distance the cotton travelled
   a by sea and river to the port of Gainsborough,
   b by river from Gainsborough to Derby,
   c by road from Derby to Belper.
2 Calculate, roughly, the time the cotton would have taken. The sea voyage would have been about three days. Allow three m.p.h. for the river and road.
3 What had happened to this load of cotton?
4 Why is it going to be hard for the Strutts to get compensation?
5 Cotton also reached the Strutts through another port and along another route. Can you suggest which these were?

Here are some figures for the Thames and Severn Canal. They show how many days the canal was closed in various years:

Year	*By Frost*	*For maintenance*	*By other causes*	*Total*
1809	21	16	14 (Thames floods)	51
1822	0	127	—	127
1826	20	26	70 (Stroudwater-Berkeley Canal junction)	116
1827	19	39 (at least)	—	58
1828	0	40	—	40
1829	4	63 (Tunnel)	—	67
1830	40	5	35 (Stroudwater repairs)	80
1839	0	28	—	28

Note: the Stroudwater Navigation joined the west end of the canal to the Severn.

1 What were the most common reasons for closing the canal?
2 What was the longest period for which it was frozen?
3 What was the longest time in any one year the canal was closed?

In 1824, a group of Liverpool business men decided to build a railway between their own town and Manchester. They formed a company and, to persuade other people to buy shares in it, they issued a Prospectus.

This extract is from the Prospectus:

The total quantity of goods passing between Liverpool and Manchester is at least one thousand tons a day. The bulk of this merchandise is carried, either by the Duke of Bridgewater's Canal, or by the Mersey and Irwell Navigation. By both these means goods must pass up the river Mersey, a distance of 16 or 18 miles, subject to serious delays from contrary winds, and quite often to actual damage or loss from storms. The average length of passage may be taken at 36 hours, longer or shorter, according to the state of the winds and tides. The average charge upon goods, for the last fourteen years, has been about 15 shillings a ton.

By the planned Rail-road, the transport of goods between Liverpool and Manchester will be carried out in four or five hours, and the charge to the merchant will be reduced by at least one third.

It is not that the canal companies have not been able to carry goods on more reasonable terms but that, strong in the enjoyment of their monopoly, they have not thought proper to do so. Against their over-charging the public has had no protection, and against its continuing they have but one security: IT IS COMPETITION THAT IS WANTED: and the proof of this may be seen from the fact that the shares in the Old Quay Navigation (i.e. the Mersey and Irwell), of which the original cost was £70, have been sold as high as £1,250 each!

But it is not altogether on account of the high charges of the water carriers that a Rail-road is desirable. The Canals are unable to carry goods regularly and punctually at all periods and seasons. In summer time there is often a shortage of water, obliging boats to go only half-loaded. In winter they are sometimes locked up with frosts for weeks together. From these problems a Rail-road would be altogether free. There is still another ground of objection to the present system of carriage by Canals, namely, the pilfering for which the privacy of such a roundabout and lengthy journey gives so many opportunities. Whereas, carriage by Railway, done in a few hours and where every delay must be accounted for, will have much of the publicity and, as a result, the safety of the King's highways.

1 According to the Railway Company:
  a How many tons of goods are carried between Liverpool and Manchester?
  b What are the two companies that carry them?
  c How long does the journey take by boat? How long will it take by rail?
  d Why have the canal companies been able to overcharge?
  e What is the way to stop them?
  f How does the weather interfere with canals?
  g Why is stealing easy on the canals? Why will it be difficult on the railway?

2 Why should we be careful not to believe everything in this Prospectus? From the other documents do you think that, on the whole, the Railway Company is telling the truth?

Study this table:

Total Trade and Coal Trade on the Thames and Severn Canal 1827–1975 (Selected Years)

Year	*Total Trade Thousands of tons*	*Coal Trade Thousands of tons*
1827	56	45
1831	66	48
1838	62	42
1840	84	54*
1841	89	52
1843	58	42
1844	70	46**
1845	80	45
1848	59	45
1851	67	54
1862	62	38
1872	50	25
1875	39	23

* Railway building to Swindon and Cirencester
** Railway building to Stroud and Gloucester

1 Plot these figures on a graph.
2 What happened to trade on the canal whilst railways were being built locally?
3 Why do you suppose traffic on the canal declined after 1845?

Written Work

1 Imagine you are a factory owner in 1810. A canal has just been built to your town. Explain how you think the canal will help you.
2 It is now 1840. You are the same factory owner. Say what problems you had with the canal. Explain why you are pleased that your town is to have a railway.

Research

1 Read about the great canal engineers, especially James Brindley, Thomas Telford and John Rennie.
2 Read the history of any canal which interests you. Choose a local canal, if there is one.

Early Railways

You will know that it is hard work to push a heavy wheelbarrow over rough ground. You will know, too, the job is a lot easier if you put down a plank and run your wheelbarrow on that. Hundreds of years ago, coalminers had the same problem and they found much the same answer. The difference was that as they used four wheeled waggons they needed two parallel boards. To keep the boards the same distance apart, they fixed them to sleepers; to keep the wheels on the boards, they fitted them with flanges. By the sixteenth century, many coal mines had simple railways like this.

Here is a description of an early railway in South Wales:

> Sir Humphrey Mackworth has a level and wind-way, commonly called a Foot-rid or Waggon-way after the manner used in Shropshire and New-castle and at great expenses continued the said waggon-way on Wooden Rails from the face of each Wall of Coal twelve hundred Yards under Ground quite down to the Water-side, about three quarters of a mile from the Mouth of the Coal-pit: the said Coal-works without the help of the Waggon-way could not be carried on at any profit. It requires Skill as well as Labour to keep the Waggons upon the Rails underground.
>
> *Report of the Case of Sir Humphrey Mackworth*, Glamorgan 1705

Note: this was a drift mine. Instead of a shaft, there was a tunnel running into the side of a hill.

1 What different names are given to this railway?
2 How far underground does it go?
3 How much of the railway is outside the mine? Where does it lead?

Early railway This railway was built to carry coal and other heavy loads from the Grantham Canal to Belvoir Castle in Rutland. Before steam locomotives it was the canals that mattered, and railways often served them in this way. People built a railway if there was not enough traffic to justify having a branch to the canal, or if the country was too hilly for one. What kind of rail is this? (See diagram on page 72). The shape of the wheels will help you decide.

Blenkinsop's 'Salamanca' 1812 See extract on page 73. Blenkinsop was worried about 'slip'. What is that, do you suppose? How did Blenkinsop overcome it? Engineers soon discovered that slip was not a problem, as long as the waggons were not too heavy. Do not imagine this locomotive had a steep slope to climb. It could not have pulled a train up a gradient of 1 in 100.

4 How important is the railway for the mine?
5 What problem is there underground? What does this suggest about the way the railway is made?

In the eighteenth century, there was an important iron works at Coalbrookdale in Shropshire. It belonged to the Darby family. In 1775 an old widow, Abiah Darby, described some changes her husband Abraham had made in the 1740's:

> They used to carry their coal upon horses' backs, but he got roads made and laid with Sleepers and rails, as they have them in the North of England. And one waggon with three horses will bring as much as 20 horses used to bring on horses' backs. But this laying the road with wood caused a scarcity and raised the price of it, so that of late years, the laying of the rails of Cast Iron was substituted; which, though expensive, answers well for wear. We have in the different works, near 20 miles of this road which costs upwards of £800 a mile.
>
> *Letter of Abiah Darby, about* 1775

1 What had been the old fashioned way of carrying coal?
2 According to Abiah Darby, how much more coal could a horse transport on a railway? Compare Abiah's figures with those on page 63. Which are you going to believe? Why?
3 Why does Abiah say wooden rails were replaced with iron? How does she seem to contradict herself?
4 According to Abiah Darby, how many miles of railway are there at Coalbrookdale? How much did it cost?

Here is another account of the Coalbrookdale railways, given by a man called Jabez Hornblower:

> Railways have been in use in this Kingdom time out of mind, and were usually formed of scantlings (beams) of good sound oak, laid on sills or sleepers of the same timber, and pinned together with the same stuff. But the owners of Caolbrookdale Ironworks decided to cover these oak rails with cast-iron, not altogether as an improvement, but in part as a measure of economy.
>
> For some reason, the price of pigs (pig-iron) became very low, and their works being very large, in order to keep the furnaces on, they thought it would be the best means of stocking their pigs to lay it on the wooden railways. It would help pay the interest by reducing the repairs of the rails, and if iron should rise in price, there was nothing to do, but to take them up and send them away as pigs.
>
> These scantlings of iron were about five feet long, four inches broad, and one inch and a quarter thick, with three holes by which they were fastened to the rails.
>
> *Evidence before a House of Commons Committee,* 1809

1 Why, according to Hornblower, did the owners of the Coalbrookdale iron company decide to cover their wooden rails with cast iron?
2 You will see that Hornblower gives a different reason from Abiah Darby. Whom do you believe? Why? (Note that both were talking about the railways long after they were built.)
3 How, according to Hornblower, were the iron plates made?

Here is the first mention of a railway in the Company's accounts. It was the earlier one, made entirely of wood:

March 28th, 1748	
Paid John Beddow & Co: Laying the Rails and making Waggons for the Lake Head foot-rid	£2.15.8½d (£2.78p)
Paid John Jones for 33½ Days Levelling the Rail Way	£1.13.6½d (£1.67½p)
Paid Thos. Rowley for Levelling 18½ Days	18.6½d (92½p)

Early railway What type of rails are these? (See diagram on page 72).

This is part of a letter written in 1823 by Bernard Dickinson, a manager of one of the Company's works:

On my return I found thy letter and have since had many dusty old Books examined and much enquiry made about the introduction of Cast Iron Rails. Most of the Old Men have agreed that it is upwards of 50 years since Iron was substituted for Wood rails, but in our Ledger we find but one *old* entry of Iron Rails which is on the 13th of November 1767 – 100 Iron rails at 7/- (35p) but no other Ledger entry do we find respecting them until 1781. Stephen Hughes an old workman who is very particular in his account of past events says it is 56 years since he first worked for the Company and that Iron rails were used about two years after, and we have a Moulders' account in which the first entry of Iron rails is in August 1768, 232 rails at 1½d (½p) each. From that date there is a regular entry every Month, so there is no doubt but they were used here in 1768 and continued from that period, but we have nothing to prove their invention here.

1 What questions do you suppose Bernard Dickinson has been asked?
2 In what three ways does he try to answer them?
3 What conclusions does he reach?
4 What does he say he cannot prove?
5 Do you think you can believe what Dickinson says? Give reasons for your answer.

In the previous four documents you have evidence about railways at the Coalbrookdale Ironworks. Collect all the important facts and arrange them under two headings:

1 Those which are almost certainly true.
2 Those about which there is some doubt.

During the eighteenth and early nineteenth centuries there were many improvements to iron rails. The diagrams on page 72 show you what they were.

This is what the Treasurer of the Liverpool and Manchester Railway said:

The Railway is by no means a recent invention: nearly two centuries have passed since the introduction of Tram-roads, rudely constructed of wood, at a trifling cost in money. The substitution of iron for wood was a great improvement: but the form of the rail was for a long time unsatisfactory, being made of flat pieces of cast iron laid on the ground, with a side flange rising two or three inches to keep the wheel to its proper track. The rails thus resting on the ground were bound to be covered with soil or sand: and it was not until the use of the edge-rail, raised above the ground, that Railways gained those advantages over ordinary roads which they are now known to possess.

An Account of the Liverpool and Manchester Railway, 1830, Henry Booth

1 What, according to Booth, are the stages in the development of the rail? Which stage does he leave out?
2 What does he say is the disadvantage of the plateway?
3 Why does he say the edge rail is better?

In the early nineteenth century there were more railways on the Northumberland and Durham Coalfield than anywhere else. A French visitor, Louis de Gallois wrote about them:

There is a network of 75 leagues of railways in a region which is 7 leagues long and 4 leagues wide. In addition 150 leagues of underground lines have been laid. All the lines which are above ground run from the pit heads of coalmines to the River Tyne and the River Wear. These two rivers can be navigated by large ships for several miles inland.

A coal waggon can carry a load of about 25 metric quintals. The smallest downhill gradient is enough to set the waggons moving on their own. Five or six of these waggons coupled together can move downhill without the aid of horses or any other form of power. A child operates a brake to slow the waggons down if necessary. Should the slope be too steep, the waggons are allowed to run down one by one. A horse is tied to the back of the waggon, and it pulls the empty waggon back up the hill.

If the hill is so steep that the waggons descend too quickly, an inclined plane is used. By means of a big pulley and a rope, the descent of a loaded waggon can be controlled, and at the same time an equal number of empty waggons can be hauled up the incline. The speed of the descent can be controlled by a brake on the pulley.

Report of English Railways, 1818

Note: A French league is 2.78 English miles.
A quintal is 100 kilograms.

1 How many miles of railway are there on the Northumberland and Durham coalfield:
a above ground **b** in the mines?
2 Where do the railways which are above ground run?
3 Say how waggons run down hill when the slope is **a** gentle **b** moderate **c** steep.
4 Who has charge of the waggons on a gentle slope?

De Gallois said this about hauling loads up hill and on the level:

Horses or steam engines are used to haul waggons up a slope. In Wales, where small waggons are commonly used, horses are employed to pull waggons up hills. The laden waggons are coupled together and a single horse pulls a number of them. But when a hill is reached the horse hauls only one waggon up at a time. When all the waggons are at the top, they are coupled together again and one horse pulls all of them. If the hill is long or very steep – and this does occur in the Newcastle district – a steam engine is installed at the top of the hill and the waggons are hauled up by means of a cable.

If the road is level, or nearly so, then a high pressure steam engine is fixed upon a waggon and this locomotive can pull as many as 20 waggons with a load of 500 metric quintals. That is the power of a locomotive built by Messrs. Losh and Stephenson and used in the Killingworth mines. The workers call these machines 'iron horses'.

The type of power used to draw waggons on rails varies according to the slope. Many different methods may be used on different sections of the same railway. The change from one method to another is made quite smoothly without delaying the service.

Report on English Railways, 1818

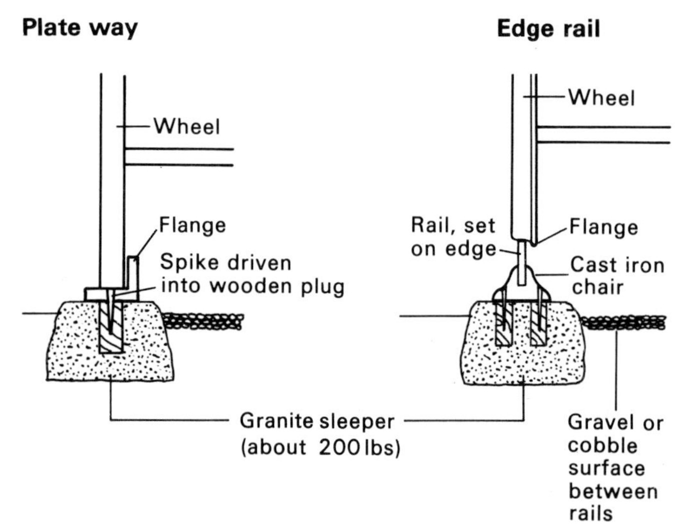

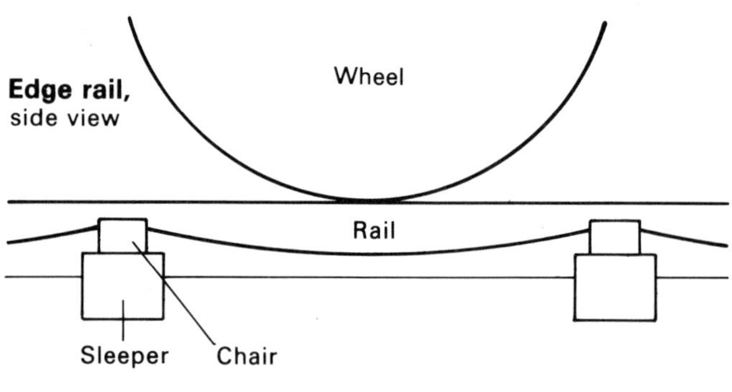

Development of the Rail The great advantage of the plate way was that the waggons using it had ordinary wheels and could run on a road. The disadvantage was that dirt collected in the angle and made it hard to pull the waggons. For that reason the edge rail gradually became more popular. It was given the 'fish-belly' shape to make it stronger. They preferred granite sleepers to wooden ones, because they had no way of preserving wood, to stop it rotting. Also it was easier to make a good track between the rails, for the horses. (See picture on page 69).

1 How are loads hauled in Wales where the slope is **a** gentle **b** steep?
2 How are loads hauled up long slopes in the Newcastle area?
3 Where are locomotives used? How much can one of them pull?
4 Where does de Gallois say there is a locomotive working? Who built it?
5 What do the workmen call locomotives?
6 Make a list of all the different methods in which waggons are moved. Say where each method is used.

Here is part of a report written in 1814 by a German visitor, Johann May;

John Blenkinsop has invented a steam locomotive. It is used to haul coal waggons on iron rails. The locomotive consists of a steam boiler which is fixed onto a carriage. Attached to the boiler are two cylinders in which there are pistons driven by steam so that they perpetually move up and down. Metal rods run from the pistons alongside the boiler and they turn a cog-wheel. The cogs on the wheel fit into notches on the rail. In this way the locomotive is propelled forward. Twenty-one waggons, linked by chains, are drawn by the locomotive. Each waggon carries 45 cwt. of coal. The total weight moved by the locomotive is:

21 × 45 cwt. of coal	945 cwt.
21 × 15 cwt. (weight of each wagon)	315 cwt.
Locomotive	140 cwt.
Total	1,400 cwt.

Before the invention of the locomotive, one horse pulled three coal waggons and so the locomotive does the work of seven horses. Three such locomotives are available. Two are always in use hauling the full waggons for a mile and a half over fairly flat ground, and then they pull the empty waggons back again. The locomotive moves so fast that one has to walk really fast to keep up with it. The third locomotive is held in reserve. The invention of the locomotive has a significant influence upon the price of coal in Leeds. Coal costs only 8/- (40p) a ton there as compared with 15/- (75p) in Manchester and Birmingham.

Report on a Journey to England, Factory Commissioner J. G. May

1 Find the various features of the *Salamanca* which May mentions, in the picture of the locomotive.
2 How many tons does the locomotive move altogether, including its own weight? What proportion of this weight is coal?
3 How many railway horses does the locomotive replace? How many packhorses would have been needed to carry the same load? (See page 63).
4 Roughly, how many miles per hour does the locomotive go?
5 Why is there a third locomotive? What does this suggest about the reliability of these early locomotives?
6 How have the locomotives helped the people of Leeds?
7 The *Salamanca* was built in 1812. Find out why it was given that name. You will need to know what Wellington did in Spain in 1812.

Here is Joseph Priestley's description of the Cromford and High Peak Railway. It ran through the Peak District which was too hilly for a canal:

The railway starts from the Cromford Canal. It is in length thirty-three miles and seven furlongs, and it reaches a height of 920 feet above the head level of the Cromford Canal by means of six inclined planes. The summit level is twelve miles three furlongs in length, and in its course it passes under a hill by means of a tunnel 638 yards in length. From the end of this elevated stretch of railway there is a fall of 740 feet to the Peak Forest Canal by three inclined planes.

The chief object of this railway is to open a nearer and more convenient link between the counties of Derby, Nottingham and Leicester, with the port of Liverpool, and the towns of Manchester and Stockport. A glance at the map will show, in less time than words can express it, the great advantages of this grand scheme for passing such a mountainous tract of country.

Historical Account of the Navigable Canals and Railways Throughout Great Britain, 1831

This diagram shows a section of the railway. It is part of its climb from the southern end to the summit:

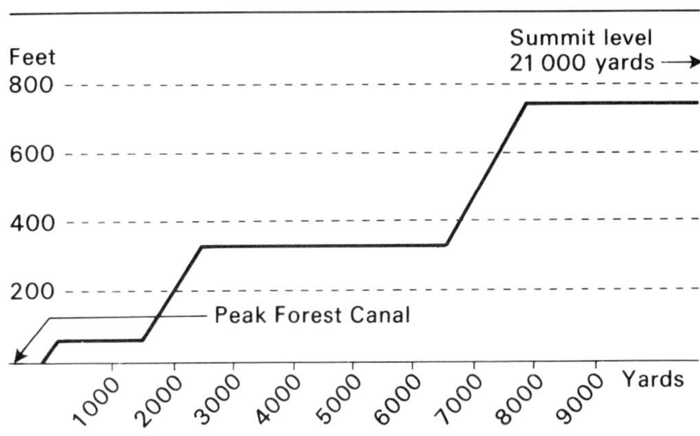

Section through the Cromford and High Peak Railway from Peak Forest Canal to Summit Level Railways had to be as level as possible for the sake of the horses. Consequently, they were built as a series of levels, joined by inclined planes. (See page 72).

1 Where does the railway start?
2 Where does it finish?
3 How high is the summit above **a** the south end **b** the north end of the railway?
4 How does the railway climb to its summit?
5 How long is the tunnel on the summit? Why was it needed, do you suppose?
6 Which towns does the railway join? How would goods finish their journey at either end of the railway?
7 In what ways is the railway like a canal? What does it have instead of locks?

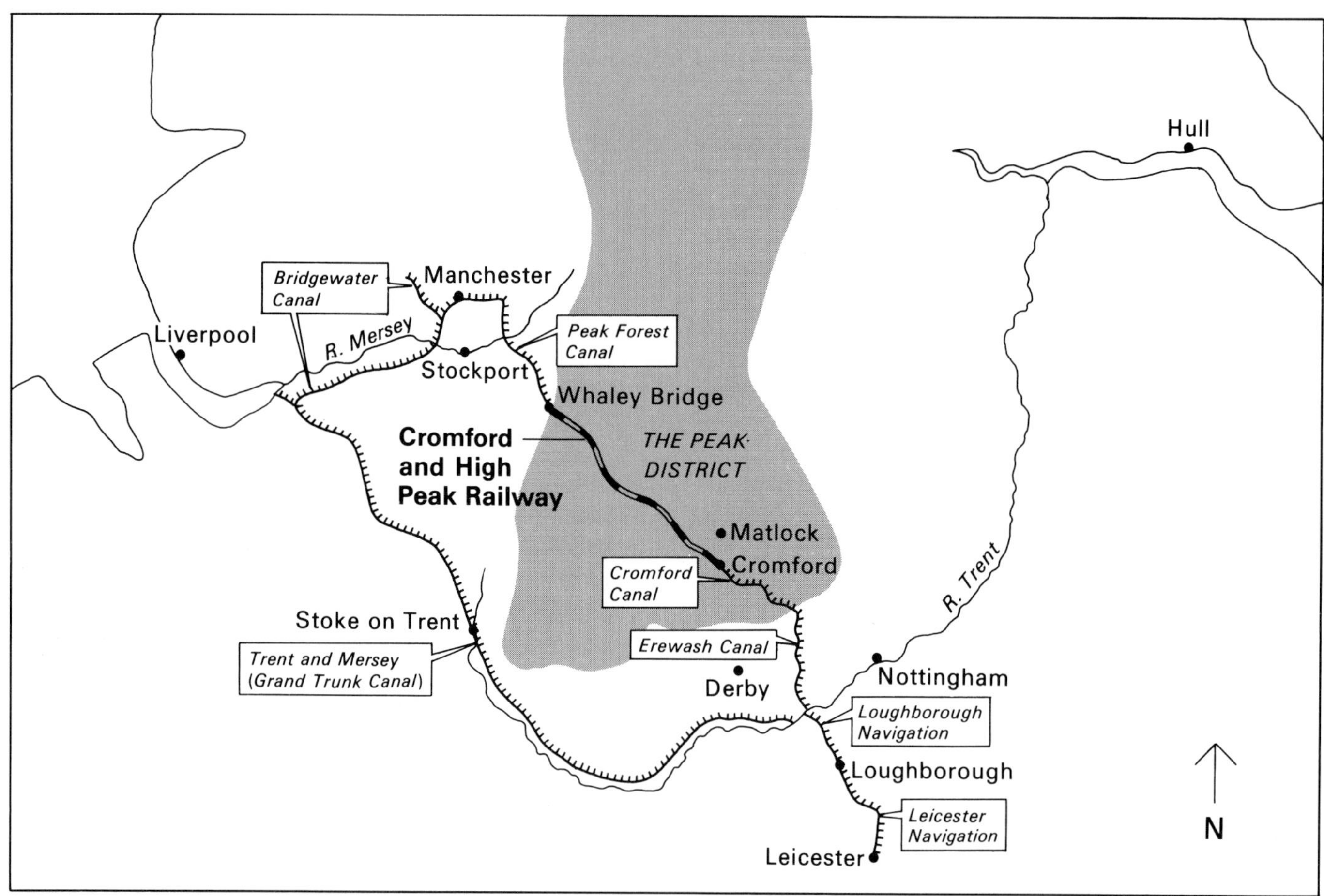

The Cromford and High Peak Railway Here we can see another way in which the early railways served the canals. The canals have been built as far as possible into the hills, and the railway links them. Why were the owners of the Trent and Mersey Canal worried when the railway opened, do you suppose? (In fact, they had nothing to fear).

This is how de Gallois finished his report on railways:

> Railways offer an intermediate form of transport linking roads and canals. They cost much less than canals and they have the advantage that they can be used at all times of the year. Costs of maintenance are low. They can link places which it would be impossible to join by canal, either because of the difficulties of the ground, or because it would be impossible to find a supply of water for the canal. Railways will one day form an additional network of communication to our existing transport system of roads and canals. They will give a public service of the greatest importance.
>
> *Report on Railways*, 1818

1 De Gallois sees railways as 'intermediate', that is coming between roads and canals. Does the table on page 63 support his view?
2 What advantage does a railway have over a canal?
3 Does de Gallois suggest railways will ever replace roads and canals? How does he see the future?
4 How does the Cromford and High Peak Railway fit in with de Gallois's ideas?
5 How, in fact, did railways affect roads and canals in the end? (See section on *Roads* and *Inland Waterways*.)

Written Work

It is 1820. Imagine that, like May and de Gallois, you have come from a foreign country to inspect English railways. Write a report of them for your government saying:

a How they have developed.
b How they work at the present day.
c List the reasons why you think your own country should have railways.

Research

1 Read about some of the men who built the early railways especially William Jessop and Benjamin Outram.
2 Find out about the history of the railway locomotive before 1830.
3 Read the story of the Stockton and Darlington Railway.

The Liverpool and Manchester Railway

By the 1820's there were about 1500 miles of railway in Britain. Most of the lines, though, were quite short and were used only to take coal from mines to the nearest river or canal. Few lines carried passengers, and none used locomotives along their entire length. Then, in 1830, the first truly modern railway opened. It was the Liverpool and Manchester.

Rolling Stock on the Liverpool and Manchester Railway Find the goods waggon, the cattle waggon and the first, second and third class carriages. One carriage is in a luxury class of its own. What do the better class carriages look like? Why is 'Wellington' written on one of the carriages? (Read *Oxford Junior History* Book 4, page 55, or any account of the official opening of the railway). Note that the track has wooden sleepers. Why was that? (See the reasons for not having them on page 72).

First read pages 71 and 73.

Now study these figures:

Population

	Liverpool	*Manchester*
1790	56,000	57,000
1821	119,000	134,000

Imports of American Cotton to Liverpool (Bales)

1792	503
1822	289,989
1823	412,020

Most of the raw cotton went on from Liverpool to the mills of Manchester.

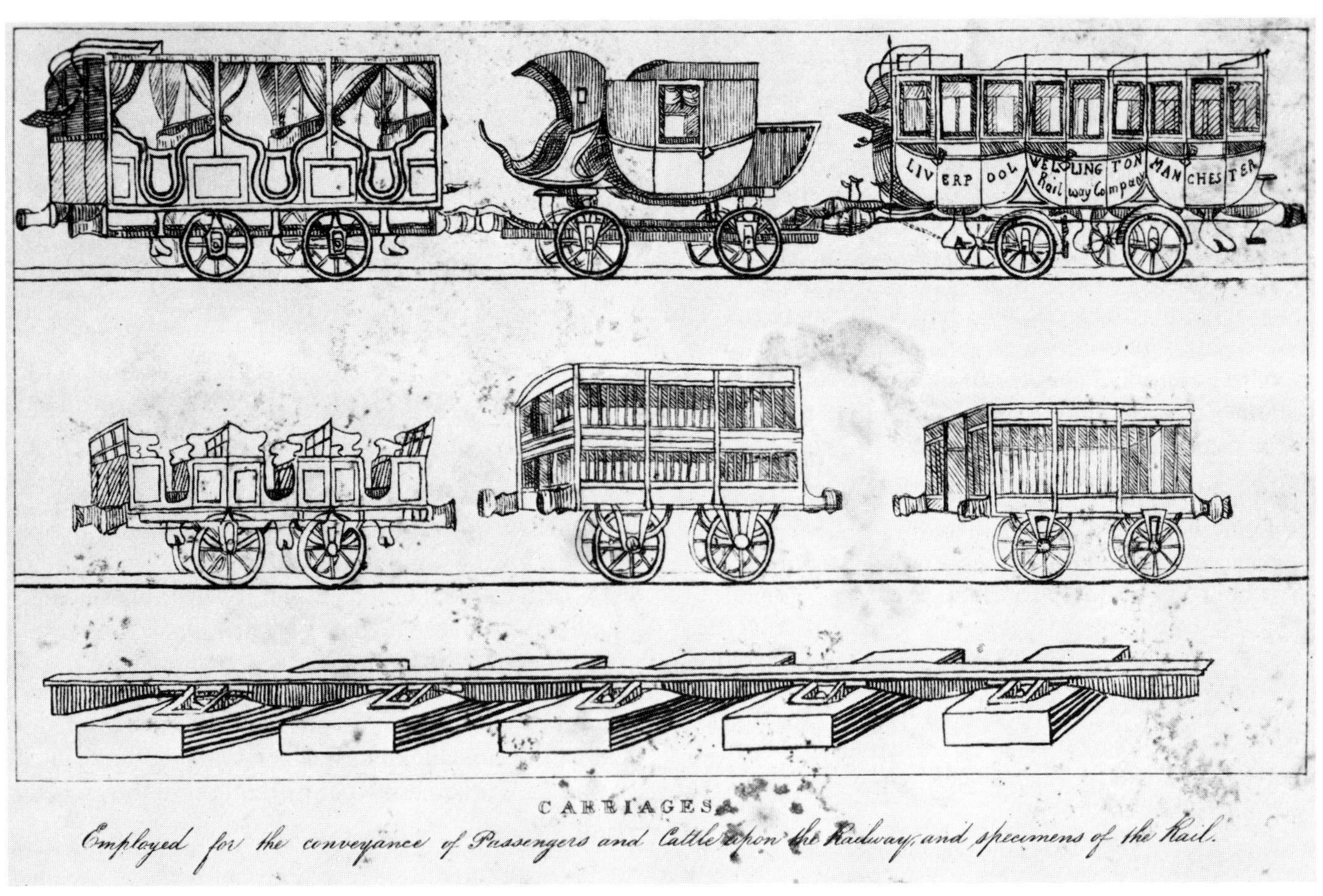

CARRIAGES

Employed for the conveyance of Passengers and Cattle upon the Railway, and specimens of the Rail.

1 Show the figures for population and cotton imports on bar diagrams.
2 Give the reasons for building a railway from Liverpool to Manchester that you have discovered so far.

This is an extract from the prospectus of the Railway Company:

> As well as the transport of goods between Liverpool and Manchester, a good deal of revenue may be expected from the transport of coals from the rich mines near St. Helens. These coals at present pass along the Sankey Canal and down the Mersey to Liverpool, a distance of about 30 miles. By the railway, the distance will be shortened by one half and the charge for transport very much reduced.
>
> *Prospectus of the Liverpool and Manchester Rail-Road Company*, 1824

1 What traffic did the Company hope to have?
2 According to the Company, what advantage will the railway have over water transport? Look at the map and see if you agree.

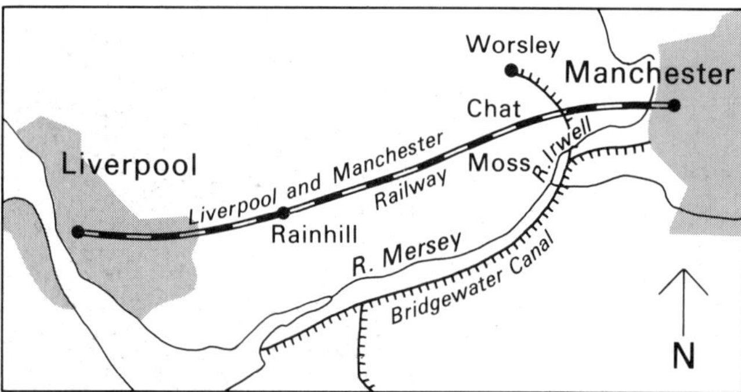

Before it could start work the Railway Company needed an Act of Parliament giving it permission. To prove to Parliament that it was possible to build the line, the Company had to make a survey of the route. The man in charge of the survey was George Stephenson. In 1824 he wrote to a friend:

> We have sad work with Lord Derby, Lord Sefton and Bradshaw, the great canal proprietor, whose grounds we go through with the planned railway. Their ground is blockaded on every side to prevent us getting on with the survey. Bradshaw fired guns through his grounds in the course of the night, to prevent the surveyor coming on in the dark. We are to have a grand field-day next week. The Liverpool Railway people are determined to force a survey through if possible. Lord Sefton says he will have a hundred men against us.

Note: Bradshaw was one of the owners of the Bridgewater Canal. The Duke who built it had died in 1803.

1 How are Lord Derby, Lord Sefton and Bradshaw trying to stop Stephenson's survey?
2 The two noblemen were against the railway because they thought it would spoil their estates. Why was Bradshaw against it, do you suppose?

It was only at the second attempt that the Company made a survey good enough for Parliament and it did not have its Act until 1826.

One of the conditions in the Act was that the railway should not annoy the people of Liverpool by running through their town. Instead, it had to go under it in a tunnel.

The Treasurer of the railway, Henry Booth, describes how the tunnel was built:

> Night and day the work went ahead, and many difficulties had to be overcome. In some places a soft blue shale was excavated: in other places a wet sand presented itself, very difficult to support till the masonry which was to form the roof was erected. In passing under Crown Street the roof fell in from the surface, being a depth of 30 feet of loose earth and sand. Sometimes the miners refused to work. Nor is this surprising considering the nature of the operation; boring their way almost in the dark, with the water streaming around them, and uncertain whether the props and stays would bear the pressure from above till the archwork should be finished. But while some parts of the Tunnel were dug with great danger and difficulty, others were hewn through a fine red sandstone, clean and dry and needing neither props nor arching.
>
> The Tunnel was made in seven or eight separate lengths, connected with the surface by upright shafts, through which the soil and rock were carried away. The exact joining of these different lengths was an object of some anxiety. The accuracy with which it was done was highly creditable to the Engineer.
>
> *An Account of the Liverpool and Manchester Railway*, 1830

1 Why was digging parts of the tunnel difficult and dangerous for the miners?
2 Which part was fairly easy? Why?
3 What method was used to dig the tunnel?
4 What might have gone wrong?
5 Why was the method chosen better than digging only from the two ends, do you suppose?

One of the main difficulties was how to carry the line over a bog called Chat Moss. The people who were against the railway line asked a canal engineer called Giles to tell Parliament what he thought of the problem:

> Be so good as to tell us whether in your judgement a Rail-road of this description can be safely made over Chat

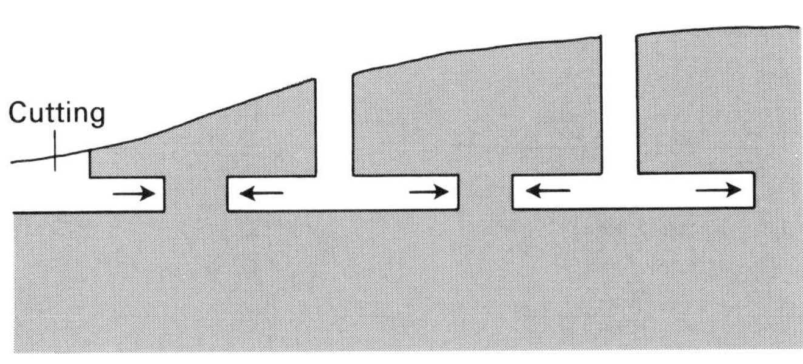

Digging a tunnel Shafts were sunk at intervals. Sections of the tunnel were then dug outwards from the feet of the shafts until they met. When the tunnel was finished, the shafts were sometimes left open, for ventilation. What mistakes might surveyors make? In fact they were often no more than a few inches out.

Moss, without going to the bottom of the Moss.

I say certainly not.

Will it be necessary, therefore, in making a Railroad which is to stand, to take out, along the whole line of the road, the whole of the Moss to the bottom?

Undoubtedly.

Will that make it necessary to cut down the 35 feet of which you have been speaking?

Yes.

And afterwards to fill it up with other soil?

To such a height as the Rail-road is to be carried.

Suppose they were to work upon this stuff, could they get their carriages to the place?

No carriage can stand on the Moss short of the bottom.

So that if you could carry a Rail-road on this fluid stuff – if you could do it – it would still take a great number of men, and a great sum of money. Could it be done, in your opinion, for £60,000?

I should say £200,000 would not get through it.

My learned friend wishes to know what it would cost to lay it with diamonds.

Proceedings of the House of Commons Committee, May 5th, 1825

Tunnel The people of Liverpool refused to have the railway running through their town so it had to pass under it. Here, the tunnel is not yet quite ready, so people are sight-seeing.

1 What does Giles say is the only way the line can cross Chat Moss?
2 How much does he say it will cost?
3 What do you suppose Giles's friends hoped Parliament would do when they heard his evidence?

Henry Booth describes how Chat Moss was in fact crossed:

Chat Moss is a huge Bog – in some places 30 to 35 feet deep – and so soft that an iron rod would sink through it. The Railway, for the most part, floats on the surface, being helped by hurdles of brushwood and heather, laid under the wooden sleepers which support the rails. The part of the Moss which gave the most difficulty was about half a mile on the east border where an embankment of about 20 feet had to be formed above the natural level. The weight of this embankment resting on the semi-fluid base, pressed down the surface. Many thousands of cubic yards of stone gradually disappeared before the line of the road came anywhere near the proposed level. By degrees, however, the whole mass beneath and on each side of the embankment became firm under the pressure, and the work was finally completed.

An Account of the Liverpool and Manchester Railway, 1830

1 Describe, in your own words, how the railway crosses Chat Moss. (Think of walking on snow shoes).
2 Which was the most difficult section? Why? How was the problem overcome?

Here are the largest items in the Company's accounts:

	£
Bridges	99,065
Chat Moss	27,719
Cuttings and Embankments	199,763
Iron Rails	67,912
Land	95,315
Parliamentary and Legal Expenses	28,465
Tunnel	34,791

Note: The total cost of the railway was about £800,000.

1 Arrange the figures in order of importance. Show them on a bar diagram.
2 Where does Chat Moss come in the order?
3 How far out was Giles in his estimate for crossing Chat Moss?

Here is what happened to Chat Moss after the railway was built:

It was, in truth, a trembling, Peaty Bog, growing only the commonest Heath Plants and even these struggling for life.

The Farmers of Lancashire knew full well the cause of its sterility and its cure. That clay and lime spread liberally on the surface would soon make it fertile, but the cost of carrying them made this impossible.

The traveller by Railway now sees, in the very middle of this great Bog, well cultivated and neatly arranged fields, flourishing crops of oats, wheat and Potatoes. Farm houses and Cottages erected, earth spreading, ditches opening and the Ploughman profitably employed where, a few months since, silence reigned undisturbed.

Cuthbert Johnson, *The Advantages of Railways to Agriculture*, 1837

The Railway crossing Chat Moss

Olive Mount Cutting

1 What were once the only plants that grew on Chat Moss?
2 What did the farmers know they must do to make Chat Moss fertile? What stopped them?
3 What changes were made to Chat Moss, after the railway was built? How did the railway help to make the changes, do you suppose?

The Liverpool and Manchester Railway Company was formed in 1824. As late as 1829 its Directors were still wondering what should draw their trains. For such a busy line horses would not do, so the choice was between stationary engines and locomotives. Some of the Directors went to see the Stockton and Darlington Railway where both were in use, but they still could not make up their minds. Henry Booth tells us what happened in the end:

Mr. Stephenson, the Company's Engineer was decidedly in favour of Locomotive Engines which he was confident would be the most economical and by far the most convenient moving power that could be employed.

The leaning on the part of the majority of the Directors was in favour of locomotives, provided they could be made of enough power, and at a less weight than the travelling Engines then in use, which were generally 8 to 9 tons in weight: the result of which was no small injury to the Railway and much expense in keeping the road in repair. The Directors determined to obtain, if possible, a Locomotive Engine that should meet these conditions. Accordingly they resolved to offer a prize of £500 for the most improved Locomotive Engine.

An Account of the Liverpool and Manchester Railway, 1830

1 Why did Stephenson say the railway should use locomotives?
2 What doubts did the Directors have about locomotives?
3 What did they decide to do as a result?

The competition was held on a level section of the track at Rainhill. It is known as the Rainhill Trials. There were four entries, but only two were serious ones. They were the *Novelty* by Braithwaite and Ericsson and the *Rocket* by Robert Stephenson and Company. Robert was the son of the engineer of the railway and the two men had worked together to build the *Rocket*.

Before the Rainhill Trials began, the locomotives ran up and down the line, showing off to the crowds. With light loads they reached the amazing speed of 30 m.p.h. The favourite was the *Novelty*. A local newspaper, the *Liverpool Mercury* reported:

It seemed, indeed, to fly, presenting one of the most perfect spectacles of human skill and human daring the world has ever beheld. It actually made one giddy to look at it, and filled thousands with lively fears for the safety of the people who were on it, and who seemed not to run along the earth, but to fly, as it were, on the wings of the wind. It is a most sublime sight; a sight, indeed, which those who beheld it will not soon forget.

Liverpool Mercury, October 9th, 1829

1 Describe in your own words the feelings of the people who watched the *Novelty*.

Henry Booth tells what happened on the day of the Trials:

The distance to be run was seventy miles: and it was a condition, that when fairly started, the Engine should travel on the road at a speed of not less than ten miles per hour, drawing after it a weight of 10 tons for every ton weight of itself. As the railway was unfinished this had to be done by moving backwards and forwards on a level plane of one mile and three quarters in length.

On the 8th of October, the *Rocket* weighing 4 tons 5 cwt. including the water in her boiler, started on her journey and performed the first thirty-five miles in three hours and twelve minutes, being nearly at the rate of eleven miles an hour. About a quarter of an hour was then taken in filling the water tank and obtaining a fresh supply of coke. The second thirty-five miles was performed in two hours and fifty-seven minutes, or at the rate of twelve miles per hour, including stops. The whole time was under six hours and a half. The speed over the ground, with the prescribed load was frequently eighteen miles per hour, and occasionally upwards of twenty. The whole performance was considerably greater than required by the terms of the competition, or than had before been accomplished by a Locomotive Engine.

The *Novelty* was the next engine which undertook the appointed task: but owing to some fault with her pipes or machinery was obliged to stop almost at the beginning. Another day was chosen and another derangement took place. Accordingly the owners informed the Judges that they withdrew from the competition having, nevertheless, full confidence in the Engine, when they should have repaired its defects.

From this date, the question between Locomotive and Fixed Engines must be considered as practically settled.

An Account of the Liverpool and Manchester Railway, 1830

1. What were the conditions of the competition?
2. How heavy was the *Rocket*? How did it compare with the *Salamanca*? (See page 73).
3. What was the *Rocket*'s maximum speed with its load? What was its average speed, roughly, for the whole distance?
4. What must have prevented the average speed being much higher?
5. What happened to the *Novelty*?
6. What did the Rainhill Trials decide, apart from the *Rocket*'s victory?

On both sides of the Rainhill level, where the Trials were held, there were slopes. The one to the west was called the Whiston incline plane. It was $1\frac{1}{2}$ miles long, and had a slope of about 1 in 100.

Henry Booth wrote:

At the time of the Rainhill trials the *Rocket* often went up the Whiston inclined plane, with a carriage holding twenty to thirty passengers, at a speed of fifteen to eighteen miles per hour; and the ease and regularity with which this was done produced a confident impression that even up the inclined planes the Locomotive would be the power used. Indeed the general feeling was that it did not matter whether the Engine travelled up an inclined plane or on a level; and various schemes were quickly started for turning turnpike roads into Railways.

An Account of the Liverpool and Manchester Railway, 1830

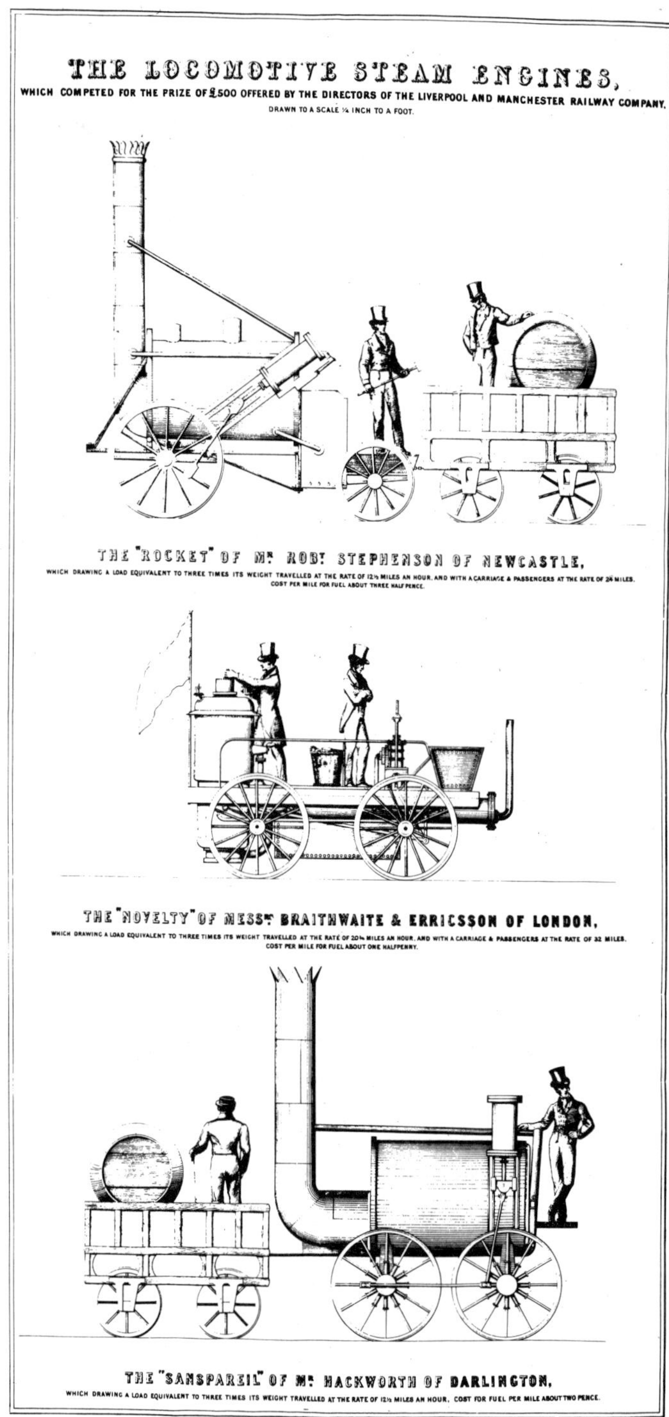

The three rivals at the Rainhill Trials Which of the three had the best performance? Why did it not win the prize? (See left hand column of this page).

1 What did the *Rocket* do at the time of the Rainhill Trials?
2 What impression did this give?
3 What plans did some people make?

However, Booth also wrote:

The *Comet* Locomotive (a new Engine on the *Rocket* principle) had to climb the Whitson inclined plane with about 26 tons behind her. With this load she reached a speed of sixteen or eighteen miles per hour on the level, before coming to the slope. Helped by this momentum, she carried out the task; her speed, however, fell from sixteen or eighteen miles to about three or four miles per hour before she reached the top.

An Account of the Liverpool and Manchester Railway, 1830

1 Draw a slope of 1 in 100 on a sheet of paper so that you can see what the Whiston inclined plane was like. Would you have any difficulty in cycling up such a slope?
2 How fast was the *Comet* going when it reached the foot of the slope?
3 How fast was it going when it reached the top?
4 What does this tell you about the power of the early locomotives?
5 How does this explain why building many of the early railway lines meant a lot of work and was very expensive? (Look at the largest single expense in building the Liverpool and Manchester Railway page 78).

Study these figures:

Passengers and Goods Carried by the Liverpool and Manchester Railway

	Passengers	*Merchandise* (Tons)	*Coal* (Tons)
1831	445,047	43,070	11,285
1832	356,945	159,443	69,396
1833	386,492	194,704	81,509
1834	436,637	210,736	99,337
1835	473,847	230,629	116,246

Mining Journal, Volume IX, 1839, page 150

1 Show these figures as block diagrams.
2 In what way was the railway an immediate success? Why was this? (See page 61).
3 In what ways was it successful after a time?

Finally, here is an extract from the diary of a wealthy lady passenger:

We had two seats in the Mail part of the train, thinking it would be easier than our own carriage, which was lashed on to a machine behind, and in which we sent the servants. Luckily, Merthyr (her husband) and I had the four places in our division to ourselves, and no strangers came in to annoy us. The thirty-six miles took exactly an hour and a half. My mamma had entreated that I should not go by this conveyance, lest some accident should befall. It would have taken us about four hours to make the journey with post horses, and the temptation of saving so much time and fatigue was not to be resisted. I never had a pleasanter journey. It is much smoother and easier than a carriage, and the sensation cannot alarm, by reason of its steadiness. My introduction to the Railway is a memorable event in my little life.

Diary of Lady Charlotte Guest, November 3rd, 1833

1 What happened to the Guests' own carriage when they took the train?
2 Where did the servants travel?
3 How long did the journey take? What was the average speed, roughly? (Lady Charlotte made a mistake. The railway was just under 31 miles long.)
4 How long does she say it would have taken by road? Is this correct? (See page 61).
5 How did Lady Charlotte's mother feel about the railway?
6 Why was Lady Charlotte pleased with the journey?

Written Work

Imagine it is 1835 and that you are George Stephenson. Write about the Liverpool and Manchester Railway. Why was it needed? What problems did you have? Why do you think the railway is a success?

Also say how people saw the future of railways before 1830, and how you see it now.

Research

1 Find out about the great railway engineers, especially Robert Stephenson and Isambard Kingdom Brunel. Also find out about Thomas Brassey and George Hudson.
2 How did railways develop after 1830? What important lines were built? When was the 'railway mania'? What did the Railways Act of 1844 say?

Chapter 4 *Social Life*

Prisons

In the eighteenth century criminals were put in prison in much the same way as cups and saucers are put in cupboards. They were just locked up, as if in store, and no-one cared much about them, apart from giving them just enough food to stay alive. There was no attempt to reform them so that they would lead honest lives when they were released. To make matters worse, criminals of every kind were put together. Dangerous robbers were locked up with children who had done nothing more than take apples from an orchard.

There were a few prisons that had been properly built. Newgate, in London, was one of these. In many other places the prison was any old building that could be used for the purpose. At Lincoln, for instance, it was a room in a tower of the ruined castle. If the place was not secure, the gaoler hammered irons on to his prisoners. That was cheaper than building a high wall.

The first extract describes what it was like in the prison at Southwell, in Nottinghamshire:

> They use the same room for every purpose, nearly 18 foot 6 inches square; of this space the beds take more than a quarter, yet in this small space have been seven to eleven men and often more: three, sometimes four and even five in one bed, lying on loose straw, without any bedclothes, except such as friends had supplied. Night-tubs, cooking utensils, plates, basins, meat cooked and raw, potatoes, coals and various articles of food or dress all jumbled together, dirty and clean, in this small room: where even the wretched prisoners complained that living with the vermin and filth was one of the worst parts of their punishment. Those who had friends were allowed to receive from them, food, money or beer; to those who knew people in Southwell, cooked dinners were regularly sent: to others coming from places further away, enough food for a week was brought: to those who were poachers, money was sent by others in their gang:

Newgate Prison This is a cartoon by Cruikshank. What is he trying to tell us about the prison?

and those who had neither friends nor money, were barely prevented from starving by the daily county allowance consisting of one pound of bread and one penny in money.

Report on the House of Correction at Southwell, Rev. J. T. Becker, 1806

1 How many square feet is the room? How many men might there be in it? How many square feet is that to a man?
2 Why is the room unpleasant, apart from the overcrowding?
3 How do the prisoners get their food? Which are the unlucky ones? What must they live on?

In 1861, a man called Walter Clay wrote a book about his father, John, who was chaplain at Preston Gaol. Here Walter is talking about the gaol in the early years of the nineteenth century, when criminals of all kinds were together:

However bad a child may be before he goes to Gaol, he generally has a certain fear of prison, and hesitates to commit any crime which might lead to it. The prison once entered, however, the little culprit finds himself surrounded by those who make him ashamed, not for what he has done, but for the *little* that he has done. It is an unhappy truth that many young delinquents soon want to excel in crime.

The Prison Chaplain, 1861

1 According to Walter Clay, how does a child feel before he goes to prison?
2 How do his feelings change when he is there? Why?

It was, of course, not only children, but adults too, who could be led astray by hardened criminals. By the end of the eighteenth century numbers of people were worried that criminals were coming out of prison worse behaved than when they went in. They wanted the prisons to be reformed so that they, in their turn, could reform criminals. Obviously the buildings had to be much better, and this was not too difficult. How, though, was it possible to turn a criminal into an honest man? Here is what the Rev. Sydney Smith had to say:

I would banish all the looms of Preston Gaol, and substitute nothing but the tread-wheel or the capstan, or some kind of labour where the labourer could not see the results of his toil – where it is as monotonous, irksome and dull as possible – pulling and pushing instead of reading and writing – no share in the profits – not a single shilling. There should be no tea and sugar, no assembly of female felons round the washing tub – nothing but beating hemp, and pulling oakum and pounding bricks.

Edinburgh Review, 1822

Note: When Sydney Smith was writing, Preston Gaol allowed its prisoners to work to earn money.

Oakum picking, Clerkenwell Prison, 1974 See Mayhew and Binney's description on the next page. Why were the men given this task? What system is the prison using? If you contrast this print with the one on page 82, you will have a good idea what prison reform meant in the nineteenth century.

1 What work are the people in Preston Gaol doing?
2 What does Sydney Smith want to see?

Important changes were indeed made at Preston. Here, and in many other prisons they introduced the 'Silent System'. The idea was to make life very unpleasant for criminals. It was hoped that when they were released they would behave themselves, through fear of being sent back to prison.

Walter Clay describes what happened:

The silent system is applied to a number of prisoners varying from forty to eighty. They are seated upon forms, are about nine feet apart, all facing the direction of the officer's raised desk, and all employed in unpicking cotton. At meals the same order is observed. Throughout, the discipline is not merely that the tongue is silent, but the eye and the hand are mute. No sign, no look – whether of recognition to a fellow prisoner, or of curiosity towards a visitor – is allowed. A prisoner, recently arrived, and not yet quite sober, once shouted 'Britons never shall be slaves'. A quiet smile on the faces of some of the old gaolbirds was the only result: not a single head was turned while the mutinous Briton was removed from the room.

The Prison Chaplain

1 What work are the prisoners doing?
2 How are they behaving?
3 What did they do when the new prisoner made a disturbance?
4 Why did the prisoners have to be silent, do you suppose? (See previous page).

Another prison which used the Silent System was the Coldbath Fields in London. In 1862 two men, Henry Mayhew and John Binny visited it. This is what they found in the 'oakum room':

All we could see was a closely packed mass of heads and pink faces, moving to and fro, as though the wind was blowing them about, and they were set on stalks instead of necks. There was a silence as intense and impressive as that of death itself.

Each picker has by his side his weighed quantity of old rope, cut into lengths about equal to that of a hoop stick. Some of the pieces are white and sodden looking as a washer woman's hands, whilst others are hard and black with the tar upon them. The prisoner takes up a length of rope and untwists it, and when he has separated it into so many corkscrew strands, he further unrolls them by sliding them backwards and forwards on his knee until the meshes are loosened.

Then the strand is further unravelled by placing it in the end of a hook fastened to the knee, and sawing it smartly to and fro, which soon removes the tar and grates the fibres apart. In this condition all that remains to be done is to loosen the hemp by pulling it out like cotton wool.

Criminal Prisons of London, 1862

Note: the oakum was sold to make doormats, but the men had no share of the money.

1 What work were the men doing?
2 Why was it unpleasant?

The men in the oakum room were the favoured ones. Outside, Mayhew and Binny found a row of prisoners with a pile of cannon balls, each weighing 24 lbs. They passed the cannon balls along the line, then back again, but not from hand to hand. This was how they did it:

'One', shouted the officer on duty, and instantly, all the men, stooping, took up the heavy shot. 'Two', was scarcely uttered when the whole line moved sideways, three yards, until each man had taken the place where his neighbour stood before. One hearing 'Three', then everyone bent down and placed the iron ball on the floor, and at 'Four' they shifted back, empty handed, to their original places. Thus a continual see-saw movement was kept up, the men now moving sideways and then returning to their former places, whilst the shot was carried from one spot to another.

The men grew hot and breathed hard. Some, who at the beginning had been yellow as goose-skin, had bright spots appear, almost like dabs of rouge on their prominent cheek bones.

The warder said, 'It tries them most taking it up, because there's nothing to lay hold of, and the hands get hot and slippery with the perspiration, so that the ball is greasy like.'

Criminal Prisons of London, 1862

1 What were the four movements the men made?
2 What happened to them as they worked?
3 What does the warder say is the worst part of their work?
4 A group of you could do shot drill, but use something light!

In some prisons there was an even worse punishment called the 'crank'. Mayhew and Binny describe it:

It is a narrow iron drum, placed on legs, with a long handle on one side, which, on being turned, causes a series of cups or scoops inside to revolve. At the lower part of the inside of the machine is a thick layer of sand, which the cups, as they come round, scoop up and carry to the top of the wheel, where they throw it out and empty themselves. A dial-plate, fixed in front of the iron drum, shows how many revolutions the machine has made.

Criminal Prisons of London, 1862

A prisoner had to turn the crank a number of times before he could have a meal or go to bed. This was the scale of 'fees':

Turns of the crank	*Reward*
1,800	Breakfast
4,500	Dinner
5,400	Supper
2,700	Bed

Turning the crank

It was possible to turn the crank twenty times a minute.

1 Draw a diagram of the inside of a crank to show how it worked.
2 How long did a prisoner have to turn the crank before each of his meals?
3 How many hours did he work in a day?

At Leicester, a prisoner who refused to work the crank was flogged and starved until he died.

Prisoners went to chapel every day. Mayhew and Binny wrote:

> They seemed to be aware that the only time when they might raise their voices and break through the dumbness man had imposed upon them, was when they were addressing their God, so that to them the consolation of prayer must be especially great.
>
> *Criminal Prisons of London*, 1862

1 According to Mayhew and Binny, why were the prisoners glad to go to chapel?

This is a description of the mid-day meal at the Cold-bath Fields:

> Big tubs, filled with thin gruel, had been carried into the dining sheds, and a pint measure had been poured into the tin mugs, and these, with a spoon and the $3\frac{3}{4}$ ounces of bread, were ranged down the narrow tables.
>
> The men sat still for a second or two, with the steaming gruel before then, until the order was given to 'Draw up tables'. Instantly the long, light tables were, with a sudden rattle, pulled close to the men. Then the warder, taking off his cap, cried, 'Pay attention to grace', and every head was bent down as one of the prisoners repeated these words:
>
> 'Sanctify, we beseech thee, O Lord, these thy good things to our use, and us to thy service, through the grace of Jesus Christ.' A shout of 'Amen' followed, and directly afterwards the tinkling of spoons against tin cans was heard, along with the peculiar sound like 'sniffing', that is made by people eating half liquid messes with a spoon. The 'good things', as the water gruel and bit of bread were ironically called in the grace, were soon eaten, and then the men, each reaching a little sack of books which had been hung above their heads, passed the rest of their dinner hour reading.
>
> *Criminal Prisons of London*, 1862

Note: gruel is made from oatmeal and water, just like porridge.

1 What did the men have to eat?
2 Why do you suppose they shouted 'Amen', rather than saying it?
3 What did they do after the meal?

The Rev. Kingsmill who was chaplain at another prison, Pentonville, had this to say about the Silent System:

> The position of stooping in which the prisoners work at picking oakum or cotton, gives ample opportunity of carrying on a long conversation without much chance of

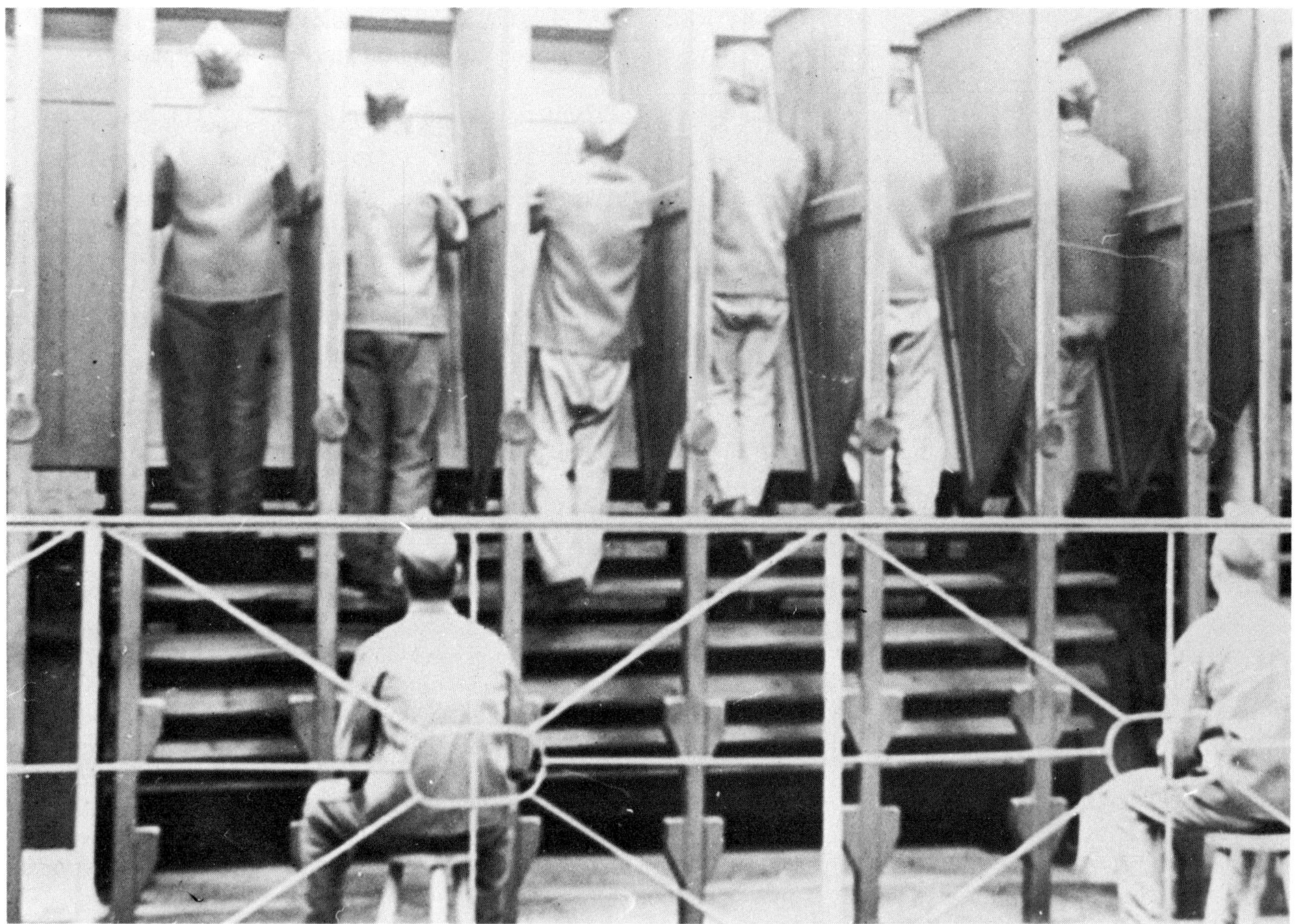

discovery; so that the rule of silence is a dead letter to many. At meals also, the rule is constantly broken. The time of exercise again affords an almost unlimited power of talking with each other; for the closeness of the prisoners to each other and the noise of the feet make talking a very easy matter. Further, the prisoners attend chapel daily, and this may be termed the golden period of the day to most of them: for it is here, by holding their books to their faces, and pretending to read with the chaplain, that they can carry on the most uninterrupted conversation.

Criminal Prisons of London, 1862

1 According to Kingsmill, what chances did the prisoners have of talking?
2 Do you agree that this is possible?
3 Do you think hardened criminals would be able to corrupt the others as Clay describes? (Page 83).

Other prisons had a different way of reforming criminals. It was called the 'Separate System'. Under this, prisoners were not only forbidden to speak to each other, but spent most of their time in 'solitary confinement'. That meant that each man was locked up in a cell, on his own. The Rev. John Clay introduced this system to Preston Gaol, Walter Clay explains why. First of all he says what he thinks goes on in a prisoner's mind while he is alone in his cell:

The Treadwheel This works like the wheel in a mouse's cage, except that the men stand outside it. Working the wheel is a bit like climbing stairs; indeed convicts called the wheel the 'everlasting staircase'. However, it is harder than that because, unlike stairs, the treads fall away beneath a man's feet and he has to make an extra effort to raise himself. By the end of the day each man will have 'climbed' the equivalent of more than 7,000 feet. Compare that with the height of Mount Snowdon. The wheel turns nothing but a huge fan which slows it down. The men know that all their time and energy is completely wasted. That is part of their punishment.

In his cell he has no temptations from without, and many wholesome warnings from within. Memory collects and brings before him everything that ever happened to him since he was a child: he traces unhappy results back to their sinful causes: the sense of sin and sorrow comes next: his thoughts turn to Him who bore our sorrows and atoned for sin; then rises up a prayer for pardon and he says, 'By God's help, I'll be a different man for the future.'

The Prison Chaplain

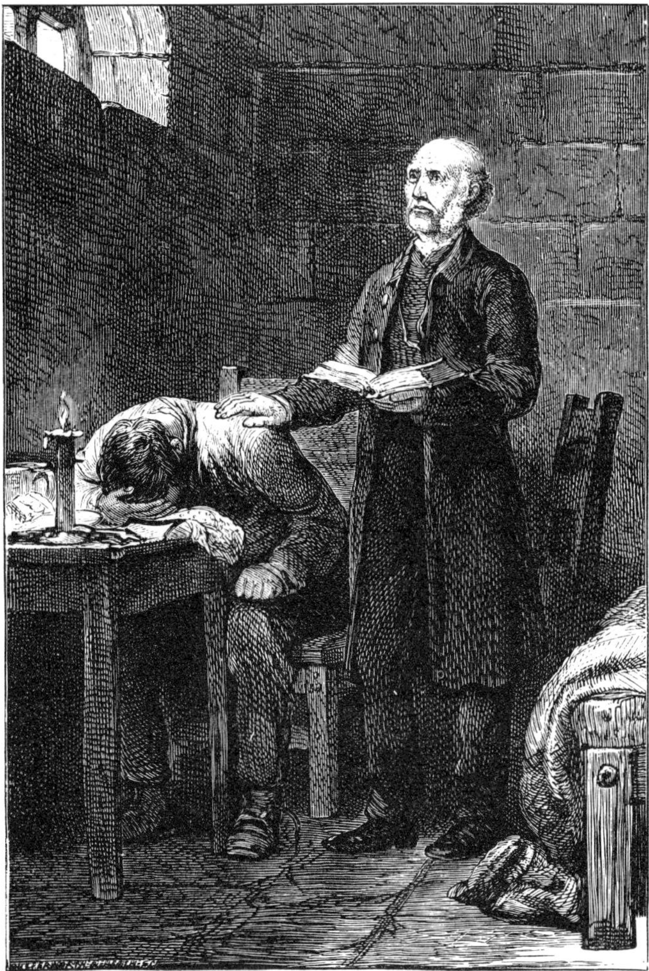

Chaplain and Prisoner This man has been held under the 'Separate System'. What has happened to him? What is the chaplain trying to do? What would Charles Dickens have said about this drawing? (see *Research*, question 2).

Here is what happened after a time:

> As a general rule, a few months in the separate cell makes a prisoner strangely weak-willed. The chaplain can then make the brawny navvy cry like a child: he can work on his feelings in almost any way he pleases: he can, so to speak, photograph his own thoughts, wishes and opinions on the patient's mind, and fill his mouth with his own phrases and language.
>
> *The Prison Chaplain*

According to Walter Clay:

1 What does the prisoner think about?
2 What does he decide to do?
3 How does he change?
4 What does this allow the chaplain to do?

One important prison which used the separate system was Pentonville, where the Rev. Kingsmill worked. Mayhew and Binny visited it. While they were there, they allowed themselves to be locked in the punishment cell for a time. Here a man was not only on his own, but in darkness:

> The air seemed as impossible to see through as so much black marble, and the body seemed positively wrapped in the blackness, as if it were buried alive, deep down in the earth itself. Though we stayed several minutes in the hope that we should gain the use of our eyes, and begin to make out bit after bit of the cell, the darkness was at the end, quite as deep as at the first. The continual straining of the eyes and taxing of the brains soon made us tired, and we could readily understand that we would end in conjuring up all kinds of terrible pictures in the mind.
>
> *Criminal Prisons of London*

1 Why did Mayhew and Binny find the punishment cell trying?
2 In what way did they think anyone would be affected after a time?

This table shows one of the main disadvantages of the Separate System:

	Number of Prisoners going Insane
Separate System	62 per 10,000
Silent System	5.8 per 10,000

Written Work

Write an account of prisons in the mid-nineteenth century.

1 Say how they were different from earlier prisons.
2 Describe the 'Silent System' and the 'Separate System'. What criticisms would you make of them?

Research

1 Read about John Howard and Elizabeth Fry.
2 Read Chapter 61 of *David Copperfield*. This will show you what Charles Dickens thought about the Separate System.
3 Read about transportation to Australia.
4 Find out what you can about modern prisons.

Care of the Poor

Until the end of the sixteenth century people who were short of food had to rely on charity. Then, in 1601, Parliament passed a law to say that each parish must look after its own poor. The ratepayers were to choose overseers, usually two in number. They collected money called the poor rate from anyone in the parish who owned land or a house. The overseers then used the money to help those in need. They called it giving 'relief'. Those who had relief from the parish were known as 'paupers'. They were of two kinds, the 'impotent' and the 'able-bodied'. The impotent were those who could do little for themselves, such as orphan children, the sick and the old. The overseers paid someone to look after the children and gave food or money to the others. The 'able-bodied' were healthy adults, and the overseers were supposed to find them work and pay them wages.

Overseers were unpaid and could only do their duties by leaving their farms or their businesses from time to time. Also, dealing with paupers could be unpleasant. This is what happened at some villages in Cambridgeshire:

> The tone of the paupers towards the overseers is generally very insolent, and often assumes even a more fearful character. At Great Gransden the overseer's wife told me that two paupers came to her husband demanding an increase of allowance: he refused, showing them that they had had the full allowance; they

A workhouse dinner 1840 When you have read the extracts, and looked at the other pictures, try to decide how far the cartoonist is exaggerating.

Christmas dinner, Marylebone Workhouse 1900 How would you feel about having your Christmas, or any other dinner, here? Why are there no women present? (See bottom of page 91 and right hand column of page 93). Compare the pictures on these two pages, with those of the prisons on pages 82 and 83.

swore and threatened he should repent of it; and such was their violence that she called them back and persuaded her husband to make them a further allowance. Mr. Faircloth, by a stricter system of relief, reduced the rates at Croydon: he became unpopular with the labourers, and they gathered in a riotous body about his thrashing machine and broke it to bits. At Guilden Morden a burning took place of Mr. Butterfields's ricks, to the amount of £1,500 damage. Mr. Butterfield was overseer.

Poor Law Commission, 1834

1 Why did paupers dislike overseers?
2 What happened at each of the villages mentioned here?

Perhaps the most difficult of the overseers' tasks was to make the able-bodied paupers work. Usually they sent them to repair the roads. Here is what happened at two Yorkshire villages:

In Pollington, they send many of them upon the highways, but they only work four hours per day; this is because there is not enough for them to do; they sleep more than they work, and if anyone but the surveyor found them sleeping they would laugh at him. In Rawcliffe, they employed a man to look over them, but they threatened to drown him, and he was obliged to withdraw.

Poor Law Commission, 1834

1 How many hours do the paupers work at Pollington? Why is this?
2 How do they spend most of their time?
3 What did the overseers try at Rawcliffe? What happened as a result?

Note: In most places the overseers gave the able-bodied money and did not even try to make them work.

During the eighteenth century some of the larger towns built workhouses. The idea was that if all the paupers were together it would be easier to supervise them and make them work. Here is Sir Frederick

This ſhews, at one view, what ſhould be the weekly Income of the Induſtrious Poor, as ſettled by the Magiſtrates for the county of Berks, at a meeting held at Speenhamland, May the 6th, 1795.	Income ſhould be for a Man.	For a ſingle Woman.	For a Man and his Wife.	With one Child.	With two Children.	With three Children.	With four Children.	With five Children.	With ſix Children.	With ſeven Children.
When the gallon loaf is s. d.	s. d.	s. d.	s. d.	s. d.	s. d.	s. d.	s. d.	s. d.	s. d.	s. d.
1 0	3 0	2 0	4 6	6 0	7 6	9 0	10 6	12 0	13 6	15 0
when - 1 1	3 3	2 1	4 10	6 5	8 0	9 7	11 2	12 9	14 4	15 11
when - 1 2	3 6	2 2	5 2	6 10	8 6	10 2	11 10	13 6	15 2	16 10
when - 1 3	3 9	2 3	5 6	7 3	9 0	10 9	12 6	14 3	16 0	17 9
when - 1 4	4 0	2 4	5 10	7 8	9 6	11 4	13 2	15 0	16 10	18 8
when - 1 5	4 0	2 5	5 11	7 10	9 9	11 8	13 7	15 6	17 5	19 4
when - 1 6	4 3	2 6	6 3	8 3	10 3	12 3	14 3	16 3	18 3	20 3
when - 1 7	4 3	2 7	6 4	8 5	10 6	12 7	14 8	16 9	18 10	20 11
when - 1 8	4 6	2 8	6 8	8 10	11 0	13 2	15 4	17 6	19 8	21 10
when - 1 9	4 6	2 9	6 9	9 0	11 3	13 6	15 9	18 0	20 3	22 6
when - 1 10	4 9	2 10	7 1	9 5	11 9	14 1	16 5	18 9	21 1	23 5
when - 1 11	4 9	2 11	7 2	9 7	12 0	14 5	16 10	19 3	21 8	24 1
when - 2 0	5 0	3 0	7 6	10 0	12 6	15 0	17 6	20 0	22 6	25 0

SECOND CALCULATION, which was adopted.

Speenhamland system Overseers used this table to decide how much 'bread money' they should give.

Morton Eden's description of the workhouse at Bristol:

The Poor of Bristol are partly supported in a work-house and partly at home by a parish allowance. The number at present in the work-house is 287. They are mostly old people and children, insane, lame, blind etc. The only work at present is picking oakum, by which very little is earned. A few years ago a workshop for spinning wool was set up, but after 3 years experiment they had lost £600 by it, and it was therefore discontinued. The master says the house was not built with a view to its present use and is, therefore, not one of the most convenient. There are 12 or 15 beds, principally of flocks, in each room: it is probably owing to this, and the number of old and diseased persons, that the house is infected with vermin, particularly bugs: to a visitor, there appears to be a want of cleanliness.

State of the Poor, 1797

1 How many people are there in the Bristol work-house? Which of the two kinds of pauper are they, on the whole?
2 Where do the other paupers live?
3 What work is done by the people in the work-house? How useful is it?
4 What work was tried for a time? Why was it given up?
5 What is wrong with the building itself?
6 What is wrong with the way it is kept?
7 In what ways was this workhouse failing to do what was expected of it?

During the Napoleonic Wars (1793–1815) there was inflation in Britain. Bread became very dear, which was a disaster for ordinary people because that was their main food (See page 101). Now it was not just the unemployed who needed help: many who had work were in danger of starving. What could be done? In 1795 the magistrates of Berkshire decided that in their county any family which did not earn enough money to buy the bread it needed should have an allowance from the parish. The allowance depended on three things, the price of bread, the size of the family, and its income. The table which the magistrates drew up is shown above.

Note: a gallon loaf weighed 8 lbs 11 ozs.

1 When the gallon loaf was 1/8d*, how much money did a man, his wife and two children need? How much would the parish give them if they earned 9/- ?
2 The gallon loaf is 1/4d. A man, his wife and five children have 12/- a week. How much will the parish give them?
3 The gallon loaf is 2/. A single man is earning 6/-. How much will the parish give him?

* One shilling = 12 old pennies = 5p;
1p is roughly $2\frac{1}{2}$ old pennies

Women in Withington Workhouse, Manchester The woman standing is the matron. Who has come to visit these women? What seems to be his attitude towards them? The shield on the wall reads 'He shall feed His flock, like a Shepherd'.

Giving allowances in this way was called the 'Speenhamland' system after the place where the Berkshire magistrates held their meeting. Soon, most of the counties in the south of England were copying Berkshire.

One result of the Speenhamland system was that the poor rates went up. They were £2.2 million in 1785 and £8.4 million in 1890. Also, people began to suspect that the poor were no longer working as hard as they should. What was the point when the parish would always make up their wages? Accordingly, in 1834, Parliament appointed a Royal Commission to look into the Poor Laws.

This is what a Sussex farm labourer, Thomas Pearce of Govington told the Commissioners:

In your parish are there many able-bodied men upon the parish?

There are a great many men on our parish who like it better than being at work.

Why do they like it better?

They get the same money and do half as much work. They don't work like me. They be'ant at it so many hours, and they don't do so much work when they be at it; they're doing no good, and are only waiting for dinner-time and night; they be'aint working, its only waiting.

How have you managed to live without parish relief?

By working hard.

What do the paupers say to you?

They blame me for what I do. They say to me, 'You are only doing it for the parish, and if you didn't do it, you would get the same as another man has, and would get the money for smoking your pipe and doing nothing.' 'Tis a hard thing for a man like me.

Poor Law Commission, 1834

1 Why are many of the men of Govington happy to take parish relief?
2 How does Thomas Pearce avoid taking relief?
3 What do the other men say to him?
4 Why do you suppose Thomas Pearce behaved as he did?
5 Most of the people who read Pearce's evidence in 1834 said he was a fine fellow. What do you think of him?

The Commission found Southwell in Nottinghamshire was very different from most other places. Here, paupers were not given money to take away and spend as they pleased. If they wanted relief, they had to come and live in the workhouse.

These were the rules of the Southwell workhouse:

1 To separate the men and women.
2 To prevent any from going out or seeing visitors, and to make them keep regular hours.

3 To prevent smoking.
4 To disallow beer.
5 To find them work.
6 To treat and feed them well.

The workhouse master said:

> If they misbehaved themselves very badly, I had authority to imprison them in a solitary cell with the consent of the overseer. But never since I have been governor have I had occasion to imprison but one person, a woman, who was a violent idiot. To the violent, turbulent young paupers who come in, swearing they would beat the parish, I gave bones or stones to break in the yard – had a hammer made on purpose.

This is what happened with three men:

> One said immediately with sulky violence, that he would never break bones for the parish when he could go out and get something for breaking stones for others, and he went out next day. The other said it hurt his back to bend so much, and he would start work the next day, which he did. A third had a hole to dig which he liked so little that he went off the third day. He had been, for nine or ten years before, one of the most troublesome men in the parish, but he went off very quietly, saying that he did not complain of the victuals or accommodation but if he was to work, would work for himself; he has never troubled the parish since, and now he gets his own living in a brick-yard.'
>
> *Poor Law Commission*, 1834

1 What was done to make life in Southwell workhouse unpleasant?
2 What punishment could the workhouse master give? How often had he done so?
3 What work did he give the able-bodied paupers?
4 What was the reaction of the three men mentioned in the extract?

When it saw the Report of the Poor Law Commission, Parliament was very impressed by what was happening at Southwell. So, in 1834, it passed the Poor Law Amendment Act. The idea behind it was to have the Southwell system all over England. A new government department, also called the Poor Law Commission, was set up to make sure this happened. Since most parishes were too small to afford workhouses, they had to join together in groups of about twelve, known as Poor Law Unions. Soon, every Union had its own workhouse, with rules very like those at Southwell.

In 1841, an economist called Nassau Senior wrote:

> No public department has had a more difficult task than the Poor Law Commissioners, and none has carried it out more successfully.
>
> Some idea of the improvement can be gained by comparing the total amount of the poor rates in 1834 with the amount in 1840. The amount for 1834 was £7,511,218: that for 1840 was £5,110,683.
>
> However, we are grateful to the Commissioners, not so much for having saved £2,400,000 a year, but for having stopped the plague and improved the morals of the people. The general result is that the labourer, finding himself no longer entitled to a fixed income, whatever his idleness or misconduct, becomes stimulated to work and honesty by the double motive of hope and fear.
>
> *Essays on Poor Relief*, 1841

1 What has happened to the poor rates since 1834?
2 According to Nassau Senior, how has the new system changed the habits of the working man?

In 1861, a French writer, Hippolyte Taine, visited a workhouse in Manchester. This is what he said about it:

> It can accommodate 1900, but at present it contains 350 only. The building is spacious, perfectly clean, well kept; it has large courts and gardens and looks upon fields and stately trees; it has a chapel and rooms with ceilings twenty feet high. There has been every effort to make it correct and useful. There is no smell anywhere; the beds are almost white and are covered with patterned bedspreads: the most aged and feeble women have white caps and new clothes. One room is set apart for the lunatics, another for the female idiots; the latter do needle work for some hours daily: during the period of recreation they dance together to the sound of the fiddle. They pull strange faces, yet they all seem healthy and not at all sad. In another room the children are taught their lessons, one of the elder children acting as monitor. The daily ration is two pounds of oatmeal, made into gruel, and a pound and a half of potatoes: four times a week, the allowance is increased by four ounces of meat. The drink is water except during illness. We were astounded: this was a palace compared with the kennels in which the poor dwell. One of us seriously asked our friend to reserve a place for him here in his old age. Recollect that a Manchester labourer can scarcely get meat once a week by working ten hours a day! Here an able-bodied pauper works about six hours, has newspapers, the Bible and some good books to read, lives in a wholesome air and enjoys the sight of trees. Nevertheless there is not an able-bodied inmate of this workhouse at this moment: it is almost empty and will not be filled till the winter. When a working man who is unemployed asks for help,

he is usually told, 'Show us you wish to work, by entering the workhouse.' Nine out of ten refuse. Whence this dislike? Today at a street corner I saw an old woman groping with her skinny hands in a heap of rubbish, and pulling out scraps of vegetables: probably she couldn't give up her drop of spirits. But what of the others? I am told they prefer their home and their freedom at any price, that they cannot bear being shut up and subjected to discipline. They prefer to be free and to starve.

Notes on England, written 1861, published 1874

1 How many vacant places are there in the work-house? When is it likely to be full?
2 In what ways is the workhouse pleasant?
3 How is it different from the Bristol workhouse of the 1790's?
4 What type of pauper is *not* in the workhouse?
5 What are people told when they come for help?
6 Why does Taine think the old woman would not come into the workhouse?
7 Why do most people refuse to come in?

Not all workhouses were like the one at Manchester. A man called G. R. Wythen Baxter collected all the nasty stories he could find about workhouses and published them in what he called the *Book of the Bastiles.* Here are two of his tales:

It appears that January last two paupers, named Lock and Dart, died in the Crediton workhouse. The report at that time was that, shortly before their death, these poor creatures had been removed to a dark out-house, and

Withington Workhouse, Manchester Judging from this picture, how seriously did the people of Manchester take the care of their poor? Why should anyone object to living here? Read Taine's description of it on these two pages.

laid on straw, without any covering but a single blanket, the temperature being at the time many degrees below freezing point: that no doctor saw them and that the officer who went with a relative of Lock into the miserable place was annoyed to discover that Dart was still alive! It was also said that these sick paupers were made to walk naked, in freezing weather, through the courtyard to the pump. Here they were washed with a mop in the same way that a carriage or a staircase might be washed – in cold water from head to foot.

An aged married couple, at Hastings, (each above 70 years old) were in need. They asked for help from the parish to which they belonged. The parish refused – and the aged pair were sent to the Bastile. They were immediately separated. The poor old woman could not eat what was put before her in the workhouse! The old man complained, 'That he missed his comfortable cup of tea in the evening with his old wife!'. The result was that they could not bear it – they went out.

Book of the Bastiles, 1841

1 In what ways were the two men in the first story ill-treated?
2 Which of the workhouse rules upset the old couple in the second story? What did they do as a result?
3 What was the original Bastille? (Note that Baxter spells it wrongly.)

In 1837 Richard Oastler made a speech in which he said:

> I tell you, if I have the misfortune to be reduced to poverty, that that man who dares to tear from me the wife whom God has joined to me shall, if I have it in my power, receive his death at my hands! If I am ever confined in one of those hellish Poor Law Bastiles, and my wife be torn from me because I am poor, I will, if it be possible, burn the whole pile down to the ground!
>
> *Damnation! Eternal Damnation to the Fiend-begotten Coarser-Food New Poor Law!*, 1837

1 Which of the workhouse rules is Oastler objecting to here?
2 What does he say he would do, rather than obey it?
3 What kind of man does this speech show Oastler to be?

Finally, here is a poem by Thomas Hardy:

The Curate's Kindness

A Workhouse Irony

I thought they'd be strangers aroun' me,
    But she's to be there!
Let me jump out o' waggon and go back and drown me
    At Pummery or Ten-Hatches Weir.

I thought: 'Well, I've come to the Union –
    The workhouse at last –
After honest hard work all the week, and Communion
    O' Zundays, these fifty years past.'

''Tis hard, but,' I thought, 'never mind it;
    There's gain in the end:
And when I get used to the place I shall find it
    A home and may find there a friend.'

'Life there will be better than t'other,
    For peace is assured,
The men in one wing and their wives in another
    Is strictly the rule of the Board.'

Just then one young Pa'son arriving
    Steps up out of breath
To the side of the waggon wherein we were driving
    To Union; and calls out and saith:

'Old folks that harsh order is altered,
    Be not sick of heart!
The Guardians they poohed and they pished and they paltered
When urged not to keep you apart.'

'It is wrong,' I maintained, 'to divide them,
    Near forty years wed.
"Very well sir. We promise then, they shall abide
    In one wing together", they said.'

Then I sank – knew 'twas quite a foredone thing
    That misery should be
To the end!... To get freed of her there was the one thing
Had made the change welcome to me.

To go there was ending but badly;
    'Twas shame and 'twas pain;
'But anyhow,' thought I, 'thereby I shall gladly
    Get free of this forty years' chain.'

I thought they'd be strangers aroun' me,
    But she's to be there!
Let me jump out o' waggon and go back and drown me
    At Pummery or Ten-Hatches Weir.

1 How did the old man feel when he first heard he was going to the workhouse?
2 What was the 'curate's kindness'?
3 What does the old man feel like doing now?

Written Work

1 Imagine it is 1840. You are a ratepayer, and neither very rich, nor very poor. Say:
   a What problems there were with the care of the poor before 1834.
   b What changes were made in that year.
   c How you feel about the New Poor Law.
2 Now imagine you are a poor man, and that you are short of money through no fault of your own. Say how you would have been treated before 1834, and how you will be treated now in 1840.

Research

1 Read about Edwin Chadwick and the work he did in connection with the poor laws.
2 Find out about the Andover workhouse scandal of 1846.
3 Read the following, all written by Charles Dickens:
   Oliver Twist, Chapters 1 and 2.
   Our Mutual Friend, Book 1, Chapter 16. Book 2, Chapter 8.
   Reprinted Pieces – A Walk in the Workhouse.
   Sketches by Boz – 'Our Parish', Chapter 1.
   The Uncommercial Traveller – 'Wapping Workhouse', Chapter 3.

Sunday Schools and Monitorial Schools

In the eighteenth century most of the children of Britain did not go to school. As soon as they were old enough, they helped their parents, and when they were 8 or 9 might even go out to work. By the end of the century, though, many of the rich were beginning to worry about the ordinary people. They seemed to be very wicked, doing all kinds of unpleasant things such as stealing, fighting and even rioting. Their immediate answer was to hang them, or transport them overseas, but there did seem to be another possibility. That was to send them to school and teach them about Christianity.

It was not easy. There were few schools, very little money and no trained teachers, while poor parents needed their children's wages. Then, in 1870, Robert Raikes started a Sunday School at Gloucester. He and his helpers taught for nothing, and the children did not lose any wages, so it seemed that the worst problems had been solved.

Soon other people were copying Raikes. One of them was a lady called Miss Hannah More. She started a number of schools for the lead miners and farm workers of the Mendip Hills. Here is a description of them which Sir Thomas Barnard wrote in 1809. He was a great admirer of Hannah More's work.

> The Mendip Schools extend over twelve parishes. They are intended not merely for the education of youth, but to instruct, improve and reform people of all ages. The early part of the Sabbath is devoted to the instruction of the young, who afterwards proceed to church in a body. Towards the close of the day the room is frequented by others: chiefly by the aged who come to take the benefit of the evening readings and discussion, and attend with great pleasure and eagerness. They derive from religion that solid relief which alone can give comfort to declining life, and smooth the path to the grave. The number of those who frequent the schools is about three thousand.
>
> Ten years ago that neighbourhood was very different. There was little to show that it was within the pale of Christianity. In the large parish of Cheddar the congregation at the parish church did not exceed the number of twenty: the regular attendants at that church are now eight hundred, and sometimes more. The teachings of Christianity were almost unknown and disregarded in that district: they are now the comfort of the aged, and the guide of the young: and observing them has been attended by a rich and abundant harvest of moral virtues of honesty, sobriety, diligence, industry and chastity.

1 Find the Mendip Hills on a map.
2 For whom were the Mendip Schools intended?
3 What did the children do on Sundays?

School of about 1800 This school would have been for the boys of quite wealthy parents. The boy is being birched on his bare bottom. Later, someone will have to pull the pieces of twig out of his wounds. Why is the victim being held in this way, do you suppose? This cartoon is by Cruikshank. What seems to be his opinion of school masters and school boys?

GOOD CONDUCT CARD
Oh, did the Son of God most high
Consent a man to be;
And did that blessed Saviour die,
Upon the cross, for me?
Accept, O ever blessed Lord,
An infant's humble praise;
Teach me to love thy holy word,
And serve thee all my days.

Good Conduct Card How would a child win a card like this? Would you think it worth winning? Compare this card with the picture on page 91. What did Victorian people hope would be a big influence on young and old alike?

4 Who attended the schools in the evenings?
5 How did the schools help them?
6 What had the Mendip area been like in the old days?
7 How did it change after the schools were opened?
8 How did Barnard measure the success of the Mendip Schools?
9 How do you measure the success of your own school?

Here now are some lines from a poem which Hannah More wrote for her schools. It is called, *The Riot: or, Half a Loaf is Better than No Bread.* **Tom is hungry and suggests a riot; Jack argues against it saying:**

On those days spent in riot, no bread you brought home;
Had you spent them in labour you might have had some,
A dinner with herbs, says the wise man, with quiet,
Is better than beef amid discord and riot.
So I'll work all the day, and on Sunday I'll seek,
At the Church how to bear all the wants of the week.
The gentlefolk too will afford us supplies,
They'll subscribe and they'll give up their puddings and pies.

1 Why, according to Hannah More, is it better to work than riot?
2 How should a poor man console himself when he is hungry?
3 What is the duty of the rich?
4 From this poem, what would you say was one of the main aims of Hannah More's schools? Does it fit in with what Barnard said about them?
5 William Cobbett who lived at the same time as Hannah More, once called her an 'old bishop in petticoats'. What do you think of that description?

Here now is an account of some Sunday Schools in Staffordshire in about 1840. It was written by a man called Horne who had been sent as a Commissioner by Parliament, to see how children were being treated in that area:

The Sunday-schools do not try to teach much. At many of them, writing is not taught at all: it is considered 'not quite proper' on a Sunday. Anyone who offers is supposed capable of teaching children to read: whereas it has probably been found that writing requires a writing master who has some practice in teaching. This is perhaps another reason.

Religion and moral instruction is all they really hope to give, and this is attempted by teaching the children to read religious books. The children learn to read these in a loud, monotonous, sing-song voice, with no attempt to heed the punctuation, and with no sort of understanding of the meaning of what they read.

Of the singing of the children at the Sunday-schools, it must be pronounced intolerable.

Most of the children are very ignorant. Many who

have attended Sunday-schools for three or four years could neither read nor write. You will find boys who have never heard of such a place as London, nor of Willenhall (which is only three miles distant), who have never heard the name of the Queen – or who have believed that Her Majesty's name was Prince Albert. You will find poor girls who have never sung or danced: never seen a dance: never read a book that made them laugh: never seen a violet or a primrose; and others whose only idea of a green field was derived from having been stung by a nettle.

The minds of most of the children are in a state of utter confusion on all religious subjects, when not in total ignorance.
(Wolverhampton)

The teachers are all unpaid. Not any of them have been trained as teachers: nor have any of them had any education, except at Sunday-school: consequently some of them cannot write – not even their own names. The head teachers are locksmiths, key-makers and other tradesmen of the place, either small masters or journeymen; and the Sunday-school at Short Heath is run by a very worthy and honest-minded butty (foreman) of a coal mine.
(Willenhall)

As to spelling her name – well, she is no scholar. Has been to school on Sundays, regular. Never heard of Job: never heard of King David: never heard of Pontius Pilate or Pharaoh. Has heard of heaven: does not know who Jesus Christ was: has heard the name.
(Answers given by Mary Garner, aged 16.)

1 Why, according to Horne, did the Staffordshire schools not teach writing? (Two points)
2 What did they try to teach? How did they hope to do it?
3 What was wrong with the children's reading?
4 Who were the teachers at the Staffordshire schools?
5 What was Horne's opinion of them? What good things can you find to say about them?
6 Why were the schools cheap to run?
7 Which of Horne's remarks could be applied to Mary Garner, do you think?
8 Can you think why Barnard and Horne should write such different things about Sunday Schools? Were the Mendip and Staffordshire Schools very different, do you suppose? Do you think Barnard or Horne exaggerated? Had they reasons for doing so?
9 Do you think that Sunday Schools were able to give a good education?

Before long people not only wanted Sunday Schools, but day schools as well. Unfortunately, they still had the problems of finding enough money and enough teachers. Two men, in particular, gave a lot of thought to the difficulties of running day schools. They were Andrew Bell, a clergyman of the Church of England, and Joseph Lancaster, a Quaker. They had little to do with each other, in fact they were rivals, but they both had the same idea. This was to employ monitors to do the teaching, while the master or mistress just supervised. The monitors were the brightest and oldest pupils, but even so they were only children, because no-one stayed at school much beyond the age of eleven. Lancaster explained the monitorial system in his book *Improvements in Education* **written in 1803:**

The Boys' School in Borough Road was started by Joseph Lancaster in 1801: it now has 700 boys who are instructed upon a Plan entirely new: by means of which ONE MASTER alone can educate 1000 boys in Reading, Writing and Arithmetic as easily and with as little trouble as Twenty or Thirty have ever been taught by the usual methods.

The whole school is arranged in classes: a monitor is appointed to each, who is responsible for teaching every boy in it. The proportion of boys who teach, either in reading, writing or arithmetic, is one to ten.

In so large a school there are many duties to be performed other than teaching, and for these duties different monitors are appointed. The boy who takes care that the writing books are ruled is the monitor of ruling. The boy who inquires after the absentees, is called the monitor of absentees. The monitors who inspect the progress of the classes in reading, writing and arithmetic are called inspecting monitors. A boy whose business it is to give to the other monitors such books etc. as may be wanted for the daily use of their classes, and to gather them up when done with: to see all the boys do read, and that none leave school without reading, is called the monitor general. Another is called the monitor of slates, because he has a general charge of all the slates in the school.

1 Why was it important one master should have as many pupils as possible?
2 According to Lancaster, how many boys could one master teach?
3 What subjects were taught at Lancaster's schools?
4 How many children did each monitor teach?
5 What monitors were there, apart from teaching monitors?
6 What impression was Lancaster trying to give of the organisation of his school?

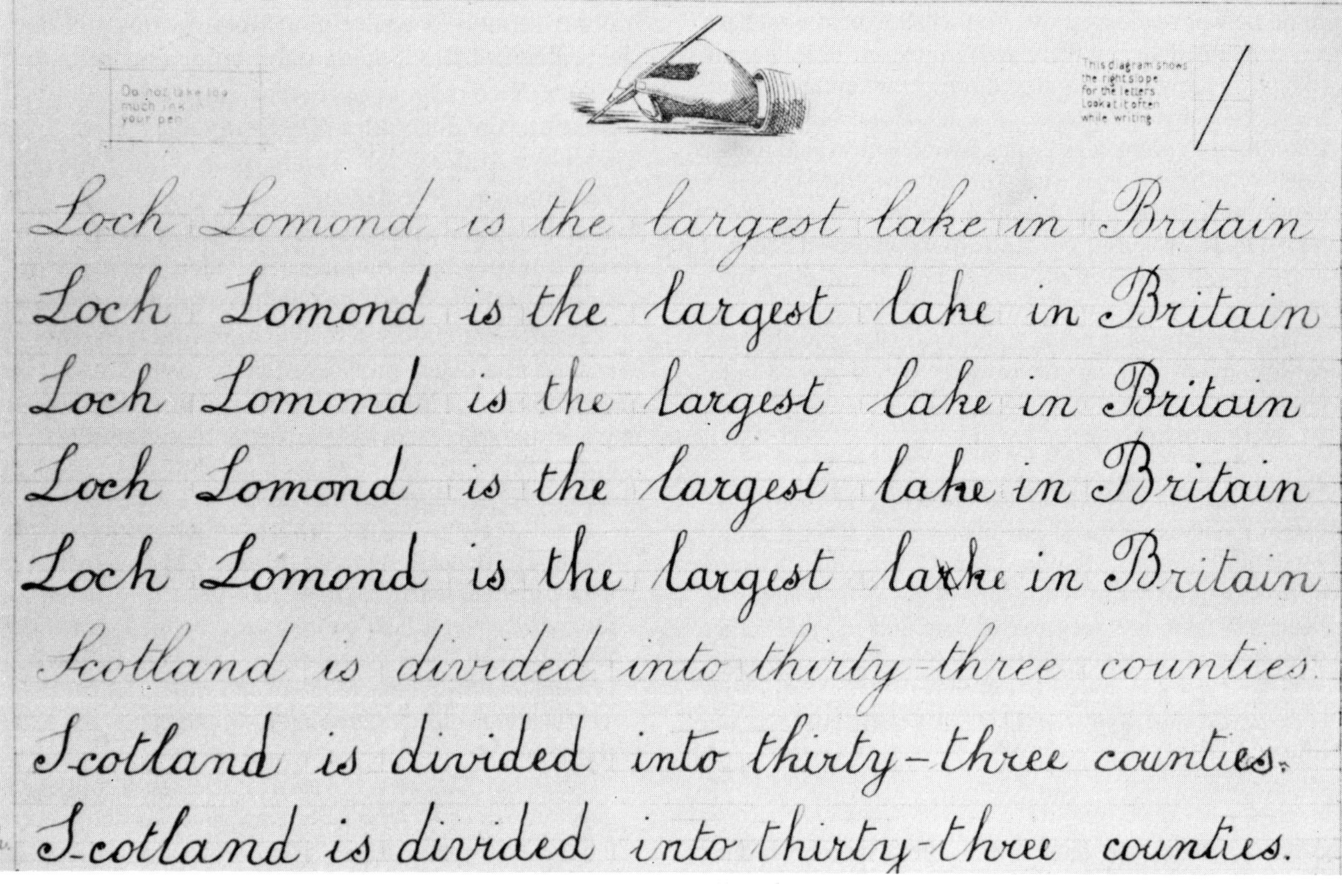
Do not take too
much ink
your pen
This diagram shows
the right slope
for the letters
Look at it often
while writing
Loch Lomond is the largest lake in Britain
Loch Lomond is the largest lake in Britain
Loch Lomond is the largest lake in Britain
Loch Lomond is the largest lake in Britain
Loch Lomond is the largest laxke in Britain
Scotland is divided into thirty-three counties.
Scotland is divided into thirty-three counties.
Scotland is divided into thirty-three counties.

Page from a Copy Book What was on this page before the pupil did anything with it? What three pieces of advice are there at the top of the page? Do you think this is a good way to teach writing? Why did the pupil make a mistake in his fourth sentence rather than his first, do you suppose? Try to do the exercise yourself. These two statements are typical of the kind of thing children in the nineteenth century learnt for Geography.

Here now is some advice from Lancaster on how to teach reading and writing:

Reading

A Method of Teaching to Spell and Read, Whereby One Book will serve Instead of Six Hundred Books.

It is desirable that the whole book should be printed three times as large as normal. Its different pages should then be pasted on board and hung by a string to a nail in the wall. From twelve to twenty boys may stand in a circle round each card: and when they have repeated the whole lesson, they are sent to practise their spelling on their slates, and another like number of boys may study the lesson in their turn: indeed, *two hundred boys* may all repeat their lesson from *one* card in the space of *three* hours.

Writing

The sand is spread on a table painted black: the sand is whitish: when the children trace the letters in the white sand, the black ground shows them to more advantage. The boys print in the sand with their fingers: they all print at the *command* given by their monitors. In teaching the boys the alphabet, the monitor first makes a letter on the sand; the boy then has to retrace over the same letter which the monitor had made for him, with his fingers, until he can make the letter himself without the monitor's help. Then he may go on and learn another letter.

It is both curious and amusing to see a number of little creatures, many not more than four or five years old, and some hardly that, stretching out their little fingers with one consent to make the letters. When this is done they sit quietly until the sand is smoothed for them, by the monitor, with a flat iron as commonly used for ironing linen.

1 Describe in your own words Lancaster's methods of teaching reading and writing.
2 Why did he suggest these methods, do you suppose?
3 What disadvantages can you see with them?
4 It has been said that Lancaster's schools were like factories. Discuss this idea.

As Lancaster was a Quaker, he did not believe in violence. There could be no caning or beating of any kind in his schools. He had other ways of keeping discipline:

If a boy persists in behaving badly he has wooden logs put round his neck, which serve him as a pillory and with this he is sent to his seat. The neck is not pinched, and while the logs rest on his shoulders they keep their balance. But on the least movement one way or the other, the logs slip to one side and act as a dead weight on the neck. Thus he is made to sit in his proper position. If this does not work, it is common to fasten the legs of offenders with wooden shackles. The shackles are a piece of wood about a foot long and tied to each leg. When shackled, he cannot walk but in a very slow, measured pace being obliged to take very small steps. Thus accoutred he is ordered to walk around the school room till tired out. Should this punishment not have the desired effect, the left hand is tied behind the back, or wooden shackles fastened from elbow to elbow, behind the back. Sometimes the legs are tied together. Occasionally, boys are put in a sack, or in a basket, suspended from the roof of the school, in the sight of all the pupils, who frequently smile at the birds in the cage. Old offenders are yoked together sometimes by a piece of wood that fastens round all their necks: and thus confined they parade the school walking backwards – being obliged to pay very great attention to their footsteps for fear of running against any object which might cause the yoke to hurt their necks. Five or six boys can be yoked together in this way.

When a boy is disobedient to his parents, uses bad language, or is dirty or untidy, it is usual for him to be dressed up with labels, describing his offence, and a tin or paper crown on his head. In that manner he walks round the school, two boys going in front of him proclaiming his fault.

Few punishments are as effective as detention. It does, however, have one drawback. In order to confine the bad boys after school hours, the master has to confine himself in school, to keep them in order. This inconvenience may be avoided by tying them to the desks in such a manner that they cannot untie themselves.

1 Make a list of the punishments Lancaster described. Which would you dislike the most?
2 Several of Lancaster's punishments are meant to make children keep still. Why was that important in his schools?
3 Why would Lancaster's punishments be forbidden in schools today?

The following is part of a letter written in 1846 by the Rev. Walter Hood, Vicar of Leeds:

The very first object which a respectable clergyman has in view when he receives an appointment, is to form a school. Let us suppose him to have persuaded some pious young man, for the love of God, to give up a trade and to undertake the school with a trifling salary. The poor young man has the sole charge of a hundred and fifty little dirty, ragged, ignorant urchins, assembled in the miserable building now dignified by the name of a National School Room, and he is expected, as by a miracle, to convert them into clean, well-bred, intelligent children. He cannot educate them all himself, and is therefore obliged to use the monitorial system: the result of which is, that while a portion of the children are vain, conceited and puffed-up, a larger proportion are left in their ignorance. I have known children who have been two years at a National School, and left it unable to read. The master seeing this, depressed in spirit, gets through the drudgery of the school hours as best he may: but has his work ceased? No, he must teach his monitors, to them he must impart some knowledge out of school hours, and his mind is still kept on the stretch.

1 Who was responsible for starting a school in a parish?
2 According to Hook, why should anyone want to be a teacher?
3 How large was the school likely to be? How did that compare with Lancaster's?
4 What were the pupils like?
5 What was the teacher supposed to do with them?
6 What system did he have to use? Why?
7 Which children, do you suppose, became 'vain, conceited and puffed-up'? Which were 'left in ignorance'?
8 What did the master feel about his work?
9 What did he have to do after school?
10 Who, do you suppose, gave the more accurate description of a monitorial school, Lancaster or Hook?

Headteachers kept log books, which were official diaries of the things that happened in their schools. Here are remarks about monitors from a number of log books:

The monitors do not improve. The children are forgetting all they know and are exceedingly idle. When I go round the class to examine the writing, I find nothing on their slates.

The two new monitors have very little command of their classes.

E. Abraham has not lighted her fire, dusted the room, nor arranged the forms. Children crying with the cold.

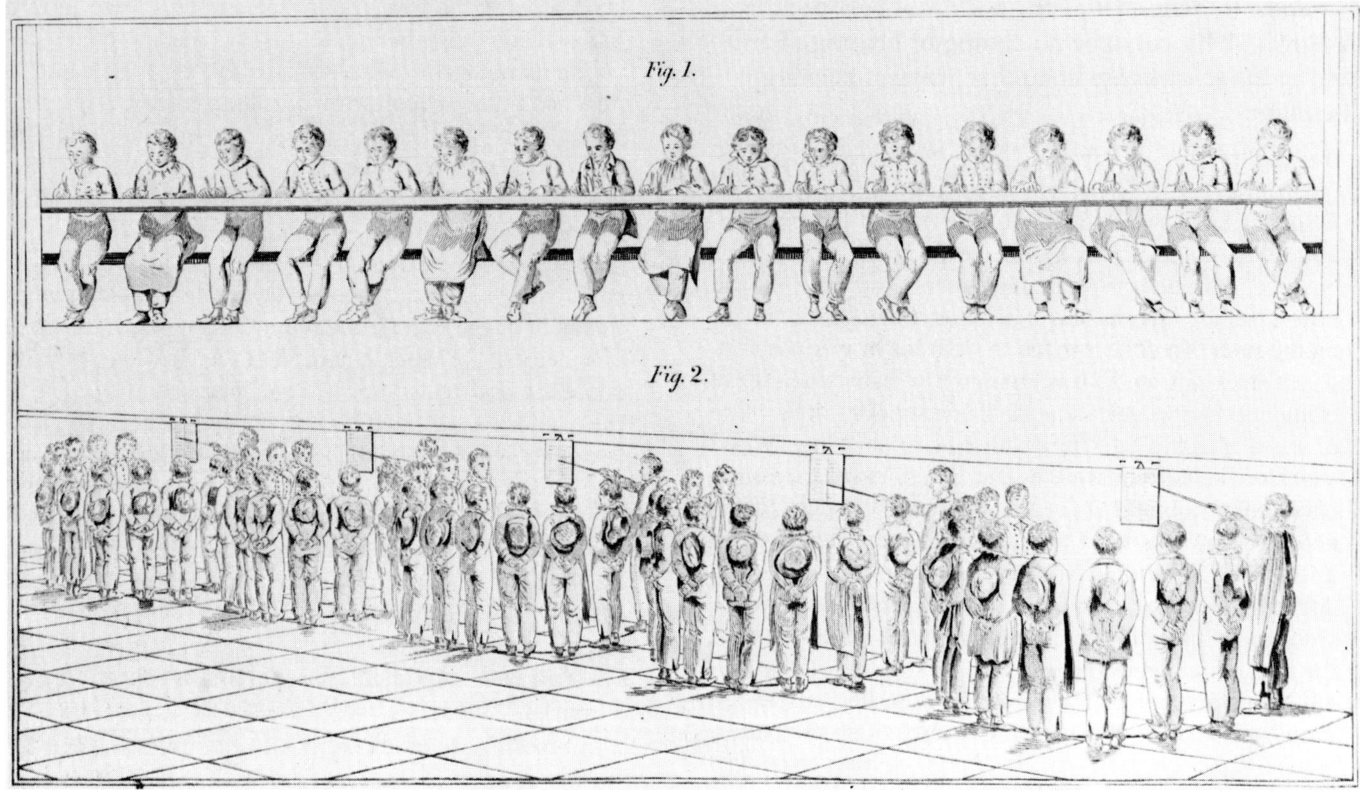

Monitorial School What two lessons are shown here? How many children does each monitor teach? Compare this picture with the cartoon on page 95. Compare both with the pictures on pages 82 and 83, and 88 and 89. Between them, these prints will give you a good idea of what nineteenth century people hoped to avoid, and what they hoped to achieve. Do you agree with their aims?

Had to reprimand the monitors twice for firing a cannon on the school premises.

Louisa Love, the monitress, dismissed for having the boys in the classroom and misconducting herself.

1 What problems were these monitors giving their headteachers?
2 What do you suppose Lancaster would have said, had he seen these entries? What would Hook have said?

These figures were published by the Census of 1851:

Numbers of Children in Schools (England and Wales)

Date	*Children in Day Schools*	*Children in Sunday Schools*	*Population*
1818	674,883	477,225	11,642,683
1833	1,276,957	1,548,890	14,386,415
1851	2,144,378	2,407,642	17,926,609

1 What is a census?
2 Draw graphs to show how the number of children in day schools and Sunday schools increased. (Before handling these statistics it would be best to correct them to the nearest 100,000).
3 How far is the increase in the number of school children due to an increase in the population?

Written Work

1 Write out the questions you think Horne asked Mary Garner (page 97). How would you answer these questions yourself?
2 Write a report on schools in the 1840's, saying what problems they are having.
3 Do you think the schools of the early nineteenth century were successful? Look at what was said in the extracts and try to decide between them. The census figures may help you make up your mind.

Research

1 Find out more about Robert Raikes, Hannah More, Andrew Bell and Joseph Lancaster.
2 Find out about James Kay-Shuttleworth and the Pupil Teacher system. How was it an improvement on the monitorial system?
3 Find out about Robert Lowe, and 'payment by results'.
4 What changes were made by the Education Act of 1870?

Food

In the early nineteenth century people, generally, were much poorer than they are today. As a result, their food was not nearly as good as ours.

First of all, we will look at an ordinary family living in Manchester in 1833. There was a husband, wife and five children. The husband worked in a cotton factory where he earned £1.0.6d (£1.2½p) a week. The only other member of the family who had a job was one of the daughters, and she earned 2s.6d (22½p) a week.

Here is what the family ate:

Breakfast	Porridge, bread, milk.
Dinner	Potatoes, bacon, bread.
Tea	Tea, bread, butter.
Supper	Porridge, bread and milk.

Sometimes meat and cheese on Sundays. Occasionally, eggs.

Here now is the family's weekly budget:

Butter, 1½ lbs at 4p a pound	6p
Tea, 1½ ozs	2p
Flour, for bread, 24 lbs	22½p
Oatmeal, ½ peck	2½p
Bacon, 1½ lbs	3½p
Potatoes, 2 score	7p
Milk, a quart a day (i.e. 7 quarts)	9p
Meat, 1 lb for Sunday	3p
Sugar, 1½ lbs	3½p
Pepper, salt etc.	1p
Coal	7½p
Rent	17½p
Clothes, school fees* doctor's bills	35p
	£1.25p

*Even poor families had to pay a little for their children's education. Usually it was no more than 1p or 2p a week.
A 'score' is 21 lbs. You can look up 'peck' in a dictionary.

1 What did this family mainly eat?

Dinner party The cost of this one meal would have fed a poor family for weeks. But then, the cost of your Christmas dinner would do the same for an African family today.

2 What else should they have eaten to stay healthy?
3 How much did the family spend on food?
4 What proportion of its income was this, roughly?
5 Ask your parents or a grown-up friend how much of their income goes on food.
6 Find out how much the food mentioned in the list would cost today. (A half a peck of oats weighs about 4 lbs.) What would the total be? How many times have prices gone up since 1833?
7 The average wage was about £1 a week in 1833. What is it today? How many times has it gone up?
8 Work out how much of the foods on the list each member of the family ate, on average. You can divide the quantities by six as one of the children was almost certainly a baby.
9 Now find out how much of the same foods each member of a family eats today on average. Put the two lists side by side and compare them. Also make a list of the things which you eat and which the family of 1833 did not.

Sometimes business was bad, and many people were unemployed. When that happened, they could not buy much food. This is what a visitor to Colne in Lancashire found in 1842:

> The food was oatmeal and water for breakfast: flour and water, with a little skimmed milk for dinner: oatmeal and water again for supper, for those who could afford three meals a day. I was told in many families that their children went without the 'blue milk' (skimmed milk) on alternate days. I saw hungry children eating rotten vegetables left behind in the market. I saw a woman nearly dead of starvation, suckling an infant which could hardly draw a single drop of milk from her exhausted breast. I asked the child's age – fifteen months. Why was it not weaned? Another mouth would be added to the number of those for whom there was not enough oatmeal.
>
> *Notes of a Tour in the Manufacturing Districts of Lancashire*, W. Cooke Taylor, 1842

1 Compare a list of the things these people were eating with the list on the previous page. What foods had they stopped buying?
2 What were some of the children eating?
3 Why did the woman not wean her baby?

At Wolverhampton in the 1840's there were many poor lock makers who found it hard to make a living. Here is a description of Wolverhampton market:

London Meat Market, 1858

Great quantities of bad meat are sold in the market, particularly veal. It is bought by the poorer locksmiths for their apprentice boys. The worst of this bad meat is not brought into the market until after dark, and is chiefly supplied by country butchers. The stalls are lighted with candles, so as to throw a strong light upon the best joints, while all the remainder is in the shade. I suspect that the lean of the stale meat is tinted up with fresh blood, and the fat parts covered with a white powder of some kind. Many of the people here do not mind eating meat, even when they know the animal died of disease. Cows, calves, sheep and pigs that die, no matter from what cause, are bought by butchers and sold in the market. Horse flesh is often sold for beef steaks.

It must be understood that the miners never buy bad meat. They always live upon the best of everything, and their boys all fare the same as the men. They keep all feast days from Shrove-tide pancakes to the Michaelmas goose. On the first day of 'ducks and green peas' the miners buy up all that there are in the market.

Children's Employment Commission, 1842

Meal in a cottage Contrast this with the picture on page 101. There is at least one similarity. Both groups intend to drink as much alcohol as they can.

1 Who buys much of the bad meat at Wolverhampton market? Who eats it?
2 How do the butchers disguise their bad meat?
3 What was wrong with much of the meat?
4 How were customers cheated?
5 Which workers bought plenty of good food?

Here is some more about miners' food:

Pitmen enjoy most of the pleasures of good living; their larders abound in potatoes, bacon, fresh meat, sugar, tea and coffee. The children eat as much of these good things as their parents; even the sucking infant is loaded with as much of the greasy well seasoned food as it will swallow. In this respect the women are most foolish, and their children are often ill.

The diet of a pitman and his family is altogether irregular. They are paid once a fortnight so an extravagant family can revel for a few days in the richest and most expensive food; after which, during the 'baff week', as it is called, they live mostly on tea and coffee.

Many pitmen have intelligent, hard-working wives who have been servants in respectable families. Without going into domestic service, the women are too often ignorant and wasteful. I have seen a huge girdle cake set edgewise on a table, leaning against the wall, from which each little urchin would help himself by tearing off what he wanted with his dirty hands: while the mother set a packet of sugar on the table, and tearing out a piece of paper with her thumb, left each to thrust his or her spoon in at pleasure.

J. R. Leifchild, *Our Coal Fields and our Coal Pits*, 1853

1 What foods do the miners like to have? Would you think them luxuries?
2 In what ways are some of the women foolish?

Some unmarried farm labourers lived in the same houses as their employers. They had low wages, but they could eat as much as they pleased. This is a description of a carter's breakfast:

The servant wench has lit the fire and set out his breakfast for him and his mate – huge basins of milk porridge and loaves as big as bee hives and as brown as the back of their own hands. Having eaten as much of these as would serve a family of six to breakfast, he then stretches out his hand to an enormous dish of cold fat bacon, of about six inches thick – nay, I once saw bacon on such a table actually ten inches thick and all one mass of fat. This is set on the top of half a peck of cold boiled beans that were left the day before, and they vanish as rapidly as the porridge and those huge hunches of bread. Well, to a certainty he has now done. Nay, don't be in such haste – he has *not* done: he has his eye on the great brown loaf again. He cuts a massive piece of the rich curly-kissing crust and a hunk of cheese. Betty sets a mug of ale before him, and as he finishes it he wipes his mouth and says to his younger companion, 'Well, Jack, we must be off, lad.'

William Howitt, *The Rural Life of England*, 1838

1 What does the carter have for breakfast?
2 Can you imagine why he ate so much?
3 Where do you think this author exaggerates?

So that you can have an idea of what wealthier people ate, here is a menu for a dinner party which someone like a doctor or a solicitor might have given:

First Course
Mock Turtle Soup
Fillets of Turbot à la Creme. Fried Fillet Soles and Anchovy Sauce.

Entrées
Larded Fillets of Rabbits. Tendrons de veau (veal) with Purée of Tomatoes.

Second Course
Stewed Rump of Beef à la Jardinière. Roast Fowls. Boiled Ham.

Third Course
Roast Pigeons or Larks.
Rhubarb Tartlets. Meringues. Clear Jelly. Cream Ice Pudding. Soufflé.

Cruikshank cartoon Before dinner and during dinner. How have these people changed? Why?

1 What are the different kinds of fish and meat in this menu?
2 How many puddings could a guest choose from?
3 From which country did some of the recipes come?

Among rich people, table manners were very important. This is what a German visitor, Prince Puckler-Muskau said about some English customs:

It is not usual to take wine at dinner without drinking to another person. When you raise your glass, you look fixedly at the one with whom you are drinking, bow your head, and then drink with the greatest gravity. Certainly many of the customs of the South Sea Islanders which strike us the most, are less ridiculous.

Of all the offences against English manners which a man can commit, the three following are the greatest: to put his knife to his mouth instead of his fork: to take up sugar or asparagus with his fingers; or above all, to spit anywhere in a room. The last named crime is viewed with such horror that you might seek through all London in vain to find a spitting box. A Dutchman who was very uncomfortable for the want of one, declared with indignation that an Englishman's only spitting box was his stomach. Had I to give a few rules to a young traveller, I would advise him thus: In Naples treat the people brutally: in Rome, be natural: in Austria, don't talk politics: in France, give yourself no airs: in Germany a great many: and in England, don't spit.

The English Tour of Prince Puckler-Muskau, 1830

1 Which English customs did Prince Puckler-Muskau find strange?
2 How far do you agree with him?

Written Work

1 Imagine you are the wife of a mill worker in the 1830's. Say what problems you have in feeding your family.
2 Why does a modern housewife find it easier to feed her family properly than one living in the early nineteenth century?
3 Suppose you had to go back in time and live with a poor family in the early nineteenth century. What food and drink would you miss most, and why?

Research

Find out what you can about kitchens and cooking equipment in the nineteenth century. Look at both poor homes and rich ones.

Drink

In the eighteenth century it was the ambition of every gentleman to be a 'three bottle man', that is, to be able to drink three bottles of wine at a sitting. Indeed, people in all walks of life were drunk quite often. In the nineteenth century most of the wealthy gave up this habit, but many ordinary working folk still drank more than was good for them.

The problem became even worse after 1830, when Parliament passed the Sale of Beer Act. Farmers were growing too much grain, but they hoped they could sell it to brewers, if only people would drink more beer. It was to encourage this that Parliament passed the Act. It allowed anyone to sell beer if he paid two guineas (£2.10p) for an excise licence. Wellington was Prime Minister at the time and he said the Act was a greater victory for him than Waterloo. Certainly it was a success. By the end of 1830 there were already 24,000 of the new beer shops, and in 1836 there were 44,000. This was in addition to the 56,000 public houses which sold every kind of drink. In some towns there was a beer shop or a public house for every twenty homes.

While the Duke of Wellington and the farmers were happy, others were not. You have already seen that there were people who were trying to make the ordinary working man into a better person. They wanted him to believe in God, to have some sort of education, to earn his own living instead of going to the parish, to be clean and healthy, and to obey the law. They also wanted him to be sober. As a result, temperance societies were formed all over Britain, and their members tried to persuade people to give up drinking. Anyone who agreed to do so signed a promise known as 'the pledge'. In Cornwall the emblem of the temperance movement was the pig: people had 'piggy banks' into which they put the money they would otherwise have spent on drink.

A lot of children drank, just like the adults, so for them the leaders of the temperance movement organised the Band of Hope. Many Sunday Schools joined it.

In 1837 a teetotal M.P. – James Silk Buckingham – persuaded Parliament to appoint a Committee of Inquiry into Drunkenness. Several of the extracts you are going to read are from the report of this Committee.

Gin Palace, 1850 What is the woman on the left of the picture doing? Who is the man with the whip? Should he be drinking? What is happening with the man in the battered top hat on the right of the picture? How are the publican and his wife shown? The artist is making his main point with the little girl at the bar, with the bottle. What is he trying to say?

First of all, though, here is what Peter Gaskell said about the poor people of Manchester:

They have no pride in their homes. There are none of the comforts of life – nothing but a hut of squalor and filth, horrible to see and to smell, and unhealthy – having few of the things which a home needs. The labourer leaves it without regret – he expects no joy on his return – he finds there nothing but want – and all these misfortunes are in large measure the result of his own bad, wasteful habits.

The worker, having no home, therefore, which can cheer him, flies for relief to the gin-vault or the beer house, wasting the money which, if properly spent, would furnish his house decently, supply his table with good, wholesome food, and provide him with ample means to make him a respectable member of society.

Artisans and Machinery, 1836

1 Why, according to Gaskell, do working people go out drinking?
2 How does he say they should spend their money?

The men who unloaded the coal ships in London were called 'coal whippers'. This is what one of them, Charles Saunders, told the Committee on Drunkenness:

I have been a coal whipper for ten years: and when I want employment I have to go to the publican to get a job, to ask him for a job; and he tells me to go and sit down, and he will give me an answer by and by. I go and sit down, and if I have twopence in my pocket, of course I am obliged to spend it, with a view to getting a job. Probably there are about fifty or sixty men come to the same person for a job. He keeps us three or four hours there: and then he comes out, and he looks round among us, and he knows those that can drink the most. Those are the men that obtain employment first. Those that cannot drink a great deal, and think more of their families than others, cannot obtain any employment. When the men are made up for the ship we go to work the next morning: but we have to take what the publican calls the 'allowance', such as a quarter of rum or a pot of beer.

In the after part of the day, when your work was over, where did you have to go then?

We had to go into the house again, for our wages.

Were you obliged to spend your money on drink?

Yes.

What would have happened if you had refused?

Then we would have had no employment.

Committee on Drunkenness, 1837

1 Where does Charles Saunders have to go to find work?
2 Why does he have to buy drink?
3 He mentions three occasions when he has to buy drink. What are they?

The Committee on Drunkenness also interviewed Michael Este who was Senior Medical Officer of the Household Cavalry:

Might the supply of spirits by the Government be stopped, for the sake of the health of the soldiers?

Spirits are not supplied by the Government except on active service.

But on foreign service is not the supply of spirits bad for the discipline of the army?

Sometimes I imagine the supply of spirits has done a lot of good, as at Walcheren, in the prevention of Walcheren fever. (Probably a form of malaria). In Egypt where I have served, I imagine the plague may have been prevented in some instances.

Committee on Drunkenness, 1837

1 Here the Committee is asking 'leading' questions. A leading question is one which suggests the answer. What answer is the Committee hoping Dr. Este will give?
2 What answer does Dr. Este, in fact, give?
3 Do you agree with Dr. Este?

Note: In those days doctors often prescribed drink, especially brandy or wine, as a medicine.

Here is part of R. H. Horne's report on Willenhall (see page 43). He is talking about the working men:

Those who do not choose to work on Monday and Tuesday will often go and sit in a tap-room for hours, though the room is empty and they have no money. They sit on a bench, looking at the fire, or leaning back half asleep, or resting with their elbows upon the table and looking over it upon the sanded floor.

I once had a conversation with three men whom I found together in a tap-room on Tuesday afternoon – a shoemaker, a gridiron maker and a locksmith. All three had been drunk: the gridiron maker had been drunk during the last four or five days: but they were recovering because they did not have the money for any more liquor. The gridiron maker, who was only able to walk in a minuet step, challenged me to produce the hand of any working man which should show more proofs of hard work than his'n. This was meant as a defence of drunkenness to which he claimed he had a right because of the hardness of his labour. The hand was certainly not like a human hand. It was coal black in the palm, the black being stained into the flesh; and the flesh was all

A drunkard comes home What is the cartoonist trying to say about drunkenness?

ragged and torn, like the sole of an old worn-out shoe, such as is flung on the road-side.

Children's Employment Commission, 1842

1 How do some of the Willenhall men spend Mondays and Tuesdays?
2 What three men did Horne meet in the public house?
3 How long had one of them been drunk? What excuse did he give?

Here now is a drinking song:

I Likes a Drop of Good Beer

Come one and all, both great and small
With voices loud and clear,
And let us sing, bless Billy, the King*
Who bated** the tax upon beer.

Chorus: For I likes a drop of good beer I do,
I likes a drop of good beer
And d—— his eyes whoever tries,
To rob a poor man of his beer.

My wife and I always feel dry
At market on Saturday night
Then a noggin of beer I never need fear
For my wife always says that it's right.

Chorus: For she likes a drop of good beer etc.

In harvest fields there's nothing can yield
The labouring man such good cheer,
To reap and to sow and to make barley grow,
As to give 'em a skinful of beer.

Chorus: For they likes a drop of good beer etc.

Long may Queen Victoria reign,
And be to her subjects dear
And wherever she goes, we'll wallop her foes
Only give us a skinful of beer.

Chorus: For we likes a drop of good beer etc.

Broadside Ballads, British Museum Library

* William IV.
** short for 'abated' which means 'reduced' or 'cut down'.

1 Who encourages this man to go drinking?
2 What different reasons does he give for drinking beer? Do you agree with them?

Peter Gaskell gave this description of people drinking in Manchester:

It is a strange sight to watch one of these dens of wickedness throughout an evening: it is a strange, a sad, yet to the thoughtful man, an interesting sight. There approaches a half-clad man, a handloom weaver, or a spinner, shivering even beneath the summer breeze which is singing around him. He comes with a faltering step, downcast eye and air of general exhaustion and dejection. He reaches the gin vault, disappears for half-an-hour and now comes forth a new creature: were it not for his filthy dress, he would hardly be recognised, for his step is elastic, his eye is brilliant and open, he is lively and happy.

Now comes a woman, perhaps his wife, carrying a sickly infant, wailing and moaning as if in pain, or hungry. She is thin, pale and badly dressed – is without bonnet, and her cap is dirty and ragged: her gown is filthy, her shoes only half on her feet, and her whole appearance forlorn and forbidding. She too disappears for a time within the gin shop, and returns equally changed. The child is now crowing in her arms, clapping its tiny hands, while its mother views it with fondness, tosses it in her arms and kisses it.

The pair have now reached home: the night is far advanced, and the effects of the drink have worn off. The child is in a stupor, and the husband and wife meet without a kindly greeting. There is no food, no fire, bickerings arise, blows, curses – till both at last sink into a drunken sleep, worn out by toil, and evil passions.

P. Gaskell, *Artisans and Machinery*, 1836

1 What are the man, woman and baby like before they go into the public house?
2 What are they like when they come out? What do you suppose has happened to the baby?
3 What happens at home, in the evening?

A man called Rowland Detrosian told this story in 1833:

A man and his wife, living in a cellar in Warrington, had three children, the eldest of which was twelve, and the others seven and eight. The parents were spendthrifts, living in a state of almost constant idleness, working only at intervals and that not very long at a time. The children worked in the factory and regularly brought home their weekly wages. The parents often locked up the three children on Saturday night and after having given them a miserable meal of tea and bread, went off to the public house together. There they spent much of the money in drink, to return home at midnight, in a state of beastly intoxication. Sometimes they even beat the poor children whose hard-earned money they had been spending so wastefully. On the following morning, Sunday, they sent the children out to beg bread, or anything they could obtain, for their breakfast.

1 What did the children do during the week?
2 What happened to them on Saturday and Sunday?

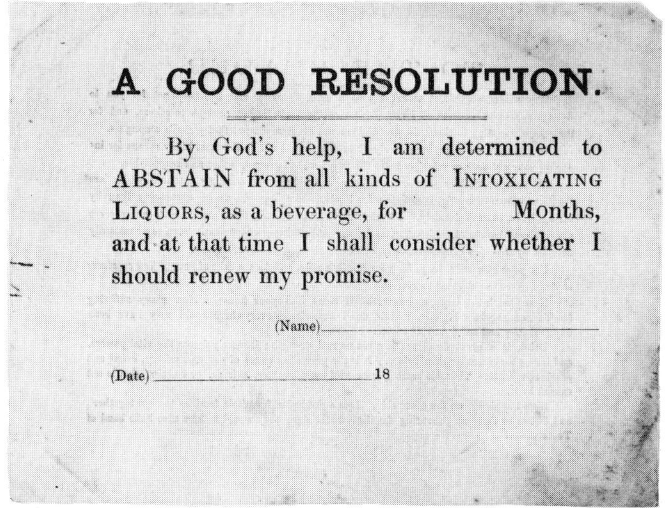

A GOOD RESOLUTION.

By God's help, I am determined to ABSTAIN from all kinds of INTOXICATING LIQUORS, as a beverage, for Months, and at that time I shall consider whether I should renew my promise.

(Name)________________

(Date)________________18

The Pledge This is the document that members of the temperance movement tried to persuade habitual drinkers to sign. How are they trying to make it easier for them? The words 'as a beverage' are there because doctors often prescribed drink as a medicine.

Here is part of an interview the Committee on Drunkenness had with Sir Charles Rowan, one of the two Commissioners in charge of the Metropolitan Police:

Does it appear to you that drunkenness is on the increase?

I should think that it is rather on the decrease.

Do you know the number of people who are arrested by the police?

Yes.

Are not the greater number of these cases for drunkenness?

They are separate entirely from the felony cases. I should not say that the crimes committed by felons are drunken cases.

With respect to robbers and pickpockets?

I should say decidedly not.

Are not other cases, such as assault, connected with drunkenness?

Many assault cases are committed by drunken people, no doubt.

Is it your opinion that drunkenness tends to produce other crimes?

I should not think that drunkenness tends to produce

felons. I should think they are too much on their guard to get drunk: they know that the success of their enterprise depends upon their discretion.

Though they may perhaps be sober when they commit their offence, is it not well known that thieves and felons employ their leisure in drunken habits?

I am not able to say, but I would doubt it.

Committee on Drunkenness, 1837

Note: A felon is a criminal who has committed a serious offence, like robbery or burglary.

1 Does Rowan think that drunkenness is increasing?
2 What crime does he say drunkards commit?
3 According to Rowan, what criminals are not drunkards? Why is this?
4 Here you can see some more leading questions. Which are they? What answers did the Committee want Rowan to give? What, in fact, did he say?

Here is what a Somerset farm labourer, George Small, said:

I am a farm labourer, am married and have six children. I work for Mr. Somers. I left off drinking cider, beer and all other strong drinks about five years ago. I have laboured hard, but I find my health now just as good as when I used to have cider. Last summer I mowed with two men from four in the morning till eight at night, but I did my share of the work quite as well as they did. They call me all kinds of names and laugh at me for not drinking cider: but I laugh at them, and ask them if they have paid their rent as I have.

Mr. Somers pays me as much as the other labourers get; only, instead of cider, he lets me have half an acre of potato ground. He manures the ground, and I put in the seed and dig up the potatoes. I wish all masters did as Mr. Somers does, for I think that if the labourers didn't drink so much, they and their families would get more to eat.

It is eight years since I had any relief from the parish: if I had been in the habit of drinking, my family would have been in rags. I am sure the drink would have been doing me no good, but without the potato ground we could not have gone on.

I went to work when I was nine years old: I had a shilling a week and three cups of cider a day. It is a bad thing for the young boys to learn to drink as they do: it is as bad with girls nearly. My eldest daughter is eighteen years old. The summer before last she went out to harvest and had half a gallon of cider a day. The farmers think people work harder with so much cider: I don't think they do.

Report on Employment of Women and Children in Agriculture, 1843

Farm labourer drinking He takes his little barrel with him every morning. Estimate how much it holds.

1 When did George Smith give up drinking?
2 How well has he worked since then?
3 What do the other labourers do to him? Why do you suppose they do this?
4 What does George Small's employer give him, instead of cider?
5 How does this help him and his family?
6 How much cider was he given as a boy? How much did his daughter have?
7 Why do farmers give their workers cider? In which other extract in this section have you found the same idea? Do you think it is correct?

This is what Mrs. Britton, the wife of a Wiltshire farm labourer said: (You will find another part of her statement on page 21).

Formerly my husband was in the habit of drinking, and everything went bad. He used to beat me. I have often gone to bed, I and my children without supper, and have had no breakfast the next morning, and frequently no firing. My husband went to a lecture on teetotalism one evening about two years ago, and I have reason to bless that evening. My husband has never touched a drop of drink since. He has been in better health and behaved like a good husband to me ever since. I have been much more comfortable and the children happier. He works better than he did. He can mow better, and that is hard work, and he does not mind being laughed at by the other men for not drinking. He now goes regularly to church; formerly he could hardly be got there.

Report of the Employment of Women and Children in Agriculture, 1843

1 How did Mr. Britton behave before he gave up drinking?
2 Why did he give up drinking?
3 How has he behaved since?

The Committee on Drunkenness asked Francis Place what he thought would be the best way to stop people drinking:

Can you suggest any laws which would be effective?

No I cannot.

Speaking of moral measures, what would you recommend?

Principally, education.

Do you think the establishment of public libraries and reading rooms, and popular lectures on subjects both entertaining and instructive might draw off a number of those who now go to public houses?

Certainly. I know that if you teach ignorant men something of geography, and something of natural history, you give them a taste for reading which hardly ever leaves them. I will give you an example. I was out walking in the spring, when the moon was up, and I overtook three lads: they appeared to be plasterers' labourers. I heard the oldest lad say, 'There is the moon.' 'Yes,' says another, 'The moon is round, do you not see?' said the largest boy. 'Yes', said the other. 'That is part of the solar system'. 'What is that?' asked his companion. 'Oh', says he, 'do you not know what it is?' The lad then explained to them the solar system, beginning with the sun in the centre and describing the planets, their size, distances etc. When I got a little farther, some vagabonds were being turned out of a gin-shop. Among them was a lad about the same age as the oldest of the three boys. He was three parts drunk and began to show off, to draw the attention of the passers-by. The conclusion which everybody must draw is that the lad who was teaching the solar system, could not have come out of a gin-shop three parts drunk and have made the same disgraceful exhibition.

Committee on Drunkenness, 1837

1 Does Francis Place think Parliament could pass any laws which would stop drinking?
2 What does he think is the best way?
3 What does the Committee suggest might be some good ways of keeping people out of public houses? Does Francis Place agree? Do you?
4 What were the three boys doing on their walk? How did the boy who was flung out of the gin shop behave? What conclusion did Francis Place draw from this? Do you agree with him?

Here now is a Band of Hope song. The tune is *Sing a Song of Sixpence*:

Sing a song of Saturday
Wages taken home,
Ev'ry penny well laid out
None allowed to roam!

Sing a song of Sunday,
A home that's black and bare,
Wife and children starving,
A crust of bread their share!

Sing a song of Monday,
Brought before the 'beak'*
Fine of twenty shillings,
Alternative 'a week'**

Workhouse for the children
Workhouse for the wife!
Isn't that a hideous blot
On our English life?

* magistrate. ** a week in prison.

1 According to the song, how should money be spent? What happens, though, if a man is a drunkard?
2 Which of the other extracts bear out what the song says? Which do not?

Written Work

Write a report on the problem of drink in the early nineteenth century. Deal with the following:

a What are the reasons and excuses which people have for drinking?
b What are the results of drunkenness?
c What are the possible ways of preventing it? Which do you think will have most sucesss?

Research

1 Read more about the Temperance Movement. Find out, among other things **a** how the firm of Thomas Cook, the travel agents began and **b** how the word 'teetotal' was first used.
2 Parliament took no notice of the Committee on Drunkenness of 1837, except to make fun of it. Later, though, laws were passed to cut down drinking. Find out what they were.
3 In 1919 the United States Congress made a law to stop the drinking of alcohol completely. This was known as 'Prohibition'. Read what happened as a result. You could start with *Oxford Junior History*, Book 6, *The Twentieth Century World*, Chapter Seven, Section 2.

Sanitation and Water Supplies

In the eighteenth century, most of the people of Britain lived in villages and small towns. They drew their water from springs, streams and wells. For lavatories they had privies, which means 'private places'. In a privy there was just a wooden seat over a hole, called a 'cess pit'. There were no sewers, so when the cess pit was full someone had to empty it. Usually, the contents went on the garden.

Then, in the early nineteenth century, the towns grew rapidly. There were many new houses, but for sanitation and water people still managed as they had done in the villages. Conditions that had been bad enough in the countryside were much worse in town.

Sanitation

A man who did a lot to help the poor was the Earl of Shaftesbury. This is what he said of the east end of London in the 1840's:

> There were a great many long alleys. They were narrow, and very long, like a tobacco pipe. In these alleys lived from 200 to 300 people, and there was but one privy for the whole of that number, and that was at the end. It was so tremendously horrible that no-one could even approach that end. The air was dreadfully foul.
>
> *Housing of the Working Class Commission*, 1885

1 How many people were there to one lavatory in this part of London?
2 What were the lavatories like, as a result?

Lavatories The lavatories discharge into the stream from which people draw their water.

In the 1840's the Blackwall Railway was built. To make a path for the railway, many houses had to be demolished in Whitechapel, a poor part of London. The houses had had cess pits lined with bricks. The chief engineer for the railway, Henry Austin, said this about them:

What were the privies like?

They were always full and often running over.

In what condition did you find the subsoil?

Filth, soaking from the cesspools had, in some cases, actually joined up from house to house.

Then the people were living on a vast dungheap were they not?

The soil under the houses was so saturated from the cess pools that it was worse than a dungheap. It amazed me that we found men willing to dig it out. When we uncovered it there were complaints from neighbours at some distance.

State of Towns Commission, 1844

1 What happened to the soil under the houses in Whitechapel?
2 What problems did this give the railway builders?

In the poorer parts of the towns, there were no drains from the houses and no sewers under the streets. We can see the results of this from the next two extracts. One describes a street in Manchester, and the other, a part of Hinckley, in Leicestershire:

The street between the two rows is seven feet wide, in the centre of which is the common gutter into which all sorts of refuse is thrown: it is about a foot deep. Thus, there is always some rotting filth poisoning the air.

Dr. Baron Howard, Manchester

How is the filth carried off?

It is generally taken away in wheelbarrows and carts. The liquid manure runs down the court. There is a kennel (gutter) in front of the houses.

Was the smell very unpleasant in hot weather?

It was so unpleasant that when the wind blew one way, the neighbours would go into the houses on the opposite side to get out of the way of it.

Interview with John Brookes, a stocking weaver
State of Towns Commission, 1844

1 What was used instead of drains and sewers?
2 How was the filth taken from the streets?
3 How might people try to escape the smell?

Here is a description of part of Glasgow in the 1840's:

We entered a dirty low passage which led into a court. Nearly all the space in it was taken by a brick container for dung, of the most disgusting kind. Beyond this court a second passage led to a second court occupied in the same way by its dunghill: and from this court there was yet a third passage leading to a third court and a third dungheap. There were no privies or drains and the dungheaps received all the filth which the swarm of wretched inhabitants could give: and we learned that a considerable part of the rent of the houses was paid by the sale of the dungheaps.

State of Towns Commission, 1844

1 Why did some people make dungheaps outside their houses?

Dr. Laurie of Greenock described what happened to the filth from the cess pools and streets of his town:

In one part of the town there is a dunghill – yet it is too large to be called a dunghill. I do not mistake its size when I say it contains a hundred cubic yards of filth, collected from all parts of the town. It belongs to a person who deals in dung: he sells it by cartfuls. To please his customers, he always keeps it for some time before selling it, as the older the filth is, the higher is the price. The heap is beside a public street: it is enclosed by a wall: the height of the wall is about twelve feet and the dung overtops it: the filthy liquid oozes through the wall, and runs over the pavement. The smell in summer is horrible. There is a housing estate nearby, and in the summer each house swarms with flies; all food and drink must be covered: if left for a minute, the flies at once attack it and it is made unfit for use, from the strong taste of the dunghill left by the flies.

Report on The Sanitary Condition of The Labouring Population, Edwin Chadwick

1 How large was the dunghill at Greenock?
2 Who owned it? Who were his customers, do you suppose?
3 How did the dunghill make life unpleasant for people living nearby?

In the richer parts of the towns the houses usually had drains which led to sewers underneath the streets. The sewers were brick tunnels, large enough for a man to go along. There was not nearly enough water from the houses to flush them, so filth collected in them until they blocked. When that happened in one of them, workmen had to break it open, dig out the filth and take it away in carts. Drains could also be faulty. A London builder told this story:

Some time ago I was asked to look at a house in one of

Nightmen These had the unpleasant task of emptying cess pools. They were only allowed to work at night. Why was that do you suppose?

the best streets in London. It belonged to a gentleman who was about to leave it because of the unpleasant smells that were continually arising. He was particularly annoyed that the smell was worst whenever he had parties. The drains had been opened and were not blocked. People imagine that when they get rid of the filth they have got rid of the smell. What they do not realise is that sewer gas, being so much lighter than air, escapes where air would not. On looking at the drains at this house, I found they were cracked and the sewer gas filtered through them. Whenever he had a party there was a stronger fire in the kitchen and stronger fires in other parts of the house. As a result, there was a greater draught and larger quantities of foul air rose up from the sewers.

State of Towns Commission, 1844

1 What problem did the owner of the house have?
2 What was the reason for it?
3 Why was it worse when he had a party?

Water Supplies

Dr. Liddle of Whitechapel said this about his poorer patients:

They get their water from a tap in the court. I cannot say whether water is scarce, or whether they are unwilling to fetch it, but the effect is that they are short of water. When I visit their rooms I find they have only a very little water in their tubs. When they are washing clothes the smell of the dirt mixed with the water is most unpleasant. They merely pass dirty linen through very dirty water. The smell of the linen when so washed is very disagreeable. They are always filthy. When they attend my surgery I am always obliged to have the door open. When I am coming downstairs from the parlour, I know at a distance of a flight of stairs whether there are any poor patients in the surgery.

State of Towns Commission, 1844

1 Where did poor people get their water?
2 Where did they keep it?
3 Why did Dr. Liddle think they were short of water?
4 How did poor people wash their clothes?
5 Why did Dr. Liddle dislike seeing his poorer patients?

A Bath clergyman, the Rev. Elwin had this conversation with a poor man:

Where do you get your water?

We have to fetch it from one of the public pumps, the distance from my house is about a quarter of a mile. It is as valuable as strong beer. We can't use it for cooking or anything of that sort, but only for drinking and tea.

Then where do you get your water for cooking and washing?

From the river. But it is muddy and often stinks bad, because of all the filth that is carried there.

Do you then prefer to cook your food in water which is muddy and stinks, to walking a quarter of a mile to fetch it from the pump?

We can't help ourselves you know. We could not go all that way for it.

Bath Chronicle

1 How far did the man have to go for pure water?
2 What did he use it for?
3 Where did he get water for everything else? Why?

In most towns there were companies which supplied water and charged their customers for it. This is a description of the one at Exeter:

The water works were established in 1694. The water they supplied was not very pure, nor was there enough of it. Moreover, the pumps were not strong enough to raise it to the higher parts of the city. The pipes, which were of wood, were always leaking. Even this poor supply was sometimes cut off by floods for five or six days, and during droughts, for periods of even three months.

History of the Cholera in Exeter, Thomas Shapter

1 When was the Exeter waterworks started?
2 In what ways was it inefficient?
3 What were its pipes made from?

Most companies were so short of water that they could only turn it on from time to time. This is what it was like for the people living in a poor street in Westminster, called Snow's Rents:

The supply of water consists in this: that sixteen houses have one stand pipe (tap) in the court. On Sunday, the water is on for about five minutes: it is on also for three days in the week for half an hour, and so great is the rush to obtain a little before it is turned off, that there is always quarrelling and pushing.

State of Towns Commission, 1844

1 How many houses were there to one tap in Snow's Rents? (How many taps are there in your house?)
2 For how much time in the week could the people draw water?
3 What happened when the water was turned on?

The rich had water brought into their homes in pipes. They stored it in cisterns, in the roof. When the water was on they hoped to fill their cisterns and

Water Carriers These people are drawing water from the River Exe, at Exeter. They will be very sparing in their use of it. Why? How will the hoops help them carry the water?

have enough to last until it came on again. Here is what happened in one house during four days. The measurements are of the depth of the water in their cistern:

> **Monday:** water 6″. Cook and housemaid on short allowance. Master's bath relinquished.
> **Tuesday:** water 1″. Boiled vegetables and tea strictly forbidden.
> **Wednesday:** cistern dry: water nowhere.
> **Thursday:** the water on. Hurrah! Listen to that rushing sound! We shall drink – we shall wash – we shall bathe! Ah, in five minutes the stream ceases, and all our hopes are blighted.

1 What did this family have to give up, through being short of water?
2 Why are they luckier than poor people?

Improvements

Being without proper sanitation and pure water was not just unpleasant, it was dangerous. It caused many diseases. People realised this and gradually there were changes for the better.

Thomas Ashton owned a cotton factory at Hyde, near Manchester. He had built over 300 houses for his workers. At first they were without water, but later he supplied it. In 1844 he had this conversation:

> How many houses have you?
> About 320.
> Have you introduced water into these houses?
> Yes, into every home.
> What happened before you had the water laid on?
> The people had to fetch it from various wells and places in the neighbourhood. They fetched it in cans. It was a lot of work for them. There were also water carriers. The poor people used to pay a penny ($\frac{1}{2}$p) per day for the smallest families; some of them paid a shilling (5p) a week and had nothing like as much water as at present.

Has the change pleased your tenants?

Very much. I know no alteration that has done so much good. They say they save money by it. Their houses are much cleaner, especially their back yards. They are much cleaner themselves.

State of Towns Commission, 1844

1 Where did Thomas Ashton's tenants get their water before it was piped to their homes?
2 How did it help them to have water in their homes?

Some town councils did their best to see that their people had enough water. This is a report about Manchester, written in 1852:

These works are now nearly finished. There will be eight reservoirs having between them an area of more than 420 acres and a capacity of 612,000,000 cubic feet. The three highest of these reservoirs are in the main valley of the Etherow.

Report of the General Board of Health

1 How many reservoirs were being built?
2 How much water will they hold? What problems would have been solved by having such large amounts in store?
3 Where are the reservoirs? Find this place on a map.

In 1848, Parliament passed a Public Health Act and set up a new Government department called the General Board of Health. This board encouraged town councils to improve sanitation and water supplies. In 1854 it reported:

The cost of water supply is an average of one and a half pence a house per week, and for main drainage one penny a house per week. The cost of the work done in the houses of the poorer classes has added one penny a week to the rent. It includes introducing a water main, putting down a sink, filling up the cesspool and substituting a water closet and house drains, and the building of a dust bin. The total average cost is three and a half pence a week, or one half penny a day.

1 What changes did the General Board of Health want to see in the houses of the poor?
2 What did it say the cost would be? (One new penny is worth about two and a half old pennies.)

By the 1850's there were glazed earthenware pipes, which could be used instead of brick drains and sewers. The General Board of Health said:

It is estimated that in 1848 there were manufactured of such pipes about 104 miles: in 1849, 416 miles: in 1850, 1040 miles: in 1851, 1820 miles: in 1852, 2080 miles: in 1853, 2600 miles.

1 Draw a graph to show how the supply of glazed sewer pipes increased.
2 Why were glazed pipes better than brick drains and sewers, do you think?
3 How did the better supplies of water help the sanitation, do you suppose?

We give the death rate by saying how many people in every thousand die in the course of a year. Today, in Britain, it is about 12 per thousand. In the 1850's it was 23 per thousand for the country as a whole. This is what the General Board of Health said about the death rate at one particular place, Lambeth Square in London:

In Lambeth Square, the deaths which, in ordinary times were above the general average, or more than 30 in 1000, had risen to a rate of 55 in 1000. By the abolition of cesspools which were within the houses, and the use of water closets, together with the introduction of self-cleaning house drains, the death rate has been reduced to 13 in 1000.

1 Draw a bar diagram to show how the death rate changed in Lambeth Square. Add a bar to show the average in the 1850's, and another to show the average today.
2 What, according to the General Board of Health, were the reasons why the death rate fell in Lambeth Square?
3 What do you suppose the Board hoped would happen when people saw this information?

Written Work

Imagine you are an old man or woman living in a big city in the 1860's. Say what the sanitation and water supplies were like when you were young. Also say what improvements have been made over the years.

Research

1 Find out what you can about Edwin Chadwick and the eleventh Earl of Shaftesbury, especially their work for public health.
2 Where does the water you use at home come from? How does it reach your house? Is it treated at all? If so, how?
3 What happens to the sewage which leaves your house? What is a 'sewage farm' and how does it work?

Cholera

There was a lot of illness in the early nineteenth century. People died of tuberculosis, typhoid fever, typhus, smallpox and other horrible diseases. The one they dreaded most of all, though, was cholera. There were a number of reasons for this. In the first place, a cholera attack is violent and kills suddenly, usually in a day or two. Secondly, over half the people who had cholera, died. Thirdly, unlike many other diseases, it was not only the poor who caught it; the rich did as well. It might strike anywhere, and during an epidemic no-one could feel safe.

A cholera patient has so much sickness and diarrhoea that his body is dehydrated, which means it loses a lot of moisture. This turns his skin blue, it gives him painful cramps, and unless he is lucky, it will kill him.

There had always been cholera in the Far East, where it stayed until the nineteenth century. At that time, there were far more traders and travellers than there had ever been before, and they carried the disease with them. Epidemics of it spread round the world. People could see the disease coming, they knew it would reach their own country sooner or later, but they could do nothing to stop it. It came to Britain in 1831–32, 1848–49, 1854 and 1867.

To prevent people catching a disease, doctors must discover what causes it. In the early nineteenth century they knew nothing about germs, so they did not really understand the diseases which were already common in Britain. Cholera, being new, puzzled them even more. In this section we will see what they thought about it.

Doctors realised that many diseases were 'contagious'. That meant you could catch them from other people, if you had contact with them. What was difficult to understand was how you could catch a disease without going near anyone who had it. Most people thought it was because of 'miasmata' or poisons floating in the air. It was believed they could kill you in much the same way as poisons in your food.

CHOLERA

MORBUS.

QUESTION.---Why is the Cholera Morbus raging in London?

ANSWER.---Because the Doctors have forbidden the use of Fruit and Vegetables.

QUESTION.---How can you prove that?

ANSWER.---The Growers can prove, that not one Case of Cholera has taken place among the thousands of poor people they employ to gather their Fruit and Vegetables, and bring them to Market, who chiefly live upon that wholesome produce of the earth; nor have the Green Grocers had any case among them or their Families.

Let there be plenty of Vegetables and Fruit used, and then the Doctors will have reason to complain of bad times, as well as all other classes of People.

It is a singular fact, that if you ask Green Grocers who are their best Customers, they will tell you that the Doctors are. Then it clearly shews that they want to avoid having the Cholera Morbus, and live to a good Old Age.

E. K. A. L. B.

Cholera poster One of the symptoms of cholera is diarrhoea. For that reason doctors advised people not to eat fresh fruit and vegetables. This poster is the greengrocers' reply. What arguments do they use? Of course, neither doctors nor greengrocers were right.

Dr. Thomas Southwood Smith, who was well-known in the 1840's talks about miasmata:

> When spread in the air, poisonous particles are carried into the system through the thin, delicate walls of the lungs. The human lungs have an almost incredibly large absorbing surface, while at every point on that surface there is a blood vessel ready to receive any substance that has been breathed in and carry it at once into the body. Hence the sudden and dreadful energy with which certain poisons act when brought into contact with the surface of the lungs.

***Punch* Cartoon 1858** The caption read 'Father Thames introducing his offspring to the fair City of London'.

Sometimes rotting filth, helped by heat or other peculiarities of the climate produces a poison so deadly that a single breath of the air in which it is spread causes almost instant death. Sometimes, where the poison is less concentrated, death follows in from two to twelve hours.

Report on the Results of a Special Inquiry into the Practice of Interment in Towns, 1843

1 How does Southwood Smith think poisons in the air enter the human body?
2 Where does he think many of the poisons come from?
3 What decides how quickly a patient will die?

In the 1840s there had been a lot of talk about making Britain's cities more healthy, but for a long time Parliament did nothing. Then, in 1848, it heard that cholera was on its way, so at once a new government department was set up, the General Board of Health.

After the cholera epidemic of 1848–9 was over the Board wrote a report on it. This extract is from the report:

The disease often attacked definite spots, confining its ravages to particular streets, the adjoining streets escaping: and even to one side of a street, scarcely a single case occuring on the opposite side. Thus, at Rotherhithe, the attacks were almost entirely confined to one side of the street, occupied by respectable private families. 'The disease', says the medical officer of this parish, 'Passed right through and across several of the streets like a cannon ball'. (Cannon balls used to bounce for long distances, killing men wherever they landed, but missing the ones in between.)

Six, eight or even more deaths were not uncommon in a particular house: but such a house did not form a centre from which the disease spread to neighbouring houses and thence over the district. On the contrary, the disease broke out at a considerable distance, the houses between escaping.

Report of the General Board of Health on the Epidemic Cholera of 1848–1849

1 How does cholera spread through a town?

Here is another extract from the same report:

When cholera first appeared in this country the general belief was that the disease spread by contact of those who were infected with the healthy. Therefore the best way to check it is by isolating the infected from the uninfected – an idea which led to strict quarantine regulations and the abandoning of the sick, even by relatives and friends. However, a closer observation has been made of this disease, and the way in which it spreads through continents, nations, cities, towns and families. It now appears that the disease is not contagious, but spreads through the air, causing a series of local outbreaks.

1 How did people first believe cholera was spread?
2 What did they do, as a result?
3 How does the General Board of Health think that cholera spreads?
4 Would Dr. Southwood Smith have agreed with the Board?
5 Does the Board's theory fit the facts given in the previous extract?

The General Board of Health also said:

Generally, it seems that the state of the air which is most likely to encourage cholera is a hot, moist, stagnant atmosphere, especially when it follows cold, dry winds.

It is important to bear in mind that it is under these conditions that unpleasant animal and vegetable refuse rots the most quickly and in which the poisons from it are carried in greatest quantity into the blood from the lungs.

1 In what kind of weather does the General Board of Health say cholera is most likely to occur? (It is the sort we have when the air pressure is high).
2 How does the Board think this weather encourages cholera?

When the people of Exeter heard the cholera was coming, this was one of the things the Corporation decided:

It was resolved that the courts and streets inhabited by the poorer classes would be watered. The water being turned on from the fire plug, ran down the gutters in a full stream, and, being dammed up at short distances by coils of straw and tarpaulin, was collected in considerable quantities. Men with large wooden shovels then threw it plentifully over the neighbouring surfaces. This method was not only effective in watering the streets, but was most useful in cleansing the gutters. The whole scene when doing this was most striking and picturesque; three or four powerful men, jack-booted, or naked as to their arms and legs, took possession of the street, and stream after stream of water flowed from their well-plied shovels.

The History of the Cholera in Exeter, Thomas Shapter

1 Why did Exeter Corporation think this kind of action would help prevent cholera, do you suppose?
2 Would **a** Dr. Southwood Smith **b** The General Board of Health, have agreed?

Note: Most other cities also cleaned their streets. Nearly always, as in London, the filth went into the river.

A man who spent a lot of time investigating cholera was Dr. John Snow. In 1855 he published a book, in which he disagreed with the ideas of Southwood Smith and the General Board of Health. Here is one of the things he said:

It is amongst the poor, where a whole family live, sleep, cook, eat and wash in a single room, that cholera has been found to spread when once introduced. When, on the other hand, cholera is introduced into the better kind of houses, it hardly ever spreads from one member of the family to another. The constant use of the hand-basin and towel, and the fact of the places for cooking and eating being separate from the sick room, are the cause of this.

The speed with which cholera spread in institutions for pauper children confirms this. In the home for pauper children at Tooting, there were one hundred and forty deaths from cholera amongst a thousand inmates, and the disease did not cease till the remaining children had been removed. The children were placed two and three in a bed, and vomited over each other when they had cholera. Under these circumstances, and when it is remembered that children get their hands into everything, and are constantly putting their fingers in their mouths, it is not surprising that the disease spread rapidly.

On the Mode of Communication of Cholera

1 According to Snow, why is cholera likely to spread to all the members of a poor family?
2 Why will it not spread in a rich home?
3 Why did so many children die in the home at Tooting?

Obviously, this particular idea of Snow's could not explain why cholera spread through a town in the way described on page 118. However, he also wrote:

If the cholera had no means of spreading, other than those which we have been considering, it would confine itself chiefly to the crowded dwellings of the poor, and would quickly die out for want of the chance to reach fresh victims: but there is another way open for it to spread itself more widely, and to reach the well-to-do classes of the community. I refer to the mixture of the cholera evacuations with the water used for drinking, either by soaking through the ground and getting into wells, or by running along channels and sewers into the rivers from which entire towns are sometimes supplied with water.

1 How does Snow say cholera can spread through a town?

Snow came to this idea after he had done some detective work. He went to a part of London where cholera had broken out in some houses and not in others. He found that the water there came from two different companies, the Southwark and Vauxhall, and the Lambeth. He also found that it was the people who drank the Southwark and Vauxhall water who caught the cholera, while those that drank the Lambeth water, nearly all escaped. The Lambeth Company took their water from fresh springs, but not the Southwark and Vauxhall Company. Snow wrote:

The Southwark and Vauxhall Company obtain their water from the River Thames. Many of the people receiving this supply were in the habit of tying a piece of linen over the tap by which the water entered the cistern. In two hours, as the water came in, about a tablespoon of dirt was collected, all in motion with a variety of water insects, while the strained water was far from being clear.

1 Where did the Southwark and Vauxhall Company get its water?
2 What came into the house, in the water?

Snow said this about the Thames:

The amount of filth in the Thames was greatly increased last autumn by the long course of dry weather. The stream of the Thames above the reach of the tide became so slender that it was difficult to navigate barges above Richmond. The Thames in London is a very large body of water, and if the whole of it flowed into the sea every day, the liquid which flows down the sewers in twelve hours would form but a very small part of it; but it must be remembered that the quantity of water which passes out to sea with the ebb of every tide, is only equal to that which flows over Teddington Lock. In hot, dry weather the river becomes a kind of prolonged lake, the same

Collecting water in the street It was water from a source like this which led to the outbreak of cholera in and around Broad Street (See page 121)

Burial of a cholera victim at Exeter There were often angry scenes at such funerals. The undertakers were anxious to bury the corpse as quickly as possible, but the mourners objected to the lack of respect. Notice how far the clergyman is standing from the grave. Why is that, do you suppose?

water passing twice a day to and fro through London, and receiving the filth of its two millions and more of inhabitants which keeps collecting there until there is a fall of rain. In time of cholera, the evacuations of the patients keep accumulating in the river along with the other impurities; and it is probably in this way that the dry weather, with a high barometer, aids in promoting the cholera as it has often been observed to do.

1 Why was the River Thames particularly unpleasant in dry weather?
2 Where would Snow have agreed with the General Board of Health (page 119)?
3 Where would he have disagreed with it?
4 What would Snow have said, do you suppose, about dumping filth from the streets into the river?

Here Snow describes what he did about an epidemic of cholera in a part of London:

The most terrible outbreak of cholera which ever occurred in this Kingdom, is probably that which took place in Broad Street, Golden Square and the adjoining streets a few weeks ago. Within two hundred and fifty yards of the spot where Cambridge Street joins Broad Street there were five hundred deaths from cholera in ten days.

As soon as I heard of this, I suspected some contamination of the water of the much-used pump in Broad Street. On going to the spot I found that nearly all the deaths had taken place within a short distance of the pump. There had been no particular outbreak or increase in cholera, in this part of London, except among the persons who were in the habit of drinking the water of the above mentioned well.

I went and told the Guardians of St. James's parish. In consequence of what I said, the handle of the pump was removed the following day.

At the same time, Snow heard that a woman from quite a different part of London had died of cholera, though she had once lived in Broad Street. Snow wrote:

I was informed by this lady's son that she had not been near Broad Street for many months. A cart went from Broad Street to West End every day, and it was the custom to take out a large bottle of the water from the pump in Broad Street, as she preferred it. The water was taken on Thursday, 31st August, and she drank of it in the evening and also on Friday. She was seized with the cholera on the latter day and died on Sunday. A niece, who was on a visit to this lady, also drank of the water; she returned to her home in a high and healthy part of Islington, was attacked with cholera and died also. There was no cholera at the time, either at West End or in the neighbourhood where the niece died.

1 How many people were dying every day in the Broad Street area?
2 What did Snow suspect was the reason?
3 How did he satisfy himself he was right? (You will find information in both extracts).
4 What did the Guardians of St. James's parish do?

Note: the cholera epidemic ended in this part of London at once.

Written Work

Pretend it is 1855. Say what different ideas there are on the way cholera is spread. Which do you think is right, and why? (Remember that in 1855 no-one knew about germs.)

Most people at the time believed the General Board of Health and famous men like Dr. Southwood Smith. Hardly anyone had heard of John Snow.

Research

1 Find out how cholera really is spread.
2 Read about Louis Pasteur and Robert Koch.

Chapter 5 *Ireland*

The Irish in Britain

In the nineteenth century, many Irish came to Britain. First of all the men came on their own, and stayed just for the summer. They moved round the countryside in gangs, helping farmers with the haymaking and the corn harvest. Then, in the 1820's, whole families began to settle permanently. They could not find farming work all the year round, so they lived in the towns, especially Liverpool and Glasgow. These were also the ports where they landed.

By the 1830's some people were saying that the Irish were causing a lot of problems in Britain. Parliament wanted to know if this was true, so it appointed a Commission. This was a group of men whose job was to look into the problem. It heard evidence from all sorts of people and, in 1835, produced its *Report on the State of the Irish Poor in Great Britain.* The following extracts are from the Report.

Here is what a Liverpool man told the Commission:

I had a conversation last week with an Irish labourer named Christopher Shields. He said that the reason of his leaving Ireland was that in the county of Wexford, his own county, he could only get 6d ($2\frac{1}{2}$p) a day, and food for himself. He told me that there was a general impression among his countrymen that if they came to England their fortunes would be made, wages are so much higher here. He now gets 16 shillings (80p) a week. He also said that an important reason for them to come here was that they could find jobs for their children which they could not do at home. This man lives in a cellar. He will never return to Ireland: he has no wish to go back.

1 Where did Christopher Shields come from, in Ireland?
2 What reasons did he give for leaving Ireland?

An English view of the Irish 1824

SYMPTOMS of GOOD LIVING.
An Irish Stew.

Paving a street This is the kind of work the Irish did in Britain. What is unpleasant about this particular job? Why is the man in the top hat waving a stick, do you suppose?

3 Has he done as well in England as, perhaps, he had hoped?

Here is a list of the jobs done by the Irish in Liverpool:

Occupations	*Numbers Employed*
Mechanics	780
Brickmakers	270
Sugar boilers (Hot unpleasant work)	200
Builders' labourers	1,200
Chemical works (unpleasant and dangerous)	600
Sawyers (Sawing up trees into planks, by hand)	80
Labourers employed in smithies, lime kilns, plasters' yards and by paviors (Laying paving stones)	340
Lumpers about the docks who discharge vessels and reload them	1,700
Porters employed in warehouses	1,900
Coal-heavers	430
Total	7,500

1 Arrange these occupations in order of importance.
2 Show the information with a bar diagram.
3 Roughly, how many Irishmen in every ten were doing skilled work? (There is only one skilled occupation in the list, and you must first decide what it is.)
4 How would you describe the work done by most of the Irish?

Here is some evidence from George Williamson. He was the Procurator Fiscal, that is, the chief magistrate of Greenock:

The Irish deal in old things of all kinds, bone, old tools, old clothes. All the hawkers of earthenware, fish, oysters, salted meat and eggs, and dealers in hareskins and shells from the West Indies and Honduras are Irish. They turn their hands to every kind of low trade. The Irish dealers in second-hand articles are, in a good many cases, receivers of stolen goods.

The Irish never seem to do well, except the dealers in old clothes. I never knew any Irish to be mechanics, or to bring up their sons to mechanical trades – nor even their daughters to service: they would sooner make them hawkers of second hand clothes and of fruit or fish. The small coal carried about in carts is also sold by the Irish. The rearing of pigs in the town is likewise carried on by the Irish to a great extent: many of them have kept pigs up stairs and in cellars.

Slum houses It was in places like these that the Irish lived.

1 If you do not know where Greenock is, find it on a map.
2 What do many Irish buy and sell?
3 Why do they do not deal in such goods as new clothes, furniture or watches, do you suppose?
4 In what way does George Williamson say the Irish are dishonest?
5 What unhealthy habit does he say they have?
6 What mistake does he make about the Irish? (Look back to the list on page 123).

This is what the Rev. Thomas Fisher said. He was a Roman Catholic priest in Liverpool:

A large number of the Irish in my flock are in a very bad state, living in cellars and attics. Their furniture is very poor, a straw mattress, a stool, sometimes a table, an iron pot and a frying pan, a jug for water, a few plates and a pewter spoon. They live on potatoes and stirabout (porridge): now and then they may get a herring or a little bacon.

1 What does the Rev. Fisher say about the homes, the furniture and the food of the Irish in Liverpool?

When the Commission wrote its Report, this was one of the things it said:

The Irish settled in England have little to do with the local people, except at work. They form separate communities in the midst of the English. This separation is due partly to the difference of habits, partly to the difference of religion (as most of the Irish are Roman Catholics) partly to the difference of country and sometimes to the difference in language. Finding the English unwilling to mix with them they naturally herd together in particular quarters or streets of the large towns.

1 What differences are there between the Irish and the English?
2 Why do the Irish live in their own part of each town?

William Dillon, a shopkeeper, described part of Liverpool:

There is a place in Liverpool called Little Ireland, for the most part inhabited by Irish. It was a great place for drinking smuggled whisky, and for fighting, quarrelling and killing each other, or any person who happened to come there. It is filthily dirty, and covers a small space in which a great many people live, perhaps as many as three families in a house.

1 Little Ireland was a 'ghetto'. If you have not heard this word before, look it up in a dictionary.
2 What did Dillon say was bad about Little Ireland?

This evidence came from Edward Davies who was Superintendent of the Manchester Watch. Today, we would call him the Chief Constable.

There is a great deal of illicit distillation among the Irish in Manchester. They're usually stills holding from thirty to forty gallons: the spirit made is very bad: it is said to be made of molasses, and potato peelings, and bottoms of beer, that is, beer that has been spoiled. There are a number of houses where the illicit whisky is sold, and these places are crammed with Irish the whole of Saturday night. Parties of men come mad drunk out of these places and patrol the streets in order to assault any person whom they may meet, but especially Irish from other provinces.

When we go to take a still, we are forced to go armed. They often make resistance, collect mobs of hundreds and throw bricks, stones and dirt and everything they can get. It is a very dangerous service.

1 Find out what 'distillation' is.
2 What ingredients did the Irish put in their stills?
3 What spirit did they make? (What does 'illicit' mean?)
4 How did they behave after they had been drinking it?
5 What happened when the police went to destroy a still?

Here now is what John Barret, the Superintendent of the Watch at Stockport, had to say:

There is a great deal of crime among the Irish of this town. Burglaries are not common among them, but of the highway robberies which occur, the majority are committed by the Irish. Manslaughters are also common among them. Serious assaults committed in a state of drunkenness are particularly frequent. They fight with weapons as fire-pokers, pieces of iron or shillelaghs, and rarely with fists. These fights are usually among Irish from different provinces and not so often between English and Irish. The women very often join in the fights.

1 If you do not know where Stockport is, find it on a map.
2 What crimes did the Irish commit the most?
3 Who, usually, were their victims?

This is the evidence of Thomas Arnitt, Overseer of the Poor in Manchester. He looked after the unemployed people in the town. He gave them what he called 'relief', which was much the same as National Assistance today. As with our National Assistance only folk who were in real need were supposed to have relief.

The Irish in Manchester have no other aim or plan than to hang on the poor laws. If they ever had any energy, it seems taken away when they have once had relief. After that they are always plaguing us: they expect us to find everything, bedding, clogs, clothing, food, medicine and medical treatment: and they will be saucy besides.

One of the greatest evils of the poor law is that it creates so much deceit. The Irish do not think it a sin to tell a lie to deceive an overseer. They pretend to have no work, make false returns of their wages, borrow children, pretend that the husband has gone when he is in town, and sham sickness. They clear away everything, beds, blankets etc., if they have any idea that a poor law visitor is near. In all these ways, the Irish deceive more than the English.

1 What help do the Irish in Manchester expect?
2 What will they do in order to have this help?
3 How, according to Thomas Arnitt, are the Irish worse than the English?

Here is the evidence of John Robertson, who was a doctor at the Lying-in Hospital in Manchester. This was a hospital where poor women went to have their babies.

I am sure there are more deaths of Irish babies than of English ones in Manchester. This is owing to bad houses, poor clothes and unwise feeding. The Irish are also in the habit of giving spirits to infants, often out of mistaken kindness.

With regard to small-pox I will state a fact which came under my notice. In the summer of 1832 I was standing at my window, looking at the annual procession of the Sunday-school children. When a certain group passed by I was surprised to see that unusually large numbers were marked with small-pox. These, I found, were the Catholic scholars who were chiefly Irish.

At the hospital, on Tuesdays, where we vaccinate free of charge, very few, if any, Irish bring their children to be vaccinated.

Passenger steamer There was not a lot of immigration to Britain before the development of the steamer. With luck, this vessel would cross the Irish Sea in fourteen hours. A sailing ship might take a week, if the wind was against her.

Page from Census of 1851 Describe the families living at 37 and 78 Trafalgar Place, using all the information you can gain from the census form. An 'annuitant' is someone living on a pension. What is a 'scholar', in the sense used here?

Parish or Township of Liverpool		Ecclesiastical District of			City or Borough of Lpool		Town of Lpool	Village of	
No. of Householder's Schedule	Name of Street, Place, or Road, and Name or No. of House	Name and Surname of each Person who abode in the house, on the Night of the 30th March, 1851	Relation to Head of Family	Condition	Age of Males	Age of Females	Rank, Profession, or Occupation	Where Born	Whether Blind, or Deaf-and-Dumb
36	Gt Howard St	Margt Donohugh	Wife	M		30	——	Ireland	
"	" "	William Rogers	Lodger	Um	16		Labourer	Do	
"	" "	Barthlow Donough	Do	Um	6		Scholar	Do	
37	Trafalgar Place Gt Howard St	Patk Cummings	Head	M	37	-	Dock Labourer	Ireland	
		Cth Do	Wife	M		37	——	Do	
	" "	James Do	Son	Um	14		Scholar	Do	
	" "	Patk Do	do	do	12		Do	Do	
"	" "	James McDonough	Lodger	M	35		House Joiner	Do	
"	" "	Ann Do	Do	M		26	——	Do	
"	" "	Mary Do	do	Um		1	——	Lancashire ~~Do~~	Lpool
38	Do Do	Hugh Hurley	Head	M	40		Dock Labourer	Do	
"	" "	Margt Do	Wife	~~Widr~~		34	——	Do	
"	" "	Eleanor Do	Dr	Um		8	Scholar	Lancashire Lpool	
"	" "	James Do	Son	Um	6	~~6~~	Do	Do Do	
"	" "	Mary Do	Dr	"	"	3	Do	Do Do	
"	" "	George Do	Son	"	½ Year		——	Do Do	
"	" "	Ellinor Do	Visitor	Widow		60	Annuitant	Ireland	
"	" "	Thos Winn	Lodger	M	44		Shoemaker	Do	
Total of Houses	I 2 U / B		Total of Persons		4/10	[illegible]			

1 Why, according to John Robertson, do more Irish babies die than English ones?
2 What disease does he say is more common among Irish children than English children? Why is this?

Alexander Carlisle, who owned a cotton mill at Paisley, had this to say:

It would be most harmful to this town were the Irish immigration stopped. Ireland is our market for labour. This has been particularly so since steam ships began plying between the two countries. They make it easy for us to bring over extra hands. The boundless coalfields beneath us and the boundless mines of labour, so to speak, existing for us in Ireland, are the reasons for the prosperity of this part of Scotland. We are in the lucky position of being able to have an increase in the number of our workers at any time we want. We can do this without paying higher wages or wasting any time.

1 If you do not know where Paisley is, find it on a map.
2 Why was Alexander Carlisle pleased about the Irish coming to Britain?
3 How did steamships help?

Charles Scott, a timber merchant from Greenock, told this story:

Last August the sawyers in my yard went on strike. They were earning from 35/- (£1.75p) to 40/- (£2) a pair per week, frequently as much as £3. We refused their terms and employed common labourers, chiefly Irish, to fill the pits. By degrees they learnt the trade and are now earning from 30/- to 35/- a week: some up to 40/-. The men who struck are now begging to be employed at their former wages and have entirely dissolved the union they formed.

1 How did Charles Scott find Irish workers useful?
2 What do you suppose the men he sacked felt about them?

Finally, here is the evidence of James Holmes of Birmingham, who employed a team of plasterers and their labourers. Not only is a plasterer highly skilled, but he has to work fast, because plaster sets quickly. He must never be without freshly mixed plaster, so the labourer who helps him must work very hard to keep him supplied.

I have generally eight to sixteen Irish labourers in my employ. They work as plasterers' labourers, to do the heaviest work, to fetch and carry and to attend to the plasterers. I have one Irish plasterer, a very civil, steady man: you would hardly think he was an Irishman. The Irish labourers will work any time. Most of them are very hardworking and very honest. I have some who worked for me ten years. They are much trusted about houses, and there are no complaints against them. If one of them is caught stealing, the others will avoid him. I consider them very valuable labourers and we could not do without them. By treating them kindly they will do anything for you. Before I came to Birmingham I could not bear the thoughts of an Irishman: now I would sooner have an Irishman than an Englishman for a labourer. An Englishman could not do the work they do. When you push them, they have a willingness to oblige, which the English have not. They would die at anything before they would be beat. They are very charitable to one another. One man working for me saved 10/- (50p) a week out of 15/2 (76p) and when he had saved £3 he sent it to his father in Ireland.

I think that the prejudice in England against the Irish labourers arises from not knowing them.

The English labourers don't like the Irish: they say if it was not for them, they would have good wages.

1 How many Irish labourers did John Holmes employ?
2 What work did they do?
3 How many of his skilled men, that is his plasterers, were Irish?
4 Write out a list of the good qualities which John Holmes said the Irish had.
5 What did he think about the Irish before he came to Birmingham?
6 Give two reasons why he thinks some English people do not like the Irish.
7 The last three people – Carlisle, Scott and Holmes – have something in common. Can you see what it is?

Written Work

One thing which Parliament had to decide in 1835 was whether it should stop any more Irish people coming to Britain. Write a report. Say what problems the Irish seem to be causing and how they seem to be helping. What would you advise Parliament to do? (In the event it did nothing to stop the Irish coming to Britain).

Research

1 Find out what you can about life in Ireland in the early nineteenth century.
2 Find out what you can about the 'navvies' who built the canals and railways in Britain. Many of them were Irish.

Famine in Ireland: 1 *The Famine Strikes*

The population of Ireland grew rapidly during the nineteenth century. The same thing happened in Britain, but there, most of the extra people moved to towns to work in factories. The Irish could not do this, as they had few large towns and hardly any industry. Almost everyone had to stay and work in the countryside. As a result, farms were divided again and again so that before long, many families were trying to live off a plot of land no bigger than a football pitch. The only crop which would give them enough food was the potato, so they grew potatoes, and nothing else.

Most of the land in Ireland belonged to wealthy Englishmen who lived in their own country. They were known as 'absentee landlords'.

To look after their Irish estates the English Landlords appointed agents. One of these was a man called Steuart-Trench. He worked for the Marquis of Lansdowne who had an estate at Kenmare in County Kerry. This is what Steuart-Trench found when he arrived there:

> The estate of the Marquis of Lansdowne had been much neglected by its agent. Nothing had been done to stop the subdivision of land. Boys and girls married, each at the age of seventeen or eighteen, without thinking it necessary to have anything beyond a shed to live in, and a small plot of land whereon to grow potatoes. Countless squatters had settled themselves in huts on the mountain sides and in the valleys. They sowed their patches of potatoes early in spring, using sea-weed only as manure. Then, as the scarce seasons of spring and summer came on, they nailed up the doors of their huts, took all their children along with them and wandered all over the countryside. They trusted to their cleverness in begging, to keep the family alive till the potato crop came in again. Thus, as a result of neglect or weakness the agent allowed numbers of strangers and young married couples to settle on the estate. The character and condition of the property were at a very low ebb indeed. The estate, in fact, was swamped with paupers.
>
> *Realities of Irish Life*, 1868

Funeral during the Famine Why are the bodies not in coffins, do you suppose?

1 At what age did many of the Irish marry?
2 What did a young couple hope to own?
3 How did they live when they had eaten all their potatoes?
4 What complaint does Steuart-Trench make about the agent who had been there before him?
5 What does he say was wrong with the estate?

Here is what it was like in Limerick, another part of western Ireland. The extract is some of the evidence which John McMahon gave the Committee on Agriculture in 1833. McMahon was one of the few wealthy farmers in his area:

Do the peasantry eat wheaten bread at all?
Never except two days in the year.
What are those days?
Christmas Day and Easter Sunday.
What do they live upon?
Potatoes and milk.
Nothing else?
Nothing else.
How is the labourer worse off than he was?
In not having work. Many have told me they would be the happiest people that there could be in the world if they could have work six months in the year at eightpence a day (3p).
Have all those labourers little patches of land of their own?
Yes.
How much?
Generally an acre.
What do they pay?
The fortunate man will have to pay from £5 to £8 a year, but will have to sell his pig to pay his rent.
Do they all wear shoes and stockings?
They do, most of them, but boys of 15 or 16 years you may see not wearing a shoe or a stocking.
In the hilly or mountain districts is that the case?
In the mountain districts there are great numbers of them bare legged, men and women.

Committee on Agriculture, 1833

1 What do the Irish peasants live on?
2 How much a week is it their ambition to earn? (Allow six days a week).
3 How much land does each peasant have? What is his rent? How does he pay it?

Now study this table:

	Calories	*Protein (grams)*	*Calcium*	*Vitamin C*
Ten pounds of potatoes	3459	45	1.92	444
1 pint of milk	393	19	0.71	171
Total	3852	64	2.63	615
Minimum needed by human body	3000	70	0.56	525

Potatoes and milk also contain ample Vitamins A, B and D.
Ten pounds of potatoes was the average daily consumption.

1 Is it possible to live on potatoes and milk alone?

So far we have been looking at the west of Ireland. The east was different. Large towns in England, like Liverpool and Manchester, needed food and it was possible to bring it cheaply and easily from Ireland. In the counties closest to England, farms were quite big, and farmers made a good living growing food for sale. Edward Roberts, a merchant who lived in Waterford, talks about the food exports from his town. In 1813 there were no steamships: by 1833 there were many.

I have taken an average from seven years, ending in 1813, and seven years ending in 1833: and it appears that the export of bacon, for seven years ending in 1813 was 223,369 flitches, and for the seven years to 1833, 361,704, which is an increase of more than one third. Butter is increased by more than one third, from 95,000 to 140,000 firkins. Wheat has increased double, from 67,000 to 143,000. In flour there has been a wonderful increase: it is a new trade with us. In the seven years ending 1813 there were only 36,036 cwt exported: in the seven years ending 1833 there were 348,715 exported. Then the export of live cattle is a new thing altogether: there were none exported in the year ending 1813, and in the year 1833 the exports have been very great indeed: pigs, 37,723: cattle 3,961: and sheep, 7,978.

Committee on Agriculture, 1833

1 Draw bar diagrams to show how the exports of different foods from Waterford increased, after the invention of the steamship.
2 Why do you suppose there were no exports of live cattle, in the early days?

In 1845 a strange new disease attacked the potatoes in most countries of Europe. It is called 'potato blight'. First of all spores of the disease destroy the leaves and, if it rains at all heavily, these spores are

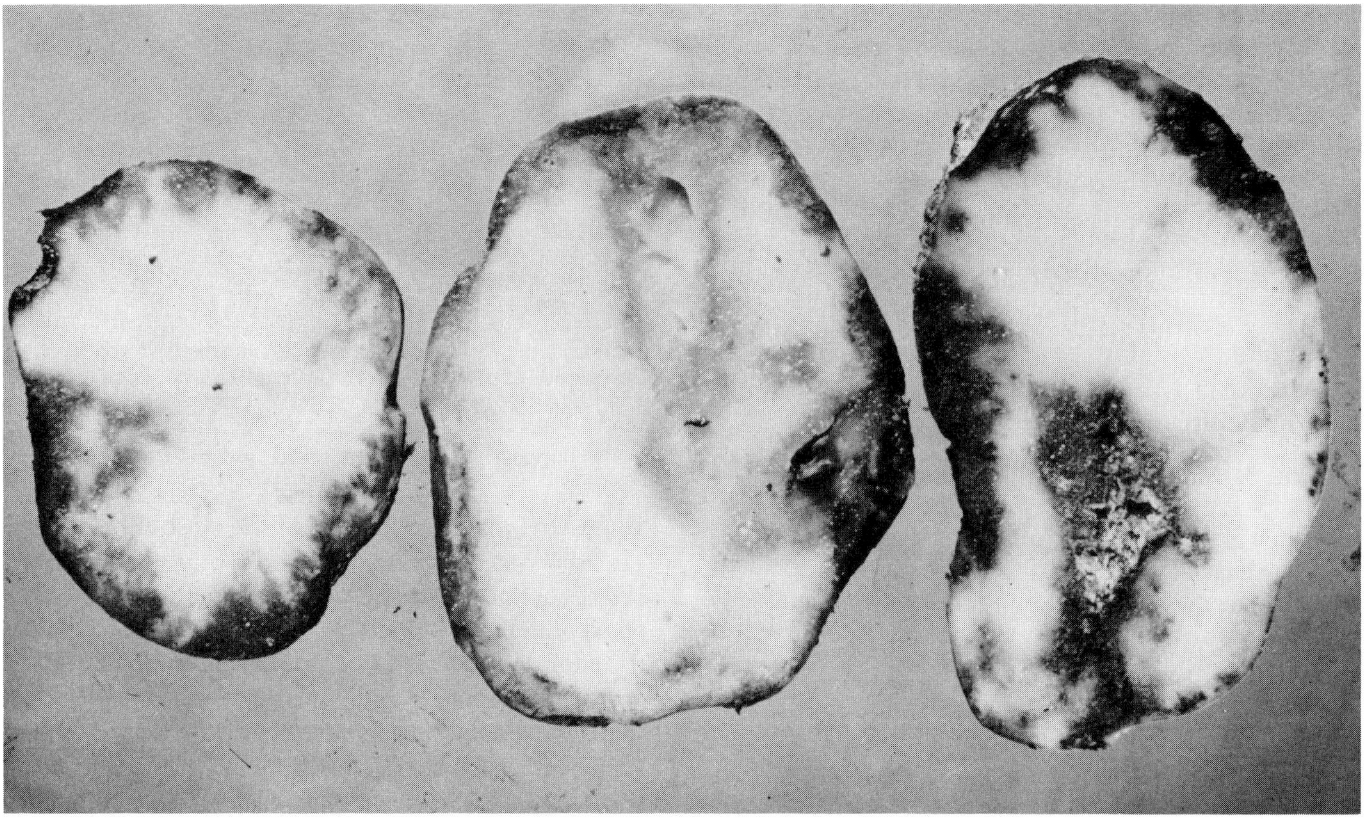

Potato Blight The foliage wilts and the potato itself rots. This photograph is modern. The drawing of the leaves is from the *Illustrated London News* of 1846.

washed into the ground and on to the potatoes. The potatoes soon become a black, stinking mess. Today, we understand potato blight and can control it. In 1845, it was a complete mystery. In Ireland it ruined most of the crop that year, and all of it in 1846 and 1848.

An Englishman called Henry Clifford wrote this letter:

> I ranged all the West and I can assure you I was in utter astonishment and dismay, too. The picture is a truly sad one – for since Wednesday last, the *green* country has become *black* – I did not see but one green field of Potatoes in the West – I scarcely would believe that four or five days would have made such a change – every field is gone. The potatoes under the blackened stalks are all more or less diseased and all kinds of Potatoes are affected by it.

1 Where did Henry Clifford travel?
2 What did he see?
3 What different feelings did he have?

Many people in England sent help to the Irish, especially the Quakers. This is what one of them, William Bennett, found in a village:

> We entered a cabin. Stretched in one dark corner, scarcely visible from the smoke and rags that covered them, were three children huddled together, lying there because they were too weak to rise, pale and ghastly, their little limbs completely wasted away, eyes sunk, voice gone, and obviously in the last stage of starvation. Crouched over the turf embers was another form, wild and all but naked, scarcely human in appearance. It stirred not, nor noticed us. On some straw, sodden upon the ground, moaning piteously was a shrivelled old woman, imploring us to give her something. Above her, on something like a ledge, was a young woman with sunken cheeks, who scarely raised her eyes in answer to our questions, but pressed her hand upon her forehead with a look of absolute anguish and despair. We entered upwards of fifty of these little houses. The scene was one and the same, differing in little but the number of sufferers. Many were remnants of families crowded together in one cabin: orphaned little relatives taken in by the equally destitute and even strangers, for these poor people are kind to one another to the end. In one cabin was a sister, just dying, lying by the side of her little brother, just dead. They did but rarely complain. When asked what was the matter, the answer was alike in all – 'Tha shein ukrosh' – 'indeed the hunger'. We learned the terrible meaning of that sad word 'ukrosh'.
>
> *Narrative of a Recent Journey of Six Weeks in Ireland*, 1847

Irish hut It was in homes like this that William Bennet found the dying people.

1 Estimate the number of people who were starving in the village.
2 How were they behaving towards each other?

Obviously, starving people could not pay their rents. An English official called Hibberd described what happened to many of them. He wrote this letter from Galway on December 29th, 1847:

> I am writing to give you particulars about the poor who arrived here from Mr. C. St. George's property at Lettermore, the most of whom were ejected, while others were driven away by starvation, the whole of whom are at this moment upon the town of Galway – full 100 are in the gaol, others have been taken into the workhouse and very many are at this moment begging at every door; in truth a constant melancholy cry of children is to be heard in every street, at the keyholes of our doors and upon many death is in truth stamped upon their brow. This, however, is not a solitary instance, as I was yesterday informed that Mr. St. George had been clearing off tenants from the two villages in that neighbourhood and it appears he is also ejecting the people from the village of Pauluny, so that he is really making a clearance at the expense of this Union which is spoken of in strong language by the resident Gentlemen as the county is covered with *whole* families all bending their course for Galway, if only for shelter from the storm.
>
> *Public Records Office*

Note: By 'Union' Mr. Hibberd means the Poor Law Union, that is the local authority responsible for looking after the poor.

Years after the famine, an Irish officer, Sir William Butler wrote:

> One day I was taken by my father to the scene of an eviction. On one side of the road was a ruined church: on the other side stood some dozen houses which were to be pulled down, and their inhabitants evicted. The sheriff, a strong body of police and above all the crowbar brigade – a group composed of the lowest and most evil ruffians – were present. At the signal from the sheriff 'the work began. The miserable inmates of the cabins were dragged out upon the road: the thatched roofs were torn down and the earthen walls battered in by the crowbars: the screaming women, the half-naked children, the paralysed grandmother and the tottering grandfather were hauled out. I was twelve years old at that time: but I think if a loaded gun had been put into my hands I would have

An eviction Many of the landlords who ordered evictions were English.

fired into that crowd of villains as they plied their horrid trade by the ruined church of Tampul-da-voun.

Memoirs

1 What does Mr. Hibberd say Mr. St. George is doing?
2 What are the people from his estates having to do as a result?
3 Why are the people of Galway angry? (Explain: 'he is really making a clearance at the expense of this Union').
4 Describe in your own words, what William Butler saw at Tampul-da-voun.

This is a letter from an English official:

I thought it my duty to attend the meeting of the Scariff Union as a result of hearing that there was a possibility of that workhouse being closed.

The facts are these: the workhouse is about £1,500 in debt, there is a very great difficulty in collecting the rate, they have no food but such as is obtained by individual Guardians.

There are nearly 250 inmates sick of fever and dysentry who, if thus left, must certainly die, and if those in fever be removed by their friends, they will spread disease through the country.

Public Records Office

1 Why is it likely that the workhouse at Scariff will have to close?
2 Why is it having problems, do you suppose?
3 How are the people in the workhouse suffering?
4 What will happen if the workhouse does close?

Written Work

Imagine that, like William Bennett, you have visited Ireland during the famine. Write a letter saying what you have seen, and what problems the country is facing. Explain why potato blight is a much worse disaster for Ireland than England.

Research

Find out what you can about the history of Ireland in the early nineteenth century.

Famine in Ireland: 2 *Attempts to Relieve the Famine*

In the early nineteenth century many people in Britain were very poor, as you have seen from some of the other sections. None the less, Britain as a whole was the richest country in the world. She had prosperous farms, large, modern factories and an enormous fleet of merchant ships. Many individuals were very wealthy. These included men like Steuart-Trench's employer, Lord Lansdowne, who gained much of their money from the rents of their estates in Ireland.

When the famine came, the Irish looked to Britain for help. They had every right to do so. In 1801 an Act of Union had made Ireland part of Britain, just as Scotland and Wales are today. Irishmen and Englishmen were citizens of the same country. The question was, what would those fellow citizens do?

First of all the government asked Charles Trevelyan, the senior civil servant in the Treasury, to make plans. Next, Relief Committees were set up all over Ireland. These were groups of important local people like magistrates and clergymen. One of their duties was to carry out any instructions the government might send. Another was to raise money, out of the rates, and by voluntary subscriptions. The government also gave them money. The more a Committee raised itself, the more the government sent.

Soup kitchen at Cork This kitchen was run by English Quakers, who gave a great deal of help during the famine. After 1847, there were government soup kitchens as well. (See page 137).

Ration cards for soup Ration cards were used during the Great Famine under the Soup-kitchen Act of 1847. Adults were entitled to a full ration each day while children under nine years of age were given a half ration.

A great deal of money was given both in Ireland and in England. Trevelyan wrote:

> From the Queen on her throne, to the convicts in the hulks, expenses were reduced, and hardships were endured in order to swell the Irish subscriptions. There were ladies' associations without end to collect small weekly subscriptions and make up clothes to send to Ireland. The opera, the fancy bazaar, the fashionable ball all raised funds: and, above all, there were the private efforts of countless individuals.
>
> *Edinburgh Review*, 1848

1 How was money raised in England, to help the Irish?

This is what Steuart-Trench said happened to some of the money when it reached Ireland:

> In one place there was a most kindly clergyman, who having obtained large funds from England, appeared in the morning at his own hall door, and threw handfuls of shillings and sixpences among the crowd who had collected to receive the charity. Good gentleman no doubt he was: but he forgot that starving people could not eat sixpences or shillings, and the food was some ten miles off. The people had no strength nor energy to seek, purchase, or cook meal or flour, and with the silver in their hands, they died.
>
> *Realities of Irish Life*

1 How did the priest give away the money?
2 Why was this foolish?
3 What should he have done?

The senior government official in Ireland was Sir Randolph Routh. He wrote this to Trevelyan, about the Relief Committees:

> Pray, if you put forth any public document, speak carefully of the Committees, whose help you will certainly require this year. Praise if you like, but do not find fault. They are very sensitive, and so are all the Irish.
>
> *Public Records Office*

1 What advice is Routh giving Trevelyan?
2 What suggests that Routh found it difficult to deal with the Committees?

An Irishman, Sir Charles Gavan Duffy wrote:

> Relief Committees were appointed and appeals were made for money. Nearly a hundred thousand pounds were contributed at home and abroad: but voluntary contribution is a system which taxes the kindly and allows the hard-hearted, the oppressor and the absentee to escape.
>
> *Four Years of Irish History, 1845–1849*

Note: One English organisation alone raised £500,000.

1 What are 'voluntary contributions'? What does Duffy think of them?
2 Who are the 'hard-hearted, the oppressor, and the absentee'?

Duffy also wrote:

> More than a third of the potato crop throughout the island was gone, in some districts more than half: and at the same time the bulk of the remaining supplies, cattle and corn, butter, beef and pork, which would have fed all the inhabitants went on being exported to England, to pay the rent of farms which no longer gave their cultivators their ordinary food.
>
> *Four Years of Irish History, 1845–1849*

1 What does Duffy say was happening during the famine?
2 What was the reason for it?

Trevelyan and the government thought that the Irish farmers should go on selling their fairly expensive food in England. If they did not, they would be unable to pay their rents, and their landlords would evict them. But the government did hope that a lot of

YOUNG IRELAND IN BUSINESS FOR HIMSELF.

***Punch* cartoon** In 1848 an organisation called 'Young Ireland' started a rebellion. Hardly any men joined it, and a force of 40 policemen put it down with ease. What the rebellion did do, was to kill much of the sympathy which the English had for the Irish. How would this cartoon affect anyone who was thinking of sending help during the famine?

cheap food would come from America. This would be maize, which they called Indian corn, and rice. The government itself bought a certain amount of Indian corn, which it stored in depots and doled out to Relief Committees. It expected that Irish corn merchants would seize the chance of making some money and bring in a good deal more. However, Routh wrote to Trevelyan:

> As for leaving the country to the corn dealers, they are a very different class of men from our London, Bristol and Liverpool Merchants. I do not believe there is a man amongst them who would import a single cargo from abroad. The man who has made the greatest outcry, Mr. Russell of Limerick, would not hesitate to extort the highest price he could obtain. Lately, he has been sending circulars to the Relief Committees to state that the meal in charge of Mr. Coffin in Limerick is damaged and of bad quality, but that the meal at his store can safely be trusted. How can confidence be given to such a class of men?
>
> *Public Records Office*

Note: Mr. Coffin was an official who had charge of a government store.

1 What does Routh feel about Irish corn merchants in general?
2 What does he say Russell of Limerick has been doing?

In Ireland, there had always been local famines from time to time. To give the people the chance to buy food the government had started public works. The same scheme was tried again during the great famine of 1845–1848. This is what William Bennett saw at Tobercurry in County Sligo:

> We here first encountered the public works so called. These consisted in making new roads and altering old ones, in many cases worse than useless and undertaken for the mere sake of employment. Apart from the moral effects of useless labour it was sad in the extreme to see the women and girls withdrawn from all that was decent and proper, and labouring in mixed gangs on the public roads. Not only in digging with the spade, and with the pick, but in carrying loads of earth and turves, and wheeling barrows like men, and breaking stones, are they employed. The poor, neglected children were crouched in groups around the bits of lighted turves in the various sheltered corners along the line. The pay was sixpence and sevenpence per day to the girls and women, and eightpence to the men.
>
> *Narrative of a Recent Journey of Six Weeks in Ireland,* 1847

1 What public works were being done?
2 What does William Bennett think of them?
3 What worried him about the women and girls?
4 What were the children doing?
5 What were the wages?

Trevelyan wrote:

The attraction of money wages, regularly paid from the public purse, or the 'Queen's pay' as it was called, led to the neglect of all other occupations. Landlords competed with each other in getting the names of their tenants placed on the lists: farmers dismissed their labourers and sent them to the works: the clergy insisted on the claims of the members of their respective congregations: the fisheries were deserted; and it was difficult even to get a coat patched or a pair of shoes mended, to such an extent had the population of the south and west of Ireland turned out upon the roads. The average number employed in October was 114,000; in November, 285,000; in December, 440,000: and in January 1847, 570,000

The fearful extent to which the country people had been thrown for support upon the Board of Works also threatened a disastrous neglect of farming. If people were kept on the works, their lands must remain uncultivated. If they were put off the works, they must starve.

Edinburgh Review, 1848

1 Why were people anxious to work on the roads?
2 Name three groups of people who wanted the poor to work on the roads. What do you imagine were the motives of the members of each group?
3 What happened to other occupations?
4 How many people worked on the roads in January 1847?
5 How did the public works make the famine worse?

An English official called Bishop wrote to Trevelyan:

I fear the road system has taught the people to look to the government for aid in every emergency, to neglect all preparation for sowing or planting their ground and, in fact, discourage them from helping themselves.

Public Records Office

Trevelyan himself wrote:

The people in some parts of the West of Ireland neglected to lay in their usual winter stock of peat in 1847, as everyone had the impression that the Queen would supply them with coal.

Edinburgh Review, 1848

1 According to Butler and Trevelyan, how did the public works change the attitude of the Irish?

Charles Gavan Duffy had this to say:

The custom at that time was to send Englishmen to a country of which they knew nothing, and to trust them to solve problems needing minute knowledge and long experience. The English officials decided that work, whether useful or not, was the proper system. They decided also that not railways or canals, or transforming the wastes into corn-fields, but an enormous extension of the road system was what was needed. Half a million people were soon at work on this, and nearly twelve thousand persons paid to supervise their useless labour. Useful roads were torn up that they might be made anew, and new roads planned where there was no traffic.

Four Years of Irish History, 1845–1849

1 What does Duffy feel about Englishmen taking charge in Ireland?
2 What public works does Duffy feel should have been done?
3 What, in fact, was done? What does Duffy feel about this?
4 How far would Bishop and Trevelyan have agreed with Duffy?

In 1847 the government tried a new plan. It told the Relief Committees they must take money from the local rates, and use it to run soup kitchens. These would sell food to those who had money, and give it to those who did not.

This is what William Bennett saw:

All these soup kitchens were in very poor localities, at a distance of four to five miles apart. At two of the places, 3,200 quarts of soup, or rather porridge, were given out daily to upwards of 800 families, the boilers being filled four or five times. The amount of help thus given is said to be beyond calculation as was obvious even in the looks of the poor people since the soup kitchens had been in action. It was delightful, in passing along the roads, to see their orderly conduct as we met the women and girls radiating from the different centres of attraction: many a graceful figure bearing her vessel on her head, and groups collected, not unworthy of the Greek or Italian artist.

Narrative of a Recent Journey of Six Weeks in Ireland, 1847

1 What does William Bennett feel about soup kitchens?
2 How do these women and girls compare with the ones he saw working on the roads?

Here is a letter which the captain of a warship wrote to Trevelyan in February, 1847:

Dear Sir,

We started from Greenhithe this morning, and if the weather continues fair we shall be at Plymouth tomor-

Distributing clothes The starving people needed warm clothes nearly as badly as they needed food.

row where we take a Pilot. We then go on to Cork to land 22 Boilers – then to Kenmore to land 75 tons of Seed Oats and Barley, which, if we are lucky in our weather may be got into the ground by the 1st March, at any rate long before St. Patrick's Day. We shall lose no time at Kenmore, but push on to Belmullet to land our 280 tons of meal and rice.

Your most obedient servant,
W. I. Williams, Captain R.N.

Public Records Office

Note: the meal was ground maize, or Indian Corn.

1 What do you suppose the boilers were for?
2 What else was the ship carrying?
3 Find on a map the places where the ship was going to call.

Here are extracts from letters which two English officials wrote to Trevelyan from County Mayo:

Mr. Vowles said:

At Ballycastle I have met with much difficulty. The Protestant minister refuses to give any funds or join any Committee where the Roman Catholic Priest is admitted. However, I succeeded in pressing Resolutions for the establishment of *five* Soup Shops in the District and the Sub-Committees for each are now applying for subscriptions in the neighbourhood and to absentee landlords and others.

Public Records Office

1 What problem did Vowles have at Ballycastle?
2 What did he succeed in doing?

Mr. Bishop, who was in Erris, said:

There are but few resident Gentry or Men of any influence to advise or help the people. The Committee are neither willing nor able to arrange the supply or distribution of food. They were useful in placing men on the roads, but anything of practical value was entirely neglected.

Public Records Office

1 Why, according to Bishop, is the Erris Relief Committee inefficient?
2 What was it able to do?
3 What has it failed to do?

Trevelyan wrote:

Uncooked meal might be converted into cash by those who did not need it as food: and even the hungriest often sold it to buy tea, tobacco or spirits: but stirabout which becomes sour by keeping, has no value in the market, and persons were therefore not likely to ask for it who did not want it to eat themselves.

It was found that the best form in which cooked food could be given was 'stirabout', made of Indian meal and rice steamed, which was solid enough to be carried away. A pound ration thus prepared, swelled by the absorption of water, to three or four pounds.

Edinburgh Review, 1848

1 What food was given out by the 'soup' kitchens?
2 How much did each person have? How many potatoes had an Irishman eaten, on average, every day before the famine? (See page 129).
3 Why was the food cooked before being given out?

Here is what Duffy said:

Indian corn was ground in England and sold to Relief Committees at a low price. Skilfully cooked, it can make a pleasant dish: but dissolved into stirabout and served out cold and half raw to a people who had neither a fire to cook it nor knowledge of how to do so, it was the most odious mess ever designed for human food. At first the peasants could not be persuaded to touch the 'yellow meal', but the pangs of hunger gradually overcame their prejudice.

Four Years of Irish History, 1845–1849

1 What does Duffy say about Indian corn?
2 Why, according to Duffy, did the people eat Indian corn at all?
3 Is it true that the Irish had no fires? (See pages 131 and 135).
4 Do you suppose the meal was difficult to cook? (It was like porridge).

So far we have been looking at the ways in which the English tried to help. Here now is what an Irishman, Charles Duffy, said should have happened:

What was needed was not to open the ports on foreign grain, but to shut them fast on what was home grown. The Irish landlords, who knew this, and feared that the people might soon come to know of it, were taking time by the forelock. There was a larger export of grain to London and Liverpool during the month of November, 1845 than had ever before taken place in a similar period. Every Irish port was crowded with vessels carrying food out of a country threatened with famine.

Had Ireland been able to protect herself, as self-governed countries protected themselves, a famine would have been impossible. Rents for a time would have been seriously reduced, or even, in some cases lost entirely. But the grants afterwards made for useless road works and demoralising food depots would have given the landlords quite enough compensation. To close the ports was the remedy the 'Nation' wanted: to keep and eat our own food. I insisted, indeed, that if there was to be a famine, it would be a famine created not by the blight, but by the landlords: for, though the potatoes were gone, the corn remained.

Four Years of Irish History, 1845–1849

1 According to Duffy, what did the Irish landlords do as soon as they realised there was going to be a famine? Why?
2 What does Duffy think should have been done?
3 How would the landlords have suffered as a result?
4 What money could have been used to compensate them?
5 What does Duffy say was *not* responsible for the famine?
6 Who does Duffy say was responsible?
7 How far do you agree with Duffy?

Written Work

1 Make a list of the different things which were done to try and relieve the famine. With each of them say:
   a How the plan worked.
   b What problems there were.
   c How far the plan was a success, if at all.
2 Consider Duffy's criticisms. Do you think they were fair? Do you think his plan for relieving the famine was a good one? Give reasons for your answers.

Research

Read more about what happened in Ireland during the famine.

Famine in Ireland: 3 *The Emigrants*

When the famine struck, many poor people wanted to leave Ireland as soon as possible. The landlords encouraged them. Their estates were swarming with starving people from whom they had no hope of collecting any rent. Not only that, the landlords had to pay rates in order to buy food for the workhouses and soup kitchens.

Steuart-Trench went to see his employer, Lord Lansdowne, to discuss the problem. He wrote:

The remedy I proposed was as follows. That he should at once offer free emigration to every man, woman and child now in the poor-house or chargeable to his estate. That even supposing they all accepted this offer, the total, together with a small sum per head for clothes and a few shillings on landing would not exceed from £13,000 to £14,000, a sum less than it would cost to support them in the workhouse for a single year. That by this means he would put the people in a far better way of earning their bread hereafter: whereas by feeding and keeping them where they were, they must remain a millstone around the neck of his estate and prevent its rise for many years to come.

I shall not readily forget the scenes in Kenmore when I returned and said I was prepared at Lord Lansdowne's expense to send to America everyone who wanted to go. It was thought by the paupers to be too good news to be true. But when it began to be believed a rush was made to get away at once.

The mode adopted was as follows: two hundred each week were chosen of these most suited for emigration: and having arranged their slender outfit, a steady man, on whom I could depend, Mr. Jeremiah O'Shea, was employed to take charge of them on their journey to Cork. This plan succeeded admirably: and week after week, to the astonishment of the good people of Cork, and sometimes not a little to their dismay, a batch of two hundred paupers appeared on the quays of Cork, bound for the Far West.

Realities of Irish Life

1 How did Steuart-Trench persuade Lord Lansdowne to help the paupers on his estate to emigrate?
2 What was each pauper to be given?
3 How did the people react, when they had the news?

Emigrants on board ship

4 How did Steuart-Trench organise the emigration?

Steuart-Trench also wrote:

> It must be admitted that the paupers sent to America on such a sudden pressure as this, were of a very motley type: and a strange figure these wild batches of two hundred each – most of them speaking only the Irish language – made in the streets of Cork, as well as on the quays of Liverpool and America. There was great difficulty in keeping them from breaking loose from the ship in Liverpool, where the ships touched before they left for the West. Their usual trick was to escape out of the ships almost naked, to hide all their good clothes which had been given them as an outfit, and to appear only in their worst rags. In this costume they took delight in rushing through the streets of Liverpool in large bodies, to the real terror of the inhabitants. In short, I do believe that so strange, unmanageable and wild a crew had never before left the shores of Ireland. But they were all in the best of spirits: there was no crying nor lamentation as is usual on such occasions: all was delight at having escaped the deadly workhouse.
>
> *Realities of Irish Life*

1 What kind of people were the emigrants?
2 How did they behave in Liverpool?
3 How do people usually feel when they leave their native land? How did these people feel?
4 Name one problem that most of these emigrants were going to have in America.
5 How do you suppose the people in America felt when these emigrants arrived?

Steuart-Trench said this about his scheme:

> I am happy to say that the most favourable accounts have been received from every quarter to which the emigrants were despatched. Money in large quantities has been sent home by them to their friends. Happily no accident ever occurred to a single ship which carried out the Kenmore emigrants. Almost all, down even to the widows and children, found employment soon after landing: and to this hour I can never experience any other feelings but those of pleasure at having been the means of sending so many miserable beings to a land far richer and more prosperous than Ireland.
>
> The estate was also vastly improved. Great numbers of the smaller tenants gave up their plots of land and most gladly emigrated to the Far West. These plots were added to the adjoining tenants' farms, and thus the number of tenants on the rent-roll was considerably reduced. The famine was over, and Lord Lansdowne's estate was righted.
>
> *Realities of Irish Life*

1 According to Steuart-Trench, what happened to the emigrants after they arrived in America?
2 How did he feel about sending so many people abroad?
3 What happened to the plots of land the emigrants left?
4 What do you suppose Steuart-Trench was careful to prevent from then onwards? (Look back to page 128).

We do not know what really happened to the emigrants from Lord Lansdowne's estates when they left Ireland, but at least they were given some help. Others had to look after themselves. Many English shipowners saw a chance to make money, and dozens of vessels came to the Irish ports. Their captains offered to take people across the Atlantic.

Most emigrants wanted to go to the United States, but that country would only accept them if the ships that brought them were well-kept, clean and not overcrowded. Few of the ships carrying the Irish were like that, so they sailed instead to Canada. The emigrants were willing enough to go there because they knew that, once landed, it would be easy to slip over the border into the United States.

When they arrived in Canada, all emigrants had to go into quarantine on Grosse Island. This was in the River St. Lawrence, near Quebec. At the worst time, May 1847, there were 35 ships anchored in the river, carrying 12,000 passengers. Most of them were starving, and many of them were suffering from typhus.

This is what the Medical Superintendent of Grosse Island, Dr. Douglas, said about the ship ***Elizabeth and Sarah*****:**

> On boarding her I found the passengers in the most wretched state of filth and disease. No order or regulation had been kept, or any attempt at enforcing cleanliness. Their excrement and filth had been thrown into the ballast, producing a stench which made it difficult to remain any length of time below. I found twenty-six cases of fever, and received the names of twenty others, including the captain, who had died on the passage. The voyage had extended to the unusual length of seventy-two days. On landing the passengers at the sheds, I had to send fifty more to hospital, and six have died since landing. The remainder, though weak, are healthy at present, and have been made to clean themselves, their clothing and bedding, those of them that had any, but most of them are without a second change of clothes.
>
> The causes which have produced disease and death

Embarking for North America

among these passengers are those so often stated by me in my Annual Reports:

1 Want of cleanliness and lack of ventilation.
2 Lack of food and water, and that of an unwholesome quality.
3 Overcrowding.

These causes produce fever, and when once the disease sets in, the stench from the bodies of the sick, dying and dead confined in the hold (the captain was kept two or three weeks on board after death), soon made the whole atmosphere unfit to breathe. The captain, from all accounts, was a man unfit to take charge of a passenger vessel: he was in ill health, and a drunkard.

Little or no attention had been paid to the most important clauses of the Passenger Act. The passengers were not provided by the vessel with any food: their own stock was soon eaten: the bunks were badly put up, and came down on the starboard side two or three days after leaving. The vessel itself is the oldest in the North of England being 83 years old.

The number of passengers put on board exceeded by sixty or seventy the number allowed to the tonnage of the vessel.

Papers relating to Canada and to Immigration in the Provinces, 1847–1849

1 In what state was the *Elizabeth and Sarah*?
2 In what state were the passengers?
3 What reason does Dr. Duncan give for the disease on board?
4 Why was the captain unsuitable for his job? What happened to him?
5 How long did the voyage last? Can you suggest why?
6 What rules, laid down by the Passenger Act, had been broken?

A. C. Buchanan, the Chief Emigration Agent at Quebec wrote:

All the Cork and Liverpool passengers are half dead from starvation and want before embarking, and the least bowel complaint, which is sure to come with a change of food, finishes them without a struggle. I never saw people so indifferent to life: they would continue in the same bunk with a dead person until the seamen dragged out the corpse with boathooks. Good God! what evils will befall the cities where they alight.

Papers Relating to Canada and to Immigration in the Provinces, 1847–1848

1 Why, according to Buchanan, do the emigrants fall ill very easily?
2 How do they feel at the end of their voyage?
3 Why is Buchanan worried for the cities where the emigrants will go?

Duffy wrote:

More than a hundred thousand souls fled to the United States and Canada. The United States had sanitary regulations for ships which were effective to a certain extent. But the emigration to Canada was left to the individual greed of ship-owners. Crowded and filthy, carrying double the number of passengers, who were ill-fed and badly clothed, and having no doctor on board, the holds were like the Black Hole of Calcutta, and deaths occurred in myriads. The survivors, on their arrival in the new country, continued to die and to scatter death around them. At Montreal, during nine weeks, eight hundred emigrants perished, and over nine hundred died

Monument on Grosse Island Which people are remembered on the side of the column, and which on the front? Which group seemed the more important in Canadian eyes? The side reads: 'In this secluded spot lie the mortal remains of 5424 persons who flying from Pestilence and Famine in Ireland in the year 1847 found in America but a Grave.'

of diseases caught from emigrants. No preparations were made by the British Government for the reception or the employment of the helpless multitudes. The *Times* pronounced the neglect to be an eternal disgrace to the British name. The Chief Secretary for Ireland reported to the House of Commons that of a hundred thousand Irishmen who fled to Canada in a year, 6,100 perished on the voyage, 4,100 on their arrival, 5,200 in the hospitals, and 1,900 in the towns to which they went. The Emigrant Society of Montreal said:

'From Grosse Island up to Port Sarnia, along the borders of our great river, on the shores of Lakes Ontario and Erie, wherever the tide of emigration has extended, are to be found one unbroken chain of graves, where repose fathers and mothers, sisters and brothers, in a commingled heap, no stone marking the spot. Twenty thousand and upwards have gone down to their graves.'

Four Years of Irish History, 1845–1849

1 According to Duffy:
   a How many emigrants went to North America?
   b How many died? Whose figures does Duffy quote?
   c What was wrong with the ships?
   d What did the British government fail to do?
2 Who do you think gives the more accurate picture of emigration, Steuart-Trench or Duffy?
3 Why is Steuart-Trench's account more favourable, do you think?

Here are some population figures for Ireland. They are in millions.

1780	*1821*	*1841*	*1851*	*1901*
4	6.8	8.2	6.6	4.3

Note: There was a census every ten years, after 1801.

1 Put these figures on a graph.
2 What problems resulted from the increase down to 1841?
3 How many people did Ireland lose as a result of the famine?
4 There was no more famine after 1851, but you can see the population went on falling. This was because people were still leaving the country. Why was this, do you suppose?

Written Work

1 Imagine you are an Irish emigrant who has managed to reach the United States. Explain why you left your home. Describe your journey.
2 Today, many Irish people believe that the English tried to use the famine to destroy their race. Go through the three sections on the famine and collect all the evidence you can which will support this view. Now find what evidence there is against it. Write an argument which an Irishman and an Englishman might have on the subject.
3 How do you think the English behaved during the famine? How do you think the Irish behaved?

Research

Find out what you can about the history of Ireland from the end of the famine to 1914.